Caithness
Loch, Heather & Peat

Mark Hill

Glass from the Graham Cooley Collection

Photography by Graham Rae

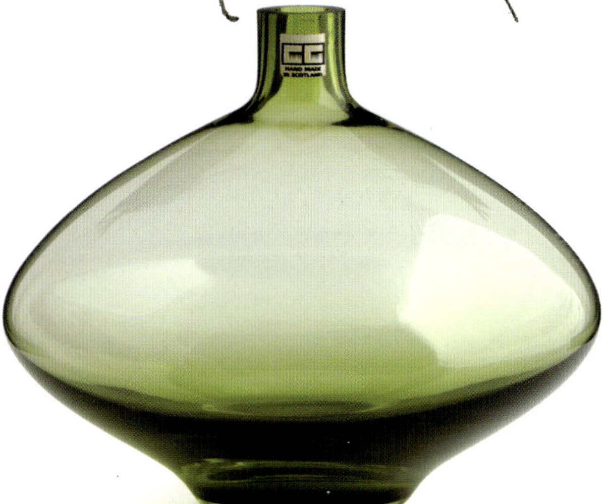

Mark Hill Publishing Ltd

First published in 2011 by Mark Hill Publishing Ltd
P.O. Box 36041, London, SW16 5XL, England
books@markhillpublishing.com
www.markhillpublishing.com
www.markhill.net

A CIP catalogue record for this publication is available from the British Library.

ISBN-10: 0-9552865-5-7
ISBN-13: 978-0-9552865-5-1

Photography by Graham Rae, www.graham-rae.co.uk
Design and pre-press production by TJ Graphics, www.tjgraphics.co.uk
Printed and bound in the United Kingdom by Cambrian Printers, www.cambrian-printers.co.uk
This publication was printed with the environment in mind, using vegetable-based inks on alcohol free presses that use printing plates processed without chemicals. The production of this publication complies with EU Eco-Management and Audit Scheme (EMAS) guidelines.

Front cover image: Four 1960s-70s Lochshiel vases, designed by Domhnall ÓBroin
Back cover image: A late 1980s Cadenza range Lantern Vase, designed by Colin Terris
Title page image: A mid-1960s-70s lamp base, designed by Domhnall ÓBroin
Contents page image: A group of 1960s-90s Barrel Vases, designed by Domhnall ÓBroin

This catalogue was published in the 50th anniversary year of the founding of Caithness Glass, and to accompany an exhibition of Caithness Glass from the Graham Cooley Collection at Broadfield House Glass Museum and at the Perth Museum & Art Gallery in 2011.

Contents

Foreword	4
Introduction	5
Clear Colour	37
Stripes & Mottles	57
Complex Decoration	73
Cut, Engraved & Sandblasted	91
Colours, Labels & Boxes	106
Selected Catalogue Pages	108
Designer Biographies	126

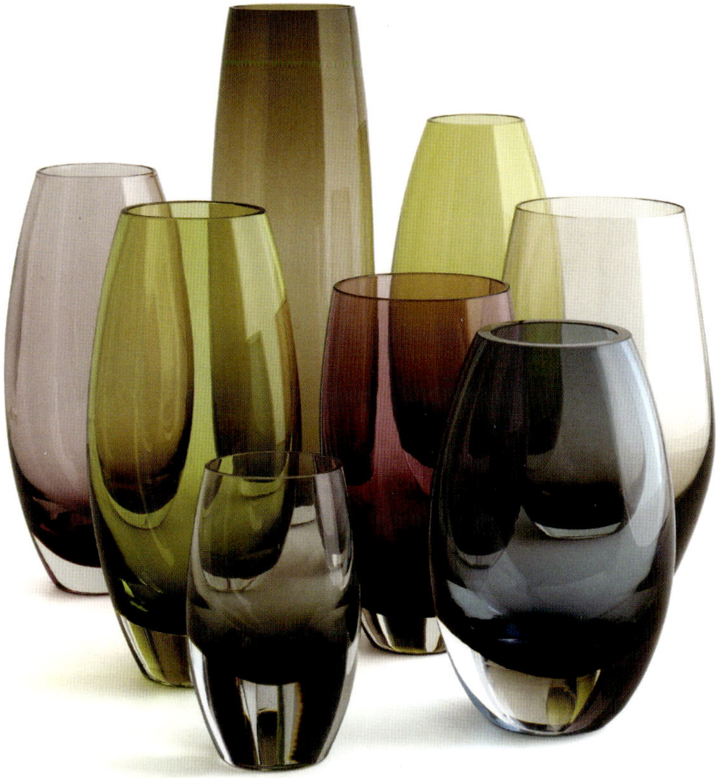

Foreword

Graham Cooley

The three individuals who made the greatest impact on the development of 20thC British glass are, in my opinion, Domhnall ÓBroin, Ronald Stennett-Willson and Frank Thrower. The similarities in their stories are striking, and symptomatic of the period in which they flourished.

All three were great glass designers in the modern style. They were determined individuals who overflowed with drive and imagination. They also had the key advantage of an entrepreneurial outlook, and each designer, together with a co-founder, was able to raise enough capital to start up and develop a business that would become a household name. These names were, respectively, Caithness Glass, King's Lynn (later, Wedgwood) Glass, and Dartington Glass.

When Caithness Glass was founded in 1961, the decorative arts were still rooted in the austerity of the 1950's, and influenced by the clean, smooth lines of German and Scandinavian design. Domhnall ÓBroin initially followed this tradition, but with a subtle difference. The tones he used were representative of the natural hues he saw in the Scottish Highlands, hence the title of my exhibition: 'Loch, Heather and Peat' – the colour names he used for his first ranges. In this sense his designs were a progressive combination of the Modern and Naturalist movements.

Until Mark's investigations, a huge gap existed in the history of Caithness Glass. Domhnall's daughter Emer Gunter was invaluable in helping us understand the earlier years. In addition, we have catalogues produced from 1980 to today. Helped further by meeting a number of key figures associated with the company, Mark has been able to put together for the first time the story of how factory designs developed from 1961 through to 2007. Mark does not claim to have discovered every story, answered every question, or filled in every gap, but through this book and my associated exhibition, I believe he has made a scholarly and enlightening reassessment of a company which is one small part of the heritage of Scotland but a huge part of its glass heritage.

Of all the British glass factories I have investigated, the story of Caithness Glass has been the most difficult to unravel. In that light, Mark's skill in marshalling all the facts and presenting the available information in a comprehensive and compelling account is all the more impressive. I got to do the enjoyable bit and ferret out all the glass.

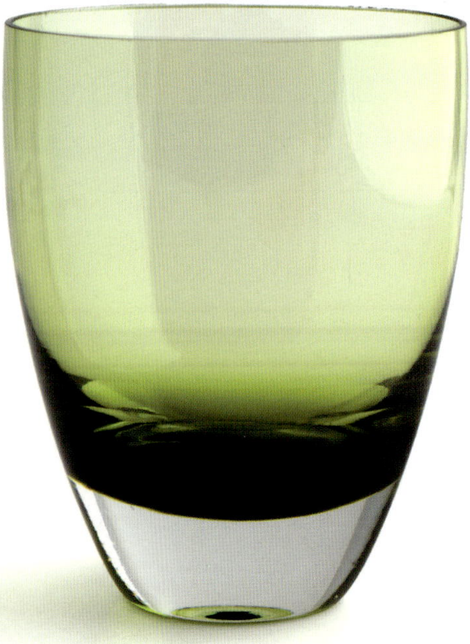

A 1960s-70s Barrel Vase, no.4019, in Moss, designed by Domhnall ÓBroin in 1961, 5in (12.5cm) high

Introduction

Mark Hill

Daniel Patrick O'Byrne was born on March 11th 1934 in Waterford, Ireland. He was the oldest of a family of five, and his parents, Thomas and Mary Anne, were a railway carter and homemaker respectively. His early education was at the Manor School and Mount Sion School in Waterford. In addition to learning Irish at school, he developed a lifelong passion for the Irish language and its preservation. From 1952, O'Byrne started using the Irish version of his name, Domhnall Padraig ÒBroin. Danny, as he was known, was a particular and precise boy who was keen to learn and apply himself. Early on, he showed great skills in art and entered and won a national drawing competition. His innate feel for line and precision also manifested itself in his unusually neat handwriting and his skills at shooting, for which he also won national awards. A concern for how he appeared to others, which was to remain with him, also developed early on, as photographs show. He always wore a tie, and presented himself neatly, with sharply combed hair. His skills allowed him to study at the Central Technical Institute in Waterford. It was here that he first came into contact with glass when, aged fifteen, the Headmaster recommended him for an apprenticeship at a newly founded glass company in the town.

The historic name of Waterford Glass had been revived three years earlier in 1947 by Czech émigré and glass entrepreneur Charles Bacik. He had invited fellow Czech cutter and designer Miroslav Havel to join him to provide the technical knowledge needed to produce the type of cut glass the company had become famous for in the 19th century. As there were no glassmaking facilities at the new company, inexpensive soda glass was imported from a Belgian factory to be cut at Waterford. Rather than initially employ experienced cutters, Havel chose to recruit a team of apprentices who could be trained. This measure brought local approval, as jobs were scarce and the company was viewed with some suspicion by many as it was owned by 'foreigners'.

Havel had developed close links with the town's Central Technical Institute from 1947, lecturing there and regularly recruiting potential talent as novice cutters left or were not able to meet the required level of skill. O'Byrne signed his indenture as an apprentice at the company in 1950. He joined the company at an exciting time. The company had recently installed a new French-made furnace, and had begun to produce its own glass that was then cut in–house. The mixed team Havel employed

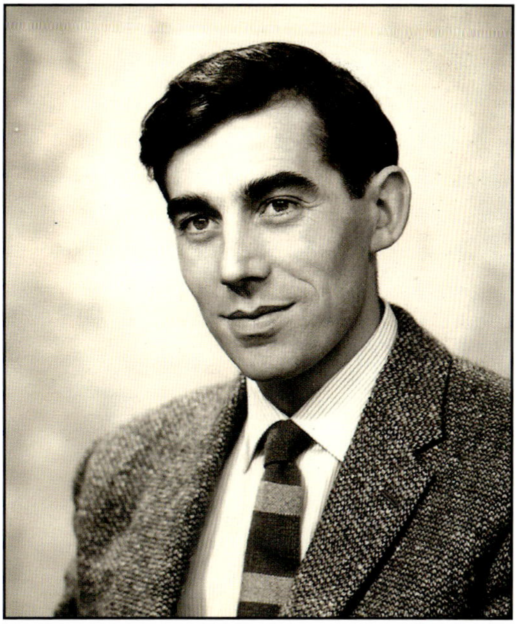

Domhnall ÓBroin in 1963, aged 29.

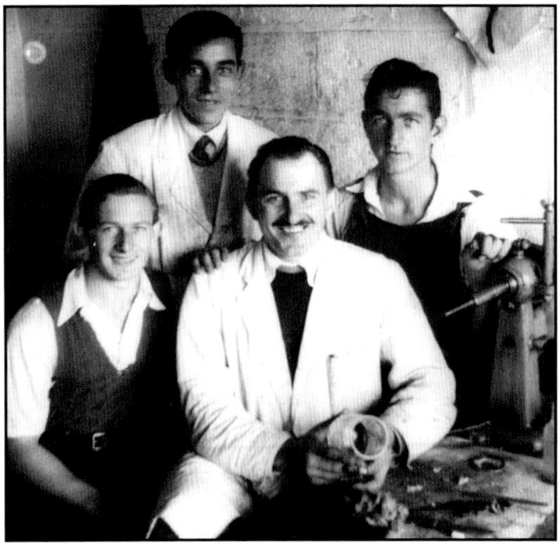

Miroslav Havel (centre) with this team of engravers, at Ballytruckle in Summer 1951. Clockwise from left: Tommy Caulfield, Daniel O'Byrne, Tommy Wall. Courtesy of Brian Havel.

comprised three experienced German cutters Bacik had hired in 1949, and a small number of locals trained primarily by Havel. Due to serious financial problems in 1950, Bacik had sold a controlling stake in the company to the owners and associates of the Irish Glass Bottle Company. This enabled the company to survive and expand into a larger, purpose-built factory at Johnstown in October 1951.

O'Byrne thrived in this small and tightly knit environment, and was exposed to all aspects of the glass design and production process. As well as learning how to cut and engrave, he saw how a small glass factory was founded and run, and how designs were taken from the drawing board through stages of production.

Havel recognised O'Byrne's skills and potential by appointing him as his assistant around a year after he joined. As a further mark of approval, he was the only other employee allowed to wear a white laboratory coat, which Havel held as a mark of seniority and status since his days working in Czechoslovakia.

This relationship with the experienced glass professional Havel was key to O'Byrne's development. Havel embarked on research trips to Swedish, Norwegian and German glass factories from 1949-51, and produced detailed reports which O'Byrne was undoubtedly able to study. More importantly, from 1952, Havel sent O'Byrne to Scandinavia for periods of time across two years to study glass design and chemistry as part of his apprenticeship. Based at Orrefors, he travelled to other factories to widen his experience. There, he saw other factory production lines, the cutting workshops, and how design and designers were handled. This exposure to the beauty and simplicity of modern Scandinavian glass bolstered what he had already experienced and learnt, and would prove invaluable in later life.

He returned to his role as Havel's assistant in 1954, and began to make larger contributions to designs, which were produced in lead crystal after the move to Johnstown in 1951. Although Havel was the controlling and driving force behind design and production at Waterford, his team

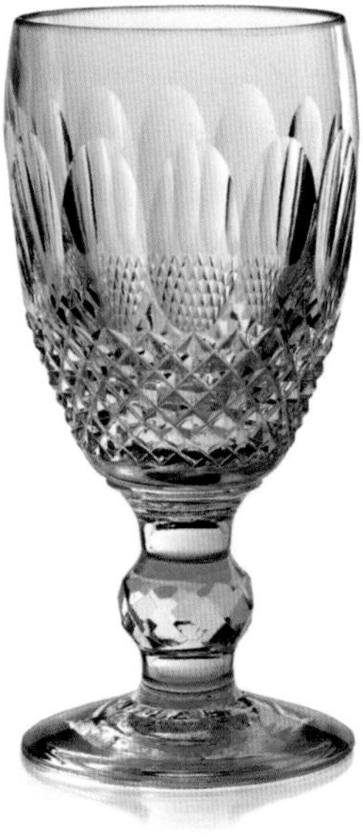

A 1950s-70s Waterford Glass sherry glass from the 'Colleen' range, designed by Miroslav Havel, 4in (10cm) high.

of five apprentices became increasingly important as his wide-ranging duties filled his time as the company grew.

During this time, O'Byrne contributed to designs including 'Innisfail', 'Sheila', 'Royal Tara', and the famous 'Colleen' suite of tableware. All were derived from Havel's drawings of original complexly cut Waterford glass, but patterns were simplified in order to allow them to be produced by the small team of apprentices and experienced cutters.

In 1955, O'Byrne completed his apprenticeship, and produced an 'apprentice piece' that displayed his skills and experience. He chose to cut and engrave a large bowl with a seated lady reading a book. The simple form of the bowl, lack of complex cut patterns, and the handling of design show that he was more strongly influenced by his visits to Scandinavia than by his experience of Havel's designs. On April 5th 1955, he received his certificate, which was numbered 'E1', indicating that he was the first engraver to successfully complete his apprenticeship.

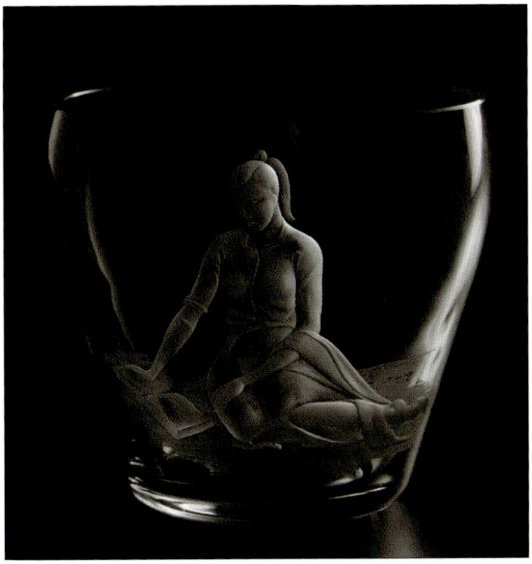

A bowl, cut with a seated lady reading a book, designed and cut by Daniel O'Byrne as his apprentice piece in 1955, 6in (15.5cm) high.

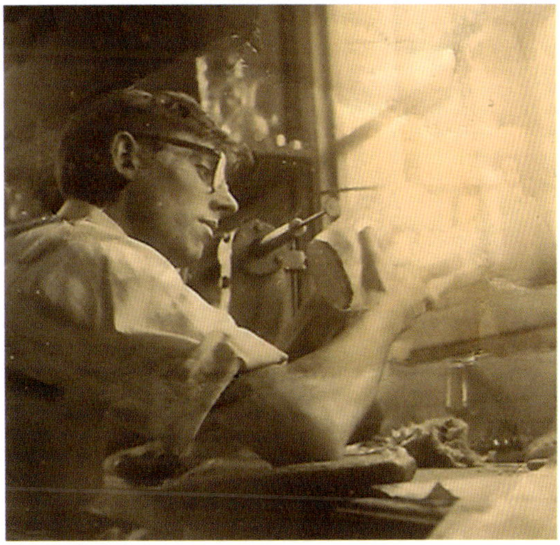

Daniel O'Byrne at Waterford in 1955, cutting his apprentice piece (below) using a copper wheel.

The 21 year old ÓBroin (as he will be called hereon) could have easily stayed at the growing Waterford, working under his mentor Havel. However, he was still young and his wide and varied experiences must have made the opportunities open to him clear. Whilst Havel remained at Waterford, ÓBroin could only progress to a certain level, whereas the outside world offered possibilities of greater experiences and success. Shortly after graduating, he won the prestigious Andrew Grant Scholarship that enabled him to study glass design and technology at the Edinburgh College of Art.

The glass department at Edinburgh had been run since 1947 by Helen Monro Turner, a noted and highly skilled glass engraver. It was one of the few educational institutions to have access to a furnace, which were the preserve of glass factories due to their high operating costs. Despite being described as 'experimental' in the catalogue of the British Artist Craftsmen's Exhibition, it clearly worked well enough to allow students to produce good results. Students thus enjoyed enormous freedom to learn and develop an array of skills in addition to engraving.

Coming from Waterford, access to a furnace was not new to ÓBroin, but it is unlikely that he would have regularly experienced hot glass directly, let alone had the opportunity to build up adequate skills to handle it successfully alone. At Edinburgh, encouraged by Monro Turner and assisted by a glassmaker, he was able to do this. He 'grasped the blowing iron with both hands', and designed and produced a small body of work that is best described as early studio glass. Although presumably not unique achievements, they are still remarkable as they were executed a few years before Harvey Littleton and Dominick Labino began their ground-breaking experiments with small furnaces at the Toledo Museum of Art in the US.

ÓBroin's surviving works from this period show a continuation and development of the 1950s Scandinavian aesthetic seen in his apprentice bowl. A small series of simple, clean-lined colourless bowls recall designs by Gerda Stromberg for Strombergshyttan in Sweden, particularly with their asymmetric and undulating machine-cut rims. They were also executed with broad freehand stripes of strong, yet muted colours, another innovation undoubtedly inspired by postwar Scandinavian glass. By comparison, British glass of the period was predominantly colourless, with styles and forms being both staid and traditional.

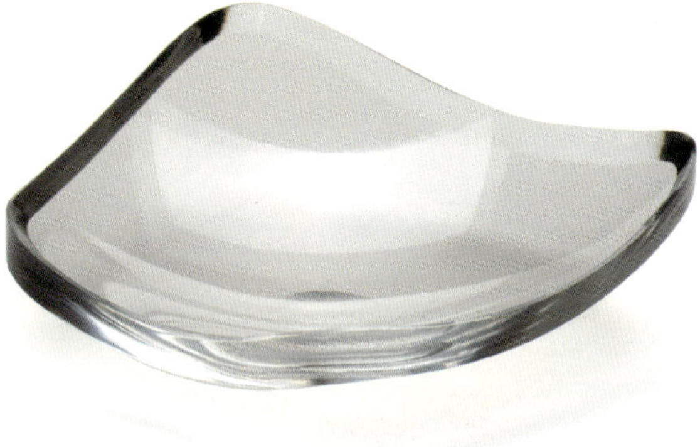

A late 1950s colourless bowl with a machine-cut rim, by Domhnall ÓBroin, 4.75in (12cm) wide.

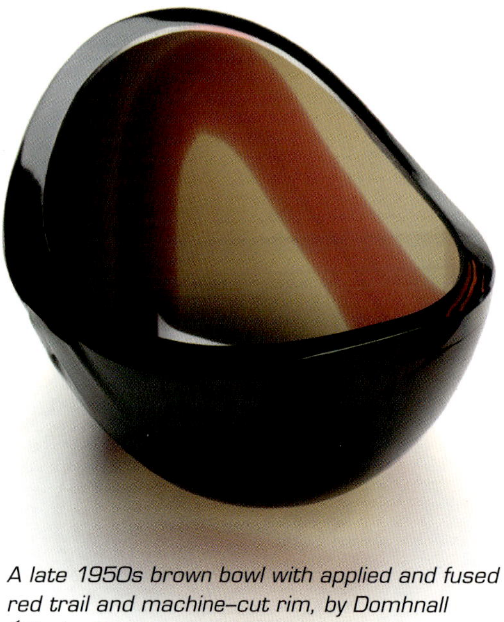

A late 1950s brown bowl with applied and fused red trail and machine-cut rim, by Domhnall ÓBroin, 7in (18cm) widest.

His progressive style also features in his two most important works executed while at Edinburgh; 'Boats' and 'The Tube'. The three shallow dishes that comprise the first work, and the attenuated tube of the second, were deemed important enough at the time to be included in the touring exhibition of British Artist Craftsmen launched at the Smithsonian Institute. From 1959-61, this collection of 175 examples of the best in British design and art, including works by Henry Moore and Louise Nevelson, toured twelve North American and Canadian cities. Both works were very large in size and were novel enough to be noted by reviewers writing for the Washington Post, House & Garden, and the Pottery Gazette, the latter pointing out their "*Scandinavian influence*".

This influence can again be seen in the third work of this group, 'Birds' (see p.10), with their asymmetric, curving and almost organic forms that are reminiscent of Per Lütken's designs for Danish factory Holmegaard.

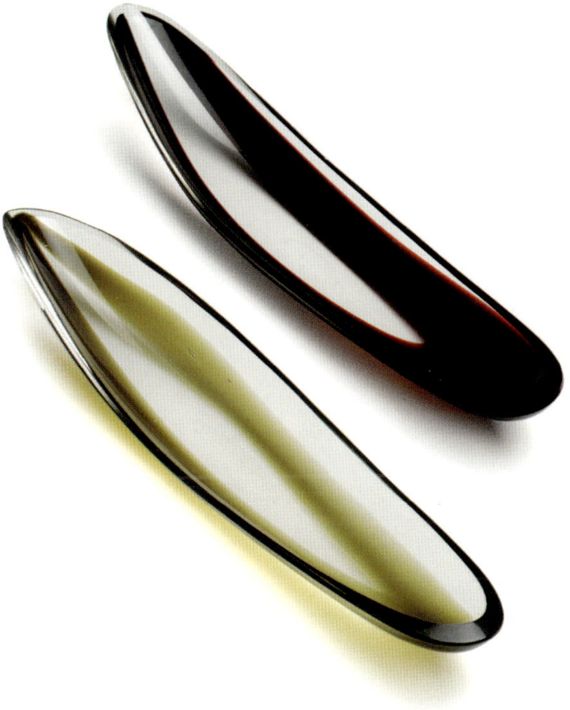

Two of the 'Boats', by Domhnall ÓBroin, c1958, included in the exhibition of the British Artist Craftsmen held across America from 1959–61. Longest 21in (53.5cm) long. The third boat, which had a deep brown stripe, was stolen when the exhibition closed and is still missing. The forms resemble Irish boats known as curraghs.

As would be expected with a teacher such as Monro Turner, much of ÓBroin's work at this time was cut or engraved. Perhaps the best surviving example is his 'Petroushka' vase (see p.10), executed c1958. The manner in which the marionette is cut into the curving form clearly echoes designs produced by Orrefors. Another, 'The Apostle', is seemingly executed on a large piece of cullet, but is in fact another echo of Scandinavian designs. In all instances, the engraving is distinctly modern in terms of subject matter, handling and execution.
Towards the end of his studies in 1959, ÓBroin was seconded to Sheffield University to study on a glass technology course put in place by W.E.S. Turner, Helen Monro Turner's husband.
It is possible that some of his works may have been executed when there. At the completion of his studies a year later he was admitted as a member of the Society of Glass Technology.
In August 1959, ÓBroin married fellow student Anne Teresa 'Nancy' O'Donnell, and their first child, Emer Maire, was born in 1960. However, it was the events of Christmas 1958 that were to have the most important impact on his professional life, and would see him and his family move to a tiny town in the northern most reaches of Scotland.

The Birth of Caithness Glass

In an obituary for the Independent newspaper, Scottish Liberal Democrat MP David Steel described Robin MacDonald Sinclair (1922-95), the second Viscount Thurso from 1970, as eschewing London society in favour of life in his country seat in Caithness, Northern Scotland. Despite his fondness for the area, Sinclair also maintained the powerful political connections built by his influential father, who was Secretary of State for Air in Churchill's government.

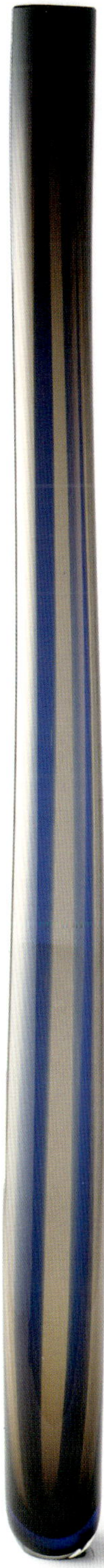

Right: 'The Tube', by Domhnall ÓBroin, c1958, included in the exhibition of British Artist Craftsmen held across America from 1959-61. In June 1968, it was entered into the 33rd annual, state–wide exhibition of The Allied Artists of West Virginia, and won both the 'Best of Show' award and the award for 'Outstanding Achievement in Glass', 53in (135cm high).

During the late 1950s, Sinclair became increasingly concerned about the number of unemployed and untrained men and women in the largely rural area he represented. A newspaper report from 1963 stated that "*...farming is small scale in Caithness, and fishing dwindles all the time...most of the men have lived on National Assistance for years and years...*". Very much like the Dartington Trust would do nearly a decade later, Sinclair decided to introduce a new form of industry to the area by founding a factory.

On his various excursions to Sweden, he had visited small glass factories and decided that the similarities between rural Scotland and rural Sweden, the lack of glass manufacture in Scotland, and the abundance of sand in Caithness made a glass factory a good idea. Legend has it that he flipped through the Encyclopedia

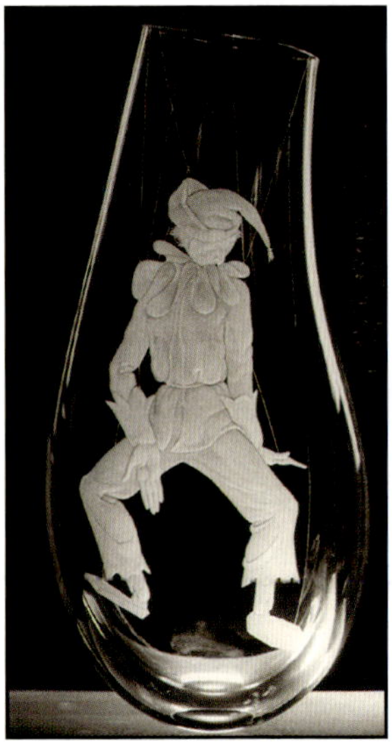

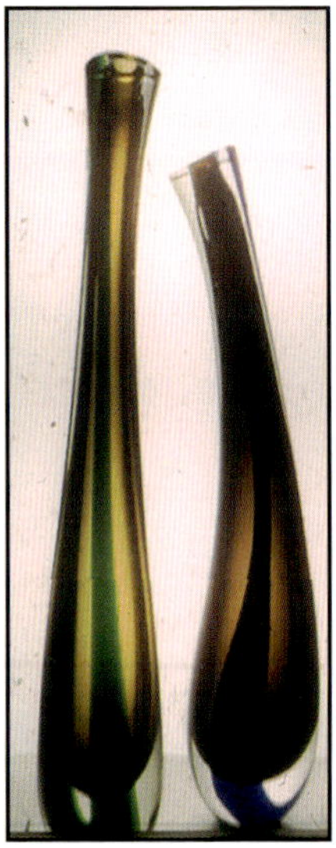

Left: The 'Petroushka' vase, designed and engraved by Domhnall ÓBroin in 1958 and exhibited at the Primavera Galleries on Sloane St, London, as part of an exhibition of work produced by members of Helen Monro Turner's Juniper Workshop in Edinburgh. It was also included in an exhibition in Nice in 1958. 12in (30.5cm) high. Right: 'Birds', with brown and yellow bodies overlaid with coloured stripes and cased in colourless glass, made by Domhnall ÓBroin in the late 1950s, tallest 21in (53cm) high.

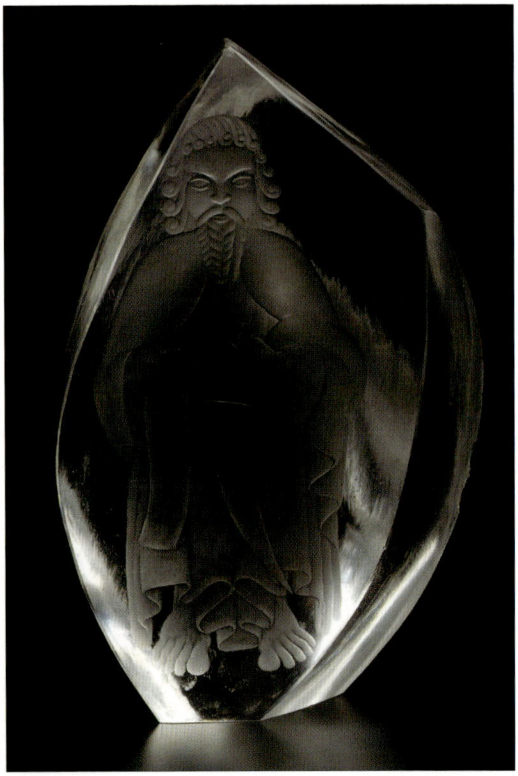

'The Apostle', designed and cut by Domhnall ÓBroin in the late 1950s, 5.5in (14cm) high.

Britannica for ideas and stumbled upon the entry for glass, exclaiming "*That's It!*".

His first stop was to contact Henry Monroe-Wilson of the Scottish Design & Industry Council, who suggested that he speak to Helen Monro Turner's 24 year old student Domhnall ÓBroin. Both young and dynamic, the pair hit it off immediately. ÓBroin stated that the £500 that Sinclair had pledged to found the factory was too little, and that it would take a sum a hundred times greater. But money was not the only issue. The workforce would be untrained, and suitably experienced glassmakers would be hard to find, let alone employ for a new, even foolhardy, venture in such a distant and rural area. Furthermore, ÓBroin's experiences at Waterford, Edinburgh, and in Sweden had given him enough indirect experience of how a factory should be laid out, how a batch of glass should be formulated, and how designs may be put through the production process, but he had never been involved himself, let alone in charge.

ÓBroin visited Wick in Caithness for the first time in December 1958. Despite any personal fears over his lack of direct experience, he agreed to take responsibility for the design of the factory, the initial designs for production, and all technical and production-based issues. Both men worked closely together to build a business plan and present it to potential investors sourced locally and from Sinclair's considerable contacts.

Raising enough money was a major challenge, especially as most investors would not believe that adequate skills could be developed in the local community, and as there was no history of glassmaking in the area. Moreover, although imported modern Scandinavian glass was becoming increasingly popular in Britain, there seemed little need for domestic production over and above that produced by established companies like Whitefriars.

Despite these difficulties, the money was raised from a large number of investors, one of the most important being Bertram Tawse of Aberdeen-based civil engineering company William Tawse. Scottish Industrial Estates agreed to build the factory and lease it back to the company.

On January 15th 1960, Caithness Glass Ltd was incorporated with Sinclair and ÓBroin joined as Directors by investors Tawse, Donald Cameron of Lochshiel, Lt-Col. Hildreth M.B.E., and Lt-Col. Lyle. ÓBroin's offical title was Supervisor of Production and Technical Director, with responsibility for "*glass chemistry...design... research and training*".

While the factory was being built at Harrowhill in Wick, ÓBroin travelled to Italy to recruit glassmakers who could produce his designs, and teach the local workforce.

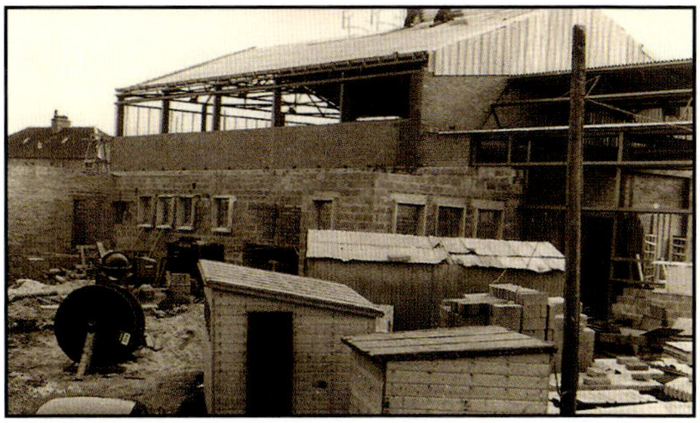

The Caithness Glass factory being built at Harrowhill, Wick, during 1960.

Locals would be employed in the finishing room with its newly acquired machinery, or attend to simple tasks in the factory, before being gradually introduced to glassmaking. He succeeded in persuading Sergio Schiavon, Justo Ferro and Pietro Fuin to leave the sunny warmth of the Mediterranean for Northern Scotland.

The factory opened in June 1961, with furnaces from Sismey & Lindforth, and the first raw materials being imported from the Continent for consistency, and because local sand contained too much iron. Despite the incredible achievement in getting that far, the general consensus was that the company was still likely to encounter problems and fail. In February 1961, the Pottery Gazette stated that ÓBroin was "*...especially experienced and well informed in all branches of domestic glass manufacture, including new techniques in regard to colour and design which he himself has developed.*

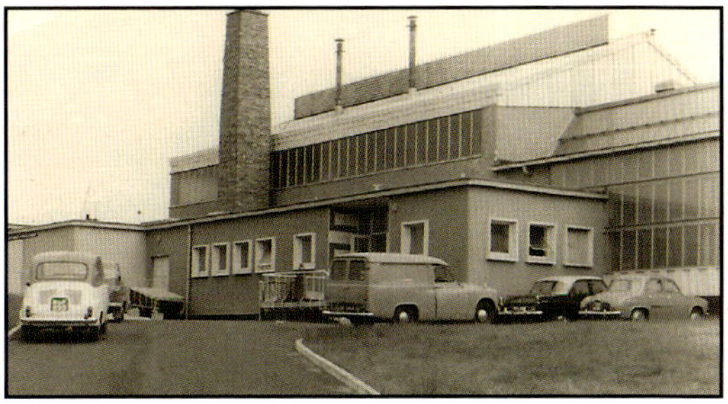

The operational Caithness Glass factory at Harrowhill, Wick, c1963.

Nobody familiar with the technical difficulties associated with crystal glass manufacture, even in well-established glassworks employing persons highly skilled and experienced, and possessing inherited knowledge going back several generations, will under-estimate the many problems that loom ahead for Mr ÓBroin and his co-directors."

In October 1962, ÓBroin required expert help and support, and recruited the famed glassmaker and designer Paul Ysart as Training Officer. ÓBroin had first met Ysart when he visited the Moncrieff glassworks in Perth during the late 1950s to have some of his designs produced. Ysart became a highly valued and important part of the team, bringing a wealth of experience and skills to the company. Most trials for new shapes were made by Ysart before production began. In January 1963, Peter Holmes, a 15 year old local, joined the company and began working closely with Ysart, effectively as an apprentice.

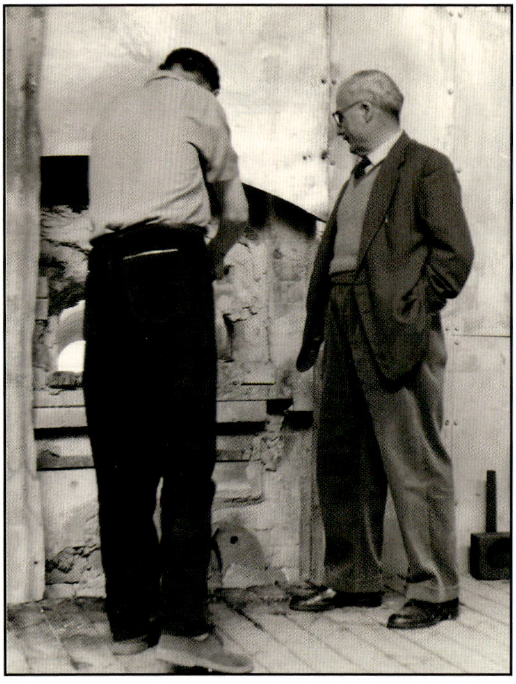

Paul Ysart (right) and a glassmaker (possibly Sergio Schiavon) in front of a furnace, c1964.

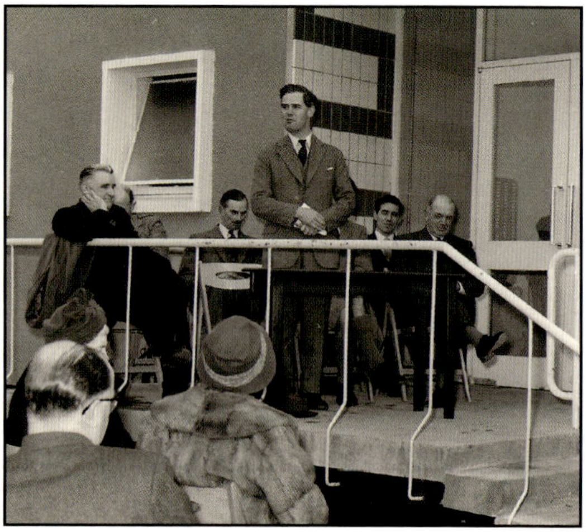

The Board of Directors and investors at the factory opening ceremony in June 1961. Domhnall ÓBroin is seated, second from right, with Robin Sinclair seated (obscured) to his right. Photograph by Jim MacDonald.

Curious about the business and keen to work and earn money, other locals joined too, and the team soon expanded.

As more inexperienced workers arrived, it became clear that Ysart and the Italians could not cope with both training them and maintaining production levels. With this in mind, ÓBroin visited Austria and Germany in late 1963 to recruit more experienced glassmakers. Following his return, Franz Pirker, Herbert Dreier and Heinz Crejci joined the company and remained there until they returned to Europe between 1965 and 1968. As well as training apprentices, their legacy was to introduce a strong production-line ethos to the team. For every fifteen trainees employed, only one would succeed, as standards set by ÓBroin and Ysart were very high.

Many trainees were very young, as the photographs here show. Those who did succeed included Chick Young, Johnny Christie, Stanley McNab, and brothers James and Tom MacBeath. Along with Peter Holmes, the latter two became amongst the most talented and able glassmakers the company trained.

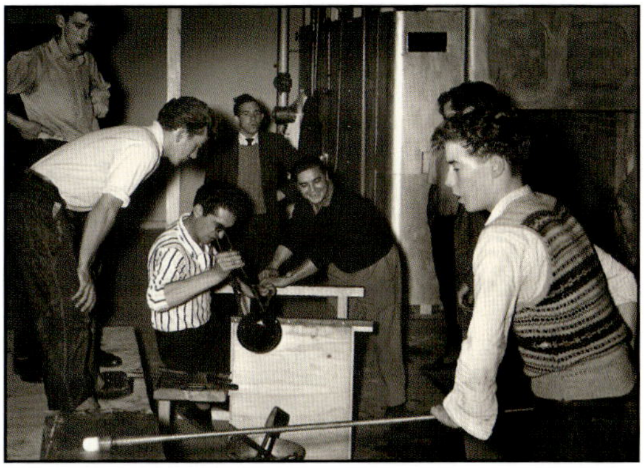

From left: Stanley McNab, Johnny Christie (leaning forward), Sergio Schiavon (with tools), Works Manager Matt Young, Peter Fuin (smiling), and two unknown glassmakers (right). c1964

Early Designs

Domhnall ÓBroin was responsible for all designs at Caithness Glass from 1961 until his departure in 1966. During this time, he finally had the freedom to pursue his own creative ambitions, and the means to see his designs put into production. Unsurprisingly, given his background and experiences, the most important inspiration was modern Scandinavian glass. This manifested itself in terms of both form and colour. Forms were simple, clean-lined and based on linear geometric shapes such as the cylinder, oval, and cone. Due to this, many have an almost austere feel, particularly in certain colours. Many bring to mind the mid-1950s designs of Kaj Franck for Finland's Nuutajärvi Notsjö, which ÓBroin saw both on his travels and for sale in the UK.

There is also a strongly Modernist aspect to his range, which was affordable, well-designed and fit for purpose, with no extraneous or unnecessary details. In 1965, he summed up his design ethic by stating that, "*our glass...is really very simple. But then no one, I feel, wants anything ornate in their home nowadays. Of course, anything used in the house should be a utilitarian object, well designed.*"

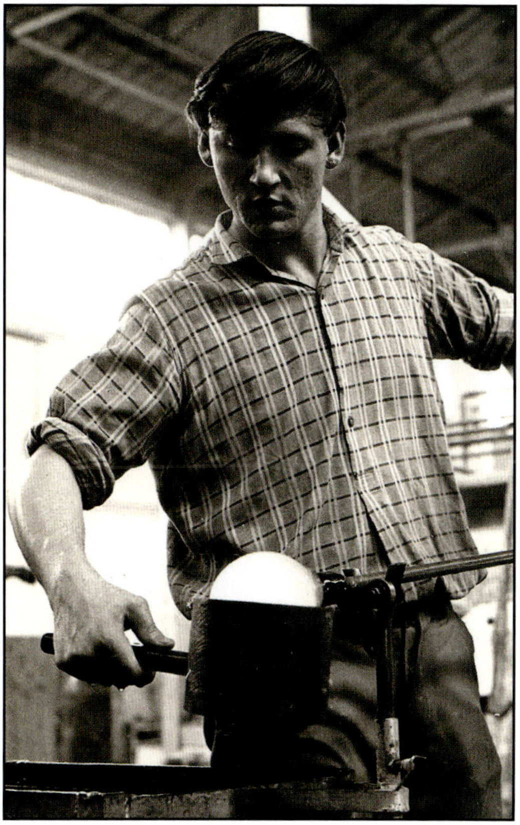

Austrian glassmaker Herbert Dreier (b.1942), in 1964, who went on to make paperweights with Strathearn Glass from the late 1960s–1981.

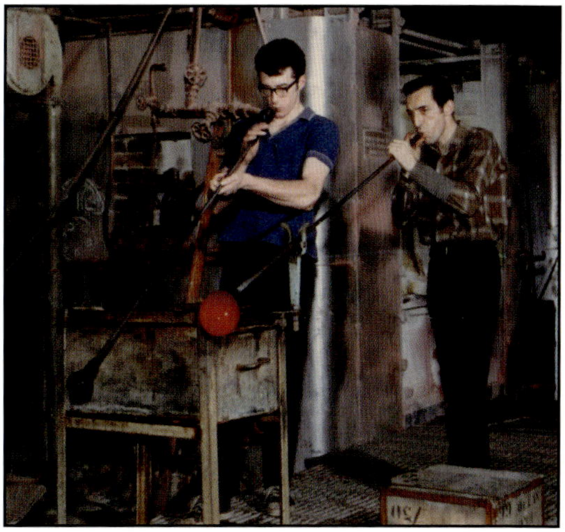

Locally recruited glassmakers Tom MacBeath (left) and Chick Young (right) in front of the mechanical lehr, c1964.

This is particularly true of his cylindrical and barrel shaped vases, which became bestsellers for the company.
Colours were also derived from Scandinavian glass, being strong, yet muted rather than bright and vibrant. They are as important to the design as the form. In order to tie his products firmly in to the country of their origin, perhaps to appeal to British buyers keen to buy fashionable 'home-grown' products over imports, ÓBroin took inspiration from the Scottish landcape around him. This was indicated in the names chosen for each of the colours he developed, which comprised the pinky-purple 'Heather', the deep blue 'Loch', the gentle green 'Moss', the earthy brown 'Peat', and the austere grey 'Soot'. ÓBroin's words were "*Since our inception we have taken our inspiration from the colours of the Scottish landscape - warm peaty tones, purple heather, golden sunsets, the grey-blue of Lochs.*"
Even though designs were identified by a catalogue number, the Scottish angle was reinforced with evocative names being given to many of the designs. These were again taken from the landscape around him, and included 'Stroma' (an island off the coast of Caithness), 'Scaraben' and 'Morven' (both hills). As well as being useful from a marketing and sales perspective, this may have been inspired by his experience at Waterford. In early 1952, Cornelius (Con) Dooley, Waterford's US salesman, decided to rename design no.600-318 'Lismore', after the Irish castle. This gave him a romantic and sentimental sales angle, as it gave the design an instant Irish heritage. ÓBroin was quoted by Meg Munro in the Evening Times in 1965 as saying, "*I brought glassmakers from Venice to start the factory, but I have tried to develop the glass in a purely Scottish way.*"
If there was one factor that limited the scope of his designs, it was the workforce who would produce them. As they were largely unskilled and were learning their trade, designs had to be easy to produce. Not only that, but they had to be simple enough to produce consistently on a production line basis to enable enough to be made for sale. Just like his feel for marketing, this commercial angle was an important aspect to his work at Caithness.

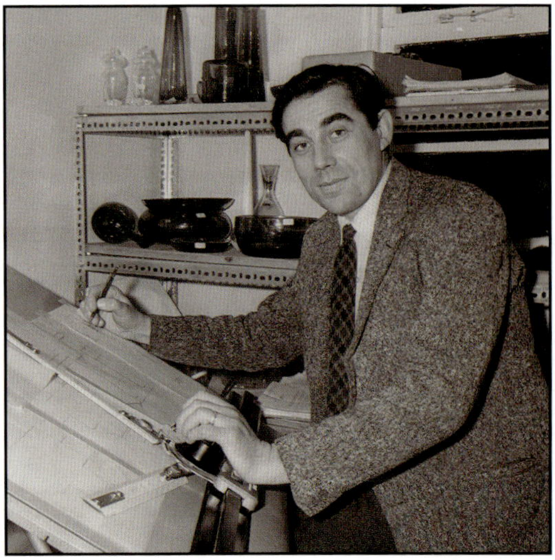

Domhnall ÓBroin at his drawing board in late 1964. Note the glass on the shelf behind him, which includes samples from other companies.

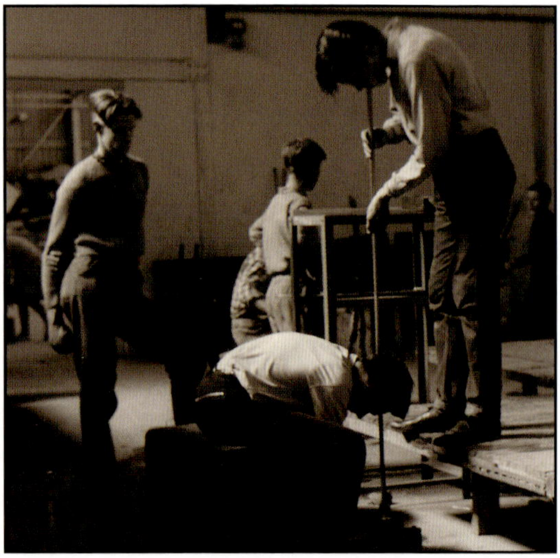

From left: An unknown trainee, Peter Holmes (seated), David MacGregor (standing), and Stanley McNab (blowing a gather into a mould), c1964.

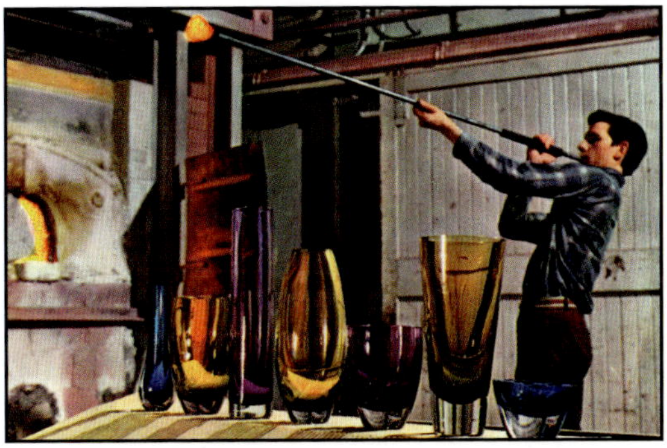

A mid-1960s postcard showing a glassblower behind a range of designs by Domhnall ÓBroin.

ÓBroin's preferred linear shapes made them perfectly suited for mould blowing. As seen on the photograph on the left, a coloured and cased gather of glass was placed from above into a dip mould. Once it had been turned and blown to ensure that the mould had been properly filled, a floor-mounted button was pushed which opened the mould by hydraulics, and allowed the finished form to be removed and put into the mechanical lehr (cooling oven). From there, they would be transferred to the finished room, where the rims were machine-cut and polished by hand.
Around 16-20 standard sized cylindrical Cased Vases (see p.46) could be made per hour by a team of two. Glassmakers were incentivised to exceed the quantity per hour decided by the company. If the agreed quantity was 20 pieces per hour, and a glassmaker produced 25 in an hour, he would receive an extra 25% of his hourly rate as a bonus.
Conversely, quality control at Caithness Glass was extremely high. As the forms were simple and undecorated, relying firmly on the purity of the colour tone, flaws such as bubbles or creases could not be tolerated. Pieces bearing flaws were 'seconded', smashed and remelted, or (later) sold in the factory's shop as seconds. Depending on their location, some flaws could be cut away in the finishing process, or large cylinders cut down to form bowls. However this was only possible with a small percentage of flawed production. This issue with the 'yield', ie; glass made from a batch across a given time period that could be deemed good enough to sell, would be a serious issue for the company throughout the 1960s and '70s. ÓBroin had set high targets for both his designs and the company's output. In 1964, he said "*We have got to be at least as good as Orrefors.*"
By 1965, over 300 items were being produced. The majority comprised drinking glasses or vases of different sizes and shapes. Tableware tended to be more finely blown than vases and bowls, and expanded in range and quantity with the arrival of the Austrian glassmakers who were able to work with the Italian glassmakers to make and apply stems and feet.

The Market & Success

ÓBroin's designs came to the market at a time when Scandinavian glass was becoming increasingly fashionable in British homes. An article in House & Garden from 1963 stated that "*It's chic to shudder at British cut glass and set your table with uncut Scandinavian instead. Many British*

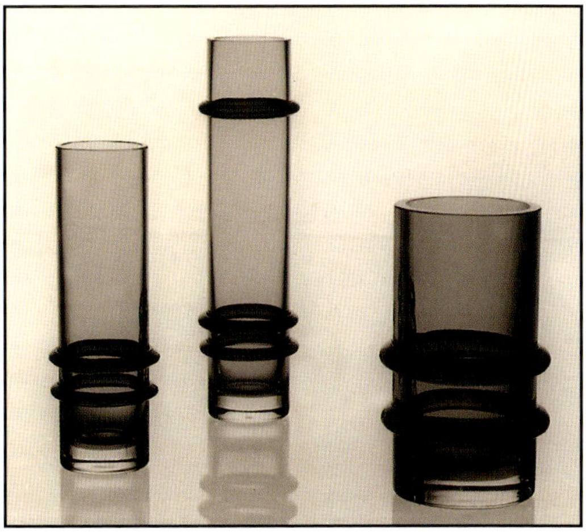

A promotional photograph, taken c1963, of the cylindrical ring vases designed by Domhnall ÓBroin during the early 1960s.

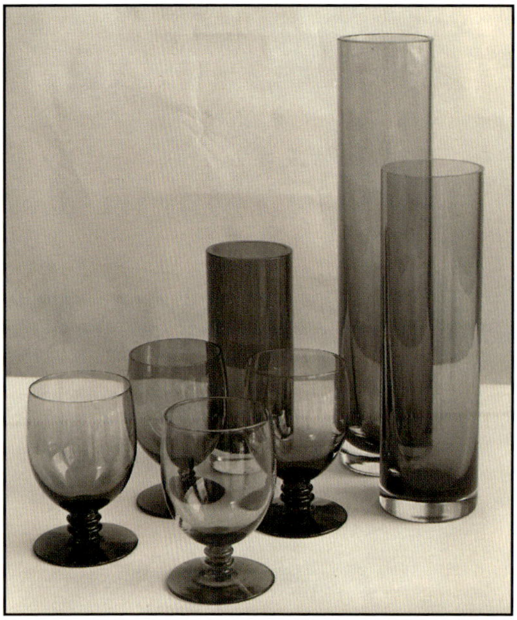

A promotional photograph, taken c1963, of a set of wine glasses with ribbed stems, and the three sizes of the cylindrical Cased Vases.

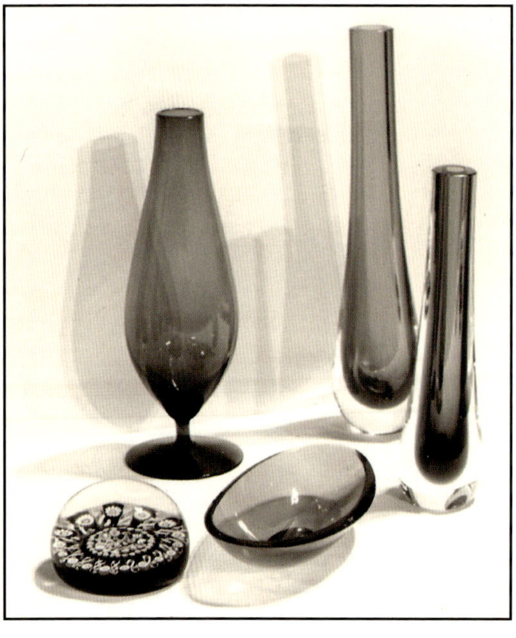

An early 1960s photograph showing a (probably) experimental goblet vase similar to Whitefriars design no.9607 from the same period, an Eclipse Bowl, and two no.4022 Bud Vases. The millefiori and cane paperweight was made by Paul Ysart.

manufacturers admit the trend, blame it on the journalists, and refuse to budge from their deeply cut trenches...saying that 'the true quality of glass is only revealed by cutting.'".

His plain and simple forms and innovative use of colour summed up the desirable Scandinavian aesthetic perfectly, and his range became instantly popular. This was modern glass for the modern postwar consumer keen to reject the traditional styles of old. The House & Garden article went on to say that "*Caithness glass is informal compared with the traditional intricacies of Stourbridge cut crystal.*"

The new company had competitors, not least from Scandinavian companies exporting their glass to the UK via agencies such as Edward Bowman and J. Wuidart & Co. ÓBroin undoubtedly hoped that the lower costs of domestic production and distribution would give him a strong competitive advantage over imported glass. It seemed to be true, with Caithness glassware being described in the national press as "*...the glassware you will like, at the price you can afford.*".

The fact that his range was produced in the UK also allowed him to appeal to the 'nationalistic' instincts of potential buyers. Although we buy goods produced in any country from across the world with impunity today, the situation was different in the early 1960s. This angle did not go un-noticed when ÓBroin was described as "*the trend-setting Irishman who interprets the spirit of Scotland so successfully through the medium of glass*". Furthermore, the Scottish angle continued to be an appealing and lucrative marketing advantage for decades to come, particularly with export markets such as the US and Canada.

ÓBroin also had a firm line in sales patter, which developed further after he was made Managing Director, with additional responsibility for sales, in October 1964. Shortly after, he stated that

"People assume that plain glassware such as ours must be Scandinavian – because it's not cut crystal – but the Scandinavians are less robust, less punchy in their designs. Our glass is bold.".

The fledgling company also had competitors within the UK. The historic and established company of Whitefriars, whose designer from 1955 was Geoffrey Baxter, was also producing table and decorative wares in a similar Scandinavian style. These also relied on the key elements of simple forms and strong colours, with Baxter's 'Blown Soda' range (released just after Caithness Glass opened) being an excellent example. However, the colours used by Whitefriars were largely different from those used at Caithness Glass, and also tended to be brighter and more vibrant than ÓBroin's more muted tones. Shapes also differed, being largely gentler and more curvaceous. Although some of Baxter's forms verge on the clean-lined and austere, they lack the linear geometricity of ÓBroin's. These differences may seem small, but must have counted at the time when, like today, a shopper may have bought a piece simply because the colour appealed to them or suited their interior, or because the shape looked practical. ÓBroin's designs were not only different in appearance, but they were also typically less expensive than those produced by Whitefriars (see p.39 & p.59). Any perceived similarity could also be deemed an advantage. Although Whitefriars may have always remained the larger and more succcesful company at the time, their success meant that a market for such glass existed. So, it was perfectly feasible for another company to take advantage of the public appetite for new and progressive glass design. If one could succeed, then another surely could. Some competitors also fell by the wayside. From 1959–60, the innovative and progressive designer Ronald Stennett-Willson produced a number of designs for Lemington Glass that bore similarities to ÓBroin's, and the range may have grown to become serious competition.

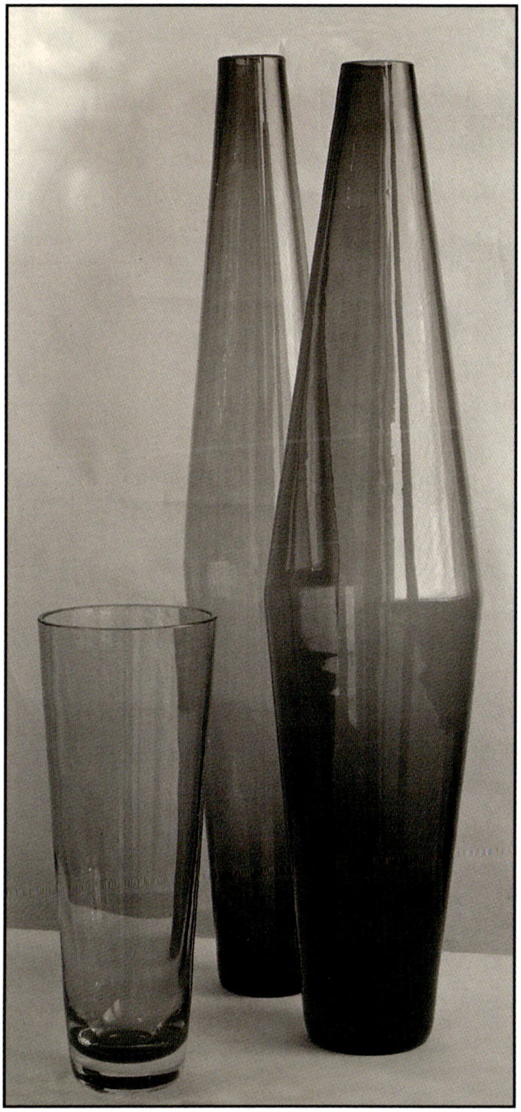

A promotional photograph, taken c1963, showing a Lochshiel vase and two experimental moulded vases that were not put into factory production.

However, the relationship was short-lived, and distribution ceased by the early 1960s. The House & Garden article continued by referring to this, saying that it was "*...time to lament Lemington and cheer Caithness.*" Stennett-Willson would however return later, launching King's Lynn Glass in 1967.

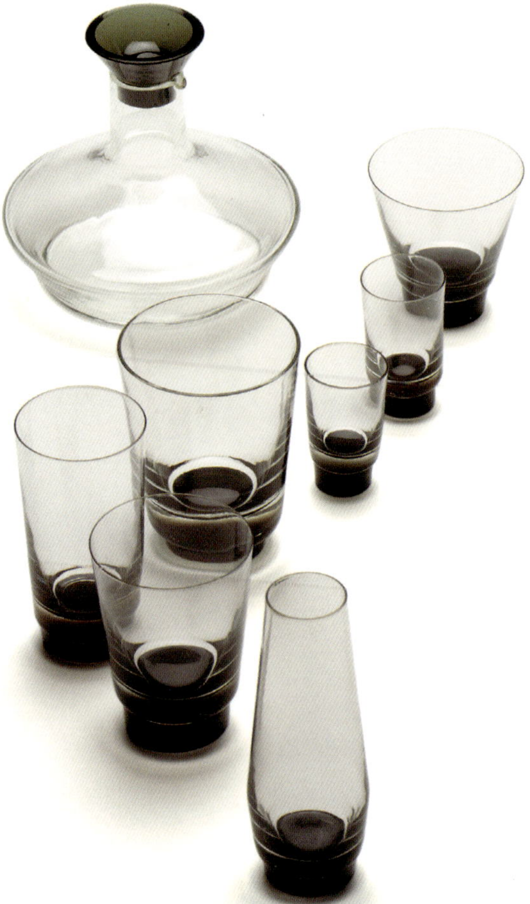

A Scaraben decanter and six glasses, designed by Domhnall ÓBroin. This layout was used to show the range of accompanying glasses in an early 1960s advertisement. The design at the bottom of the row may also be used as a vase.

ÓBroin took on the UK market with fervour, attending all the major trade fairs and building strong relationships with distributors such as Edward Bowman. In an interview with the Guardian on July 4th 1964, ÓBroin implored, "*Please don't describe us as a brave little firm struggling in the northern wilderness...We're well established now.*" He then went on to discuss the expertise of the countrywide network of sales people, who had found out what sold best where, "*in the Black Country they cry out for blue glass, but no one in Edinburgh will buy it.*"

Despite making an impact on the market, unsurprisingly the company made heavy losses in its first few years. By September 1964 however, the company managed to make its first profit, albeit a small one. This was a major achievement for such a young company, as well as being an enormous boost to morale and a firm validation of ÓBroin's designs and business plan.

The key Blackpool trade fair a few months later in February 1965 brought further good news. Not only did the company enjoy a fourfold increase in domestic orders, but it also received a large order from, surprisingly, a Swedish company based in Gothenburg. That was backed up with expansion into the Australian and German markets. Germany was entered after the Council for Industrial Design presented Chancellor Ludwig Erhard with a Scaraben decanter personally engraved by ÓBroin. A similar example was presented to the Duke of Edinburgh in the same year. Surprisingly, given his background, these comprise the best known of the engraved or cut pieces that ÓBroin executed whilst at Caithness. He did engrave some other pieces, but these were mainly given to friends and family, rather than being sold commercially or presented on behalf of the company. Exhibitions of the company's ranges followed in London, and the staff at Wick expanded to 76, 30 of whom were productive glassmakers.

All of these successes were promoted by ÓBroin in 1965 when he stated to The Scotsman that, "*We have at last become accepted as the leading company for modern design in glassware in Britain*". Although this could be deemed as another example of ÓBroin's sales spin, the national press raved in a similar manner. On January 14th 1965, Meg Monro wrote in the The Evening Times that Caithness Glass was the "*Scottish made glassware taking the world by storm...royalty love it, women the world over rush to buy it, and as a status symbol for the home, it is way out front."*

ÓBroin's Departure

If 1965 was a highpoint for Caithness Glass and Domhnall ÓBroin, the following year proved to be quite the reverse.

Even though the company was immensely successful and had made a firm impact on the market, the small profit made in late 1964 was not repeated. Certain investors such as Bertram Tawse were obliged to provide extra funds to keep the company afloat. This had to be repeated numerous times during the next decade.

In late 1964, Mr I. Thomson, a Glasgow-based management consultant, was made Chairman, reflecting the company's serious financial predicament.

Some of ÓBroin's designs were also proving time-consuming, and thus expensive, to produce. The high level of quality control demanded also reduced the yield per batch, particularly for the troublesome designs. Ranges such as the ring vases (see p 47) and Scaraben (see left) were under threat of being discontinued in the search for increased revenue against rising costs.

As the demands and challenges of the developing company changed, ÓBroin found himself at odds with certain members of the Board of Directors over a number of key issues.

From a personal angle, he also had enormous responsibility and an exhausting workload. Not only was he Managing Director, but he was in charge of sales, design, technical development, and more. He had enjoyed an enlightening and truly rewarding six years with the company, but these problems indicated that it was time to move on to new challenges, just as he had done at Waterford. Passions ran high, and a serious rift opened, leading to his resignation from the company in late 1966.

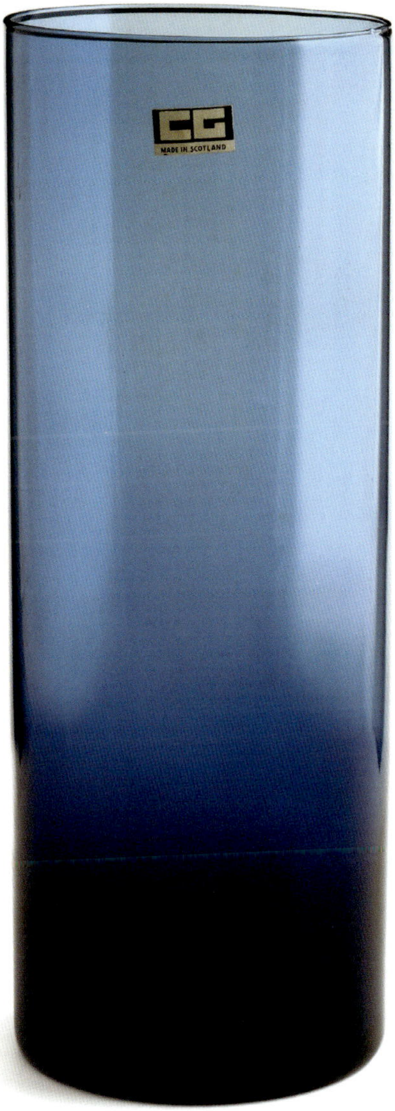

A Loch Blue cylindrical vase, designed by Domhnall ÓBroin c1961, 10.5in (26.5cm) high. Despite being simple to make, these uncased minimalist vases were discontinued by 1971.

Despite this, he remained on excellent personal terms with his original co-founder Robin Sinclair, and other members of the company such as Paul Ysart. In a later letter to ÓBroin, Sinclair made it quite clear to ÓBroin that he was welcome to return to Caithness Glass at any time.

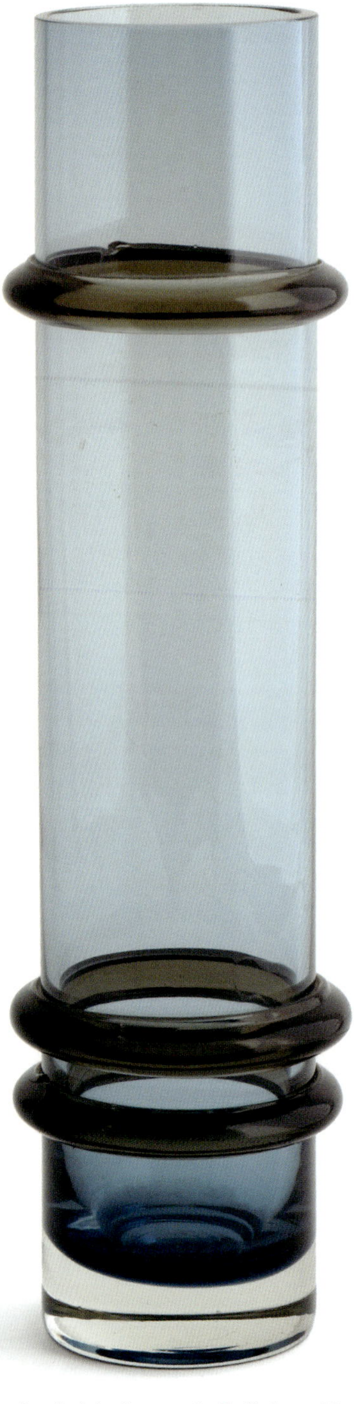

A ringed cylindrical vase, in Twilight, with applied Peat rings, designed by Domhnall ÓBroin c1961, 12in (30.5cm) high. Two colour examples such as this are scarce.

Although the company was not financially healthy, he had left a strong body of successful designs, solid technical and working practices, and an excellent team behind him as his legacy. Without his many considerable skills and talents that covered nearly all aspects of glass production and sale, the company would have undoubtedly failed. Not only that, but the company was recognised nationally and, by 1967, 95% of his designs had been approved by the Design Council.

ÓBroin after Caithness

In November 1966, ÓBroin, his wife Nancy, and their children Emer and Ciaran, left Scotland to travel to West Virginia, where a number of glass factories were based. He accepted an offer to become General Manager of Pilgrim Glass at Ceredo, with Sinclair providing a reference. There, he used his experience to improve furnace technology and efficiency, and more than double output and sales. He also produced his last designs, devising their 'Kitchen Chemistry' range of stoppered jars that bore similarities to his earlier ranges in terms of their simplicity of line and the mould blown production process. He also designed a moulded and cased stylised 'Madonna' figurine, which he gave to friends, such as Paul Ysart, and family. The highly successful Cranberry colour was also introduced under his tenure.

In 1970, he left Pilgrim Glass and joined Fenton Glass in Williamstown, firstly as the assistant to the General Manager, and then later as the Manager of Manufacturing. Furthering his experience at Pilgrim, he improved furnace efficiency by almost 60%, and installed new environmentally friendly and economical furnaces, whilst still maintaining production levels.

It was these technical aspects of glass chemistry, colours, and the efficiency of furnaces, rather than design or sales, that were to dominate the rest of his professional life. In 1980, he left Fenton to become an independent consultant. In an almost prophetic manner, he warned of the vast costs of, and the environmental damage caused by, gas-powered glass furnaces. He provided companies across the world with solutions to help them increase efficiency and overcome production issues. He also became active in a number of professional bodies, acting in an advisory capacity on an international level. An avid traveller for business and pleasure, Domhnall ÓBroin retired in 2000, and died in Costa Rica in 2005.

Caithness after ÓBroin

The void left by ÓBroin's departure would have been hard to fill. It is a credit to his organisational capabilities that the company continued operationally without serious issues. The influential George Mackie (now Baron Mackie of Benshie) took over as the driving force of the company during the late 1960s, backed by a "*public spirited Board of Directors*", that included Robin Sinclair, Bertram Tawse, and Hugo Brunner, the beneficiary of a trust built from a fortune made from industrial chemicals. The Highlands & Islands Development Fund had also become a major shareholder, and lent its support. Mackie's experience and these backers proved essential as the company hit financial problems during 1966, with shares being written down from £1 to one shilling.

The production process was streamlined and over the next few years, and designs that were poor sellers or proved time-consuming and costly to produce were phased out. In 1967 Edinburgh College of Art graduate Charles Orr was employed as the company's designer.

Rather than develop a radically new range immediately, he produced a number of designs that followed ÓBroin's aesthetic, as the look was still fashionable, and had

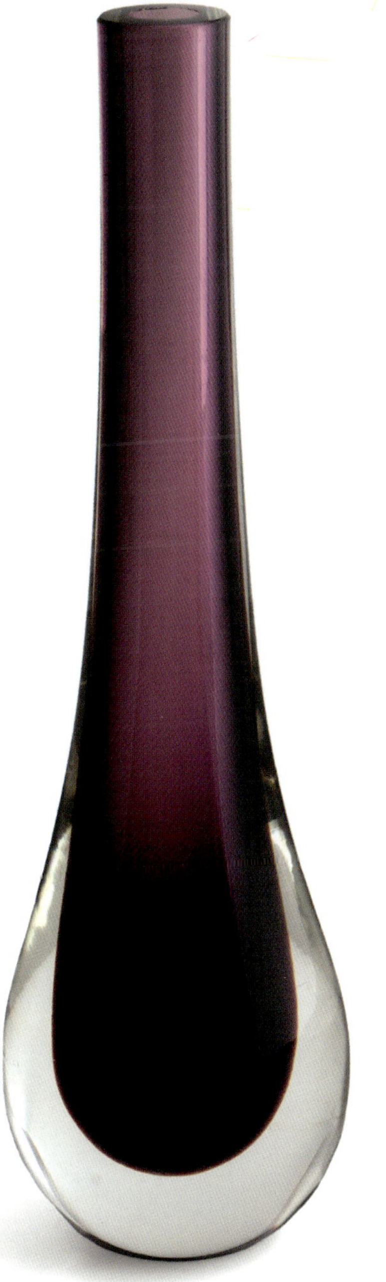

A Bud Vase, no.4022, in Heather, designed by Domhnall ÓBroin c1961, 7.75in (19.5cm) high. This design was based on his late 1950s studio glass designs 'Birds' and 'The Tube'. It was also perhaps inspired by the cased 'sommerso' work of various glass factories on Murano. Highly successful, it was produced in different colours for decades as part of the Stroma range.

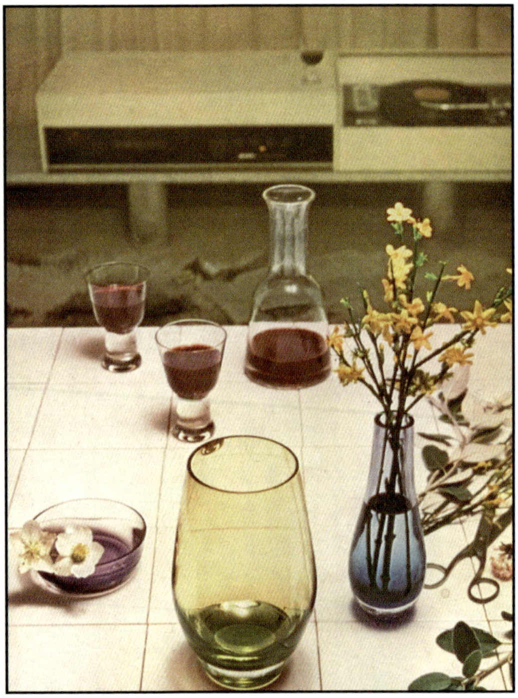

A late 1960s magazine advertisement showing a decanter, no.4026/D, and two wine goblets, no.4026/WI, from the Dunnet range designed by Charles Orr in 1967. The green vase and the blue vase, no.4033, were also designed by Orr, and the Cased Dish, no.4008, was designed by Domhnall ÓBroin in the early 1960s. All three were from the Stroma range.

a proven sales record. Furthermore, this was the look that buyers had come to expect from Caithness Glass. Changing it could be risky, especially at a time when the company needed to maximise sales. Forms remained simple, with a strong, almost austere handling of line. The angular Dunnet range of tableware is a good example. The decanter was offered with five different sizes or shapes of goblet, ranging from wine to champagne and liqueur. As well as fitting seamlessly into the company's already successful designs, their thick integral stems and feet made them easy to produce in large quantities. Less experience was required to form them than to make thin stems and feet.

Colours also remained strong. ÓBroin's original colours continued to be used, although they were often less muted in tone from this period onwards. The deeper and more vibrant Loch blue was also phased out in favour of Twilight around this time. If anything, vase forms became slightly more curvaceous as the two in the advertisement on this page show, echoing the popular Barrel Vases, and aiming to be as simple and practical as possible. One vase, shown in Heather on p.52, was formed in the same mould as the tall lampbase shown on p.55, but was cut down to make a vase. Undoubtedly, the reason behind this was the fact that the company could re-use an existing mould, rather than commission a new one.

The last design number ÓBroin produced was no.4025, the Morven decanter. Design numbers do not run in consecutive order of the date of their introduction, and a design may have been produced by ÓBroin some time before manufacture began. The catalogue from 1972 reproduced on p.108 shows a number of other vase and tableware forms with later numbers. Numbers before no.4040 are probably the work of Charles Orr, and those after are the work of Colin Terris.

The continuation of ÓBroin's successful designs, augmented by Orr's lookalikes, ensured the company weathered the second half of the 1960s. However, this relative hiatus of innovation was short-lived. The last few years of the 1960s were to prove extremely exciting for the company, as three major developments took place that were to change the direction of Caithness Glass forever.

Oban

Although Dunnet became successful, Charles Orr's greatest contribution to the company was the Oban range, designed from 1968-69, and released shortly after. Oban was a ground-breaking design for the company as it was the first to include a pattern, rather than rely purely on the simplicity of an undecorated, coloured form. Thin, multi-coloured stripes are arranged vertically down a colourless body, around the base, and back up the other side. When viewed, these stripes combine to give an interesting optical effect.

The thin coloured rods, imported from Kügler in Germany, were sandwiched between two layers of coloured glass in a process known as the 'ribbon colour' technique. Paul Ysart and Peter Holmes produced the first trial pieces for the range under Orr's direction.

Shapes remained simple and linear, primarily comprising cylinders which were initially blown into moulds adapted from industrial tubing. Orr also designed four new shapes for the range, a footed bowl with a semi-circular bowl (OG7 & OG17), a bulbous Bottle Vase (OG1 & OG2), a taller Bottle Vase (OG3), and a flattened Bud Vase (OG18). The Bottle vases were used for a number of subsequent ranges over the next few years.

Although they were bought in, rather than being mixed in-house, colours continued the Scottish theme begun by ÓBroin, focusing on the blues, greens, pinks, purples and browns of the Scottish landscape.

Behind this, the range also fulfilled other important aspects. It was easy and quick to produce on a factory production line basis, and only required a single furnace of colourless glass. It was also thought that the patterned design would reduce the number of seconds, increase the yield, and thus the revenue. In February 1970, Design magazine commented that the range was "*simple in its present form, but can be extended as the blowers gain experience.*"

This was an important point, as the new range would not be made at the existing Wick factory, but would instead be made at a new factory in Oban. Just as when Caithness Glass was founded, experienced glassmakers moved to Oban to train new staff employed locally. In this instance, Peter Fuin and David MacGregor were amongst the few who moved from Wick to Oban to oversee the introduction of the range, and train new glassmakers.

The Oban range proved to be successful after it was launched, and it was produced

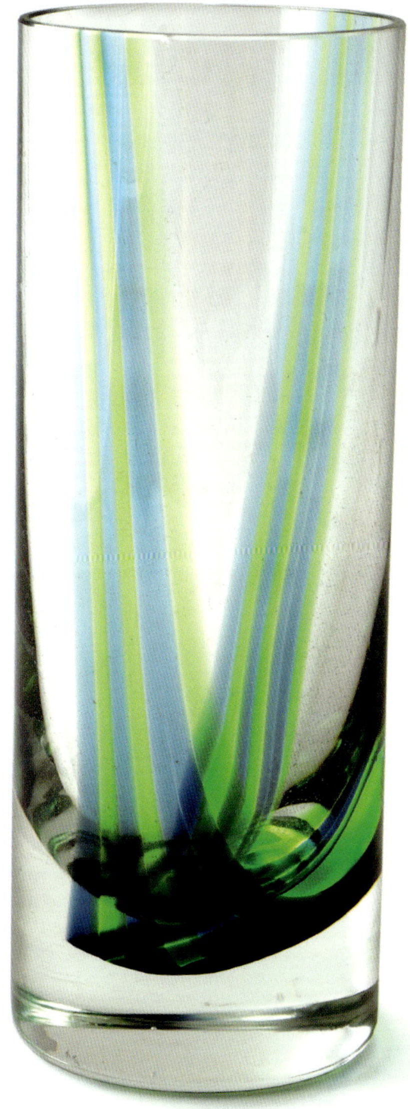

A 1970s Slim Vase, no.OG12, with blue and green stripes, from the Oban range designed by Charles Orr in 1969, 7in (17.5cm) high

in various colourways in large quantities until the mid-1980s. However, most of it had to be produced at Wick, as the Oban factory's newly installed furnace proved troublesome.

Each new batch of glass was melted over a weekend in preparation for a working week. The glassmakers soon discovered that it was too 'seedy' on Monday, meaning production was filled with tiny bubbles, leading to too many second quality pieces. On Tuesday and Wednesday, it was perfect, but by Thursday it began to become too hard to gather effectively. This tiny window of opportunity caused major problems, and production was turned over to paperweights on the problematic days, with the design being selected to suit the state of the glass, and the results it would give. The situation did not improve and, within a few years, Oban produced solely paperweights.

Nevertheless, the new factory was a successful addition from another perspective. Oban was, and remains, a popular tourist destination. A factory shop was opened to serve Scottish and other visitors who travelled there, and became an instant success, returning strong sales until its closure in 1995. Factory shops serving tourists and entertaining visitors would remain a very important income stream for the company.

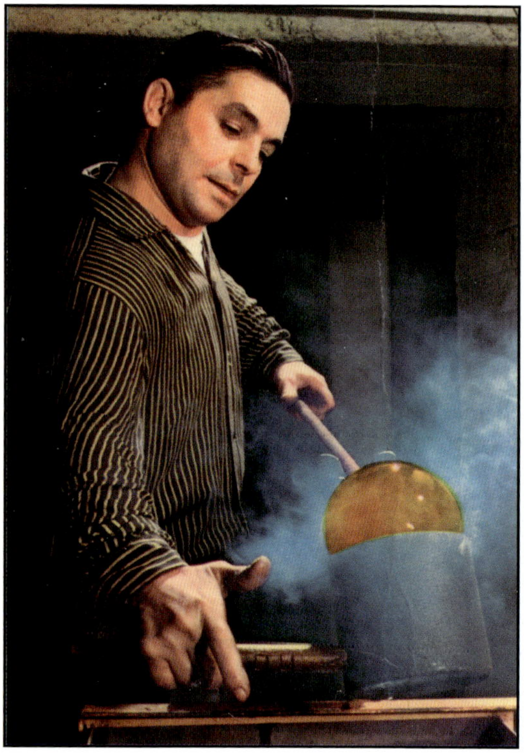

A 1960s promotional postcard showing Peter Fuin moulding a hot gather of glass.

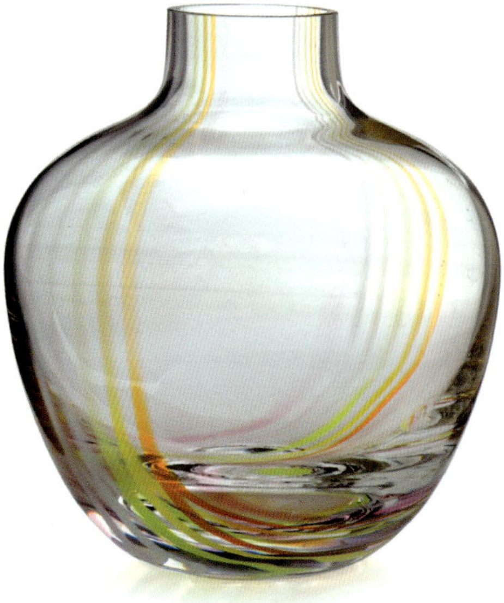

An Oban Medium Bottle Vase, no.OG2, from the 'Rainbow' range, produced from c1983-85, 5in (12.5cm) high.

Despite the innovation of Oban's striped design, Caithness Glass still remained close to the original design aesthetic set down by its co-founder in 1961. They did not produce textured glass, as their major competitor Whitefriars and new competitor Dartington Glass, were doing to great commercial success in the late 1960s and early 1970s. Even though it was an increasingly fashionable trend, led again by the Scandinavians, the company's management felt that they did not want to 'follow the pack'. Instead, they preferred to remain different and true to the look they had built up over the past decade. Three other activities were also developing that offered much more potential than that offered by the new fad of textured glass.

Caithness Jewellery

As part of the conditions of his employment, Paul Ysart was allowed to use a furnace at Wick at weekends in return for a modest fee. He used this time to experiment, and produce paperweights which he could sell privately. He also demonstrated skills and techniques to selected apprentices and glassmakers such as Peter Holmes. Once the techniques had been passed on and the demonstration was over, Ysart would smash the finished vase or bowl fearing that, if the management saw and liked it, they might ask him to put the design into production. It would turn out that this fear was justified. It was through Ysart's paperweights that the range of Caithness jewellery was developed.

In late 1969, Ysart produced a small number of brooches, pins and similar jewellery set with single tiny glass domes that resembled miniature millefiori paperweights. He gave these to selected members of staff as Christmas presents. George Mackie saw one of these pieces and immediately decided that the idea should be expanded into a new range. Ysart was tasked to produce the millefiori canes, and a team of twelve newly recruited women were employed to apply the miniature domes to sterling silver pendants, brooches, bracelets, rings, tie-pins, cufflinks, and earrings. The silver mounts, some of which were inspired by Celtic forms and motifs, were designed by a 24 year old former art student and silversmith called 'Sandy' Shand Keiss.

The range was launched with great fanfare in December 1970, and taken to the important Blackpool Gift Fair and the US the following year. Prices ranged from £3 upwards, with a ring costing from

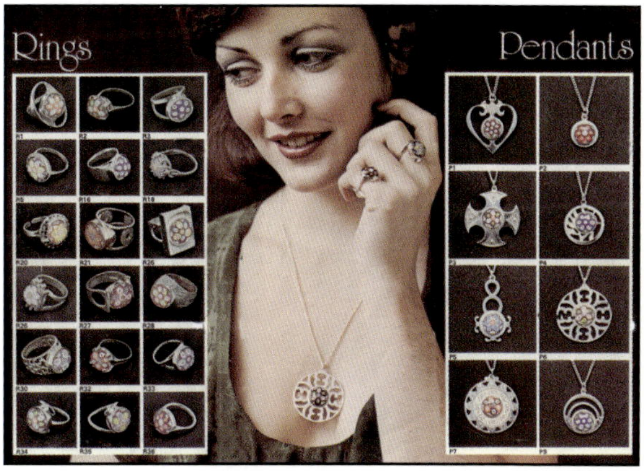

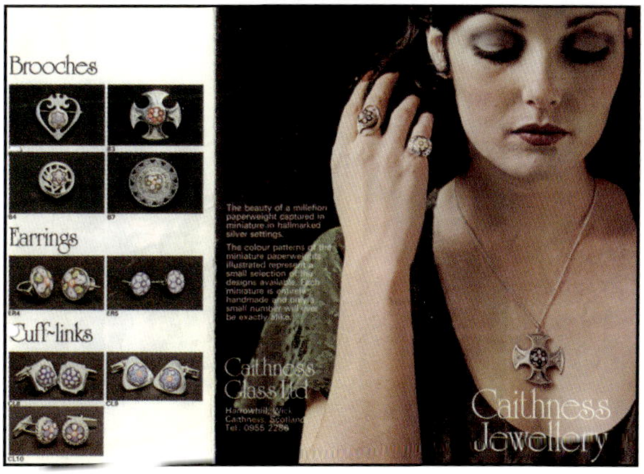

Two early 1970s catalogue pages of Caithness jewellery, designed by Paul Ysart and Sandy Shand Keiss.

£10–20, depending on the design. Caithness jewellery proved to be successful, and was produced into the 1980s.

Caithness Paperweights

Successful as the Oban range and the new jewellery range were, neither grew to be as popular or as commercially successful as the paperweights that emerged at around the same time.

Although P aul Ysart had made numerous paperweights over the years he worked for Caithness Glass, they were never developed into a production range, despite many discussions.

Ysart's influence was critical to their final introduction, and his innate skills and expertise influenced not only his colleague Peter Holmes, but also a new employee, the engraver Colin Terris. The story of the development of the company's world famous paperweights began with the legendary Planets series of 1969, which was devised by Colin Terris and Peter Holmes. This story has been detailed elsewhere and is beyond the scope of this publication, which focuses on art glass.

In 1970, a year after the Planets series was released, Ysart left Caithness Glass to found his own company nearby that focused on the production of paperweights. He concentrated on this until his retirement in 1979. He died in 1991.

The wealth of skills he left behind, combined with the talent of designers like Terris and designer glassmakers like Holmes, saw the department expand exponentially. By 1979, the national press was reporting that around half of the company's £2million turnover was derived from paperweights. As the company moved towards the millennium, this share would only increase.

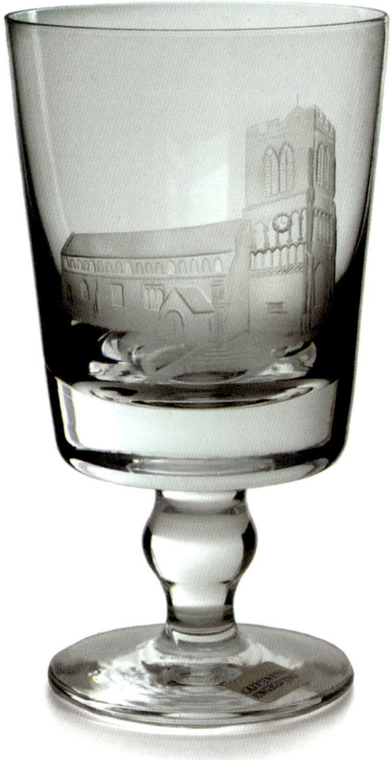

A limited edition goblet cut and sandblasted with a church design by Christine Beaton in 1974, from a series, the base inscribed 'CBeaton CG 74 5/25', 6.25in (16cm) high.

Caithness Engraving

Although paperweights became the most important product for the future of Caithness Glass, they were closely followed in terms of importance by engraved ranges. Over the next few decades, this section of the business would grow in a similarly rapid manner, bringing the company to the attention of buyers and collectors worldwide. Not only that, but it marked the company out from its competitors, making it effectively a market leader.

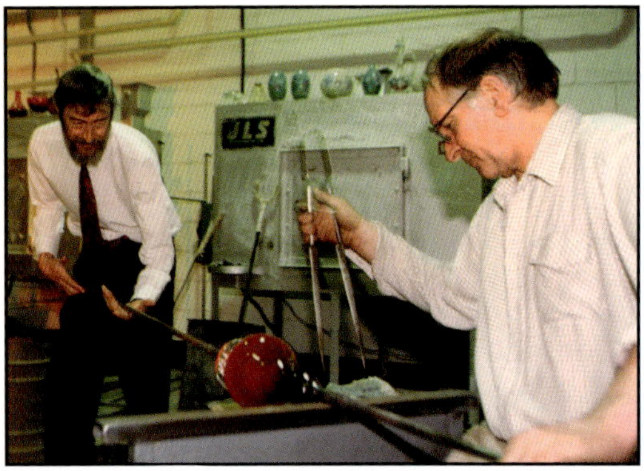

Colin Terris (left) and Franco Toffolo making glass during the late 1990s.

The engraving department was founded in 1968, when George Mackie invited Edinburgh of Art engraving graduate Colin Terris to join Caithness Glass. He immediately set about building a team of talented engravers including Anne Robertson, Denis Mann, and David Gulland. More information on these engravers, and their work can be found in the relevant section of this publication.

As well as using copper wheel and diamond point engraving techniques, they developed sandblasting techniques. This enabled 'engraved' glass to be produced rapidly, and more cost-effectively. In fact, the majority of 'engraved' Caithness Glass produced from the 1970s-2000s was actually sandblasted.

From a commercial perspective, engraved or sandblasted designs were extremely lucrative for the company. An engraved motif added perceived value to a piece, and they perfectly suited the giftware market, which became the major focus of the company from the 1970s onwards. Commemorative designs were created for weddings, anniversaries, or birthdays, or around popular themes, such as the royal family or the exploration of space. The company had enjoyed close links with the royal family after H.M. The Queen Mother had visited the factory in 1963. From then she displayed and used Caithness glass in the Castle of Mey, her nearby private home, and she granted the company a Royal Warrant in 1968.

Releasing royal commemoratives in more expensive limited editions also became popular. The costs of running a glass company were considerable, and the company had to take advantage of the public appetite for such special pieces. The Celebration range, which contained most of the anniversary–related designs, was affordable for many people. As such, it sold extremely well, as demonstrated by the large quantity available in the market today.

Entire new ranges could also be developed using existing shapes, with many of ÓBroin's shapes being perfectly suited to engraved designs.

The first dedicated engraving catalogue, released around 1970, shows tableware with themed designs including country pursuits, animals and nature, sports, ships, aviation, and historic buildings. These themes were carefully chosen to appeal to the company's target market of buyers. The designers and management decided that more avant garde or modern designs and themes would not sell.

To a lesser degree, sandblasted or engraved motifs could also be used to cover up or remove small numbers of flaws, such as bubbles or creases. This allowed a small percentage of what would otherwise be 'seconds' to be decorated and sold at full price.

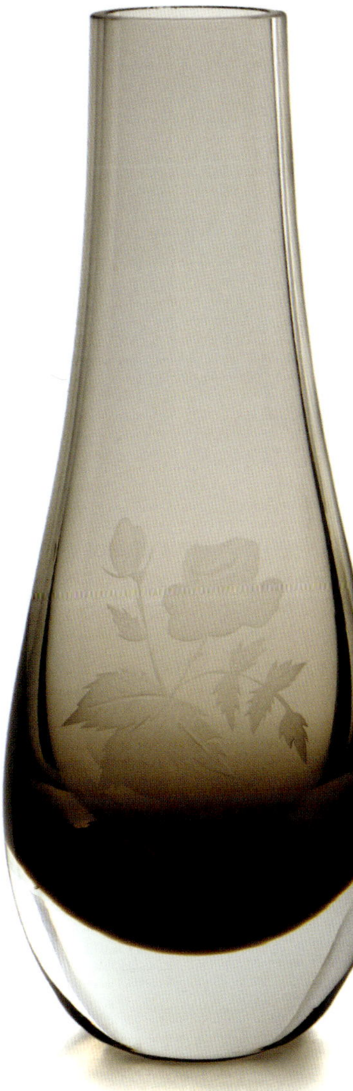

A Bud Vase, No.4033, in Peat, designed by Charles Orr, sandblasted with a rose, the base inscribed SR for an as yet unidentified engraver, 7.5in (19cm) high.

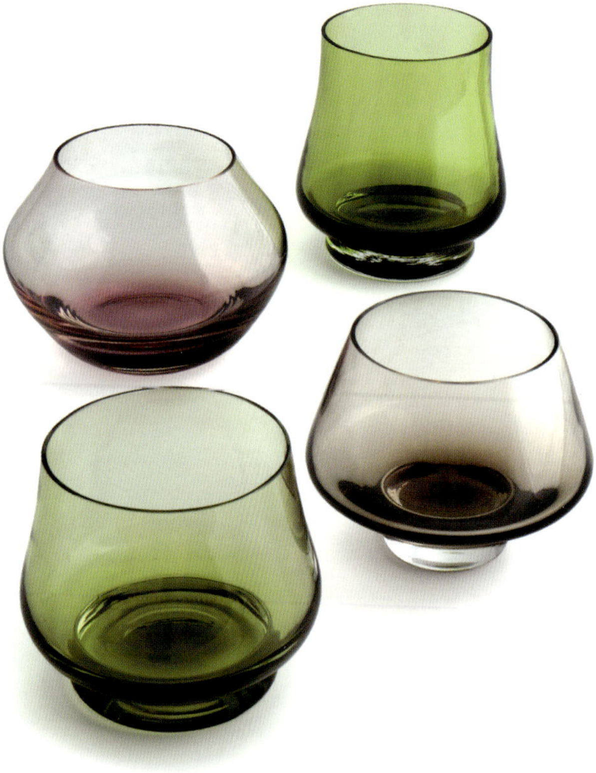

Four bowls introduced in the 1970s, and available in Moss, Heather, Peat, Twilight, Amethyst, and colourless. The Moss bowl at the top, no.4036, was probably designed by Colin Terris, as was the Moss bowl below it. The Peat bowl, no.4035, was designed by Denis Mann and was a smaller version of his famous Mastermind trophy, designed in 1972. All were introduced in 1977.

The department expanded greatly during the late 1970s, with over twenty people producing catalogue designs or corporate commissions. Some of the most successful designs, such as 'Romeo & Juliet' and 'Autumn Leaves' (see pp.102–103), were sold for over three decades. As production processes changed and improved, designs were produced using stamps, and then screen-printed transfers.

As a result of this success, many of the new shapes released from the early 1970s onwards were designed with engraving in mind. Bodies had large surface areas, and near cylindrical vases and (presentation) bowls became very popular forms. Good examples include the CT120 'Chalice' shown on p.104, and the CT4096 tapered vase shown on p.101. Goblets were also popular, and were often released in limited editions. Later, some colourless goblet forms were bought in from Sweden and British companies such as Nazeing. In terms of factory production, an increasingly large percentage of plain coloured pieces were produced for the engraving department. The skill set, team of experienced engravers, and facilities built up from the 1970s onwards would prove invaluable as designs increased in complexity by necessity during the 1990s and 2000s. Engravers-turned-designers, such as Helen MacDonald, were able to design and produce important ranges that incorporated both hot and cold-worked techniques. Some of these were made in small limited editions, or as unique pieces, often for export to countries such as the US or Japan.

The Rise of Colin Terris

By 1970, Caithness Glass was in financial trouble once again. Despite Robin Sinclair writing to ÓBroin to say that the company had made a small profit in 1970, and sales looked promising, it needed serious reorganisation and refunding. The Highlands & Islands Development Fund, by then a major backer, demanded action, as did George Mackie.

In 1971, Alistair Mair was brought in as Managing Director from Rolls Royce, where he had been a Product Centre Manager. His proven organisational skills and business acumen were perfect for the company. He worked closely with Mackie, who raised further funding together with Hugo Brunner and Bertram Tawse. Mair remained with the company until 1998, acting as Chairman for a period of time. He oversaw major expansion, the opening of new factories, a combined marketing and sales effort, and he steered the company through various changes of ownership from the 1980s onwards.

If Mair provided the organisational and business stability, it was the engraver Colin Terris who provided the critical design direction from the early 1970s onwards. By the time the 1972 catalogue had been released, Terris had taken control of all design issues, thus uniting paperweights, engraving, table and decorative wares under one guiding light.

But Terris' role was greater than just providing leadership in design. As the 1970s progressed, he also became the public face of the company. This role was made clear at events and in the company's magazine, 'Reflections', published from the 1990s onwards.

His first designs mainly comprised tableware, such as the water set of a jug and glasses (no.4040) shown in the 1972 catalogue. This was followed with a series of decanters (see p.40) with identical hollow stoppers, the most notable and successful of which was Canisbay (right), which was accompanied by a number of different sizes of goblet.

Most of Terris' 1970s designs continued ÓBroin's proven aesthetic in terms of colour and form, even if shapes were generally more rounded and curving (see pp.110-111).

As well as designing a great many paperweights, Terris also produced many of the engraved and sandblasted designs that the company was to use for the next three decades. However, it is important to note that although many shape, design and pattern numbers were given 'CT' prefixes, not all of them were by Terris.

Interestingly, ÓBroin's name was omitted from the landmark 1972 catalogue, as was Orr's. Around a year after Alistair Mair joined the company, Charles Orr left to found and run a small studio pottery nearby in Wick.

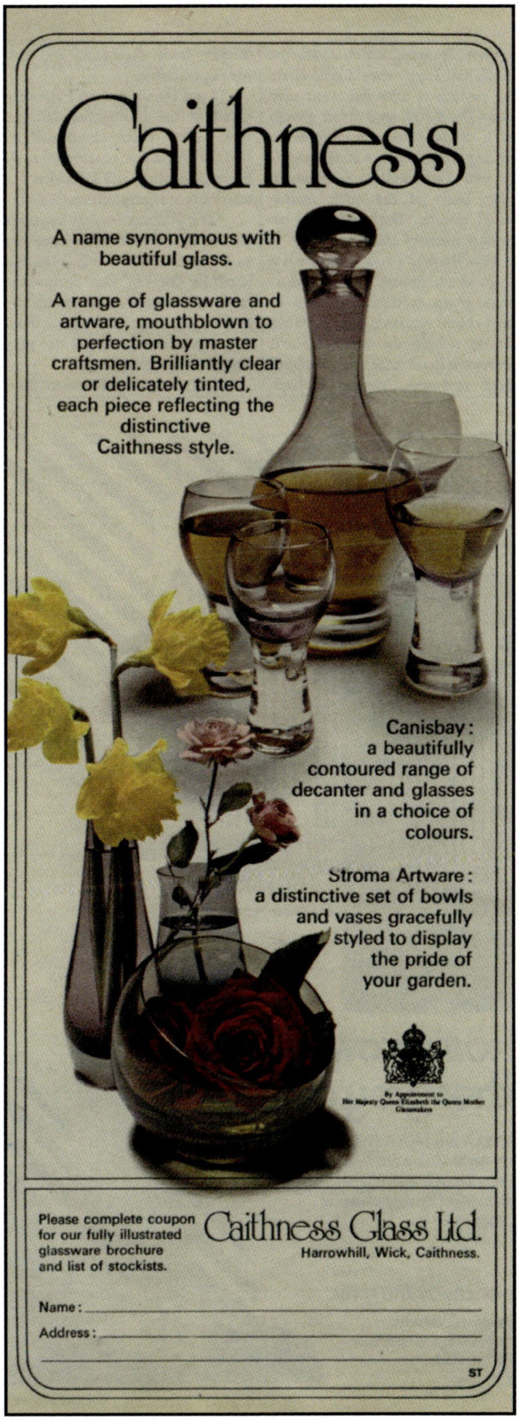

A mid-late 1970s magazine advertisement for the Canisbay range and a Rose Bowl, designed by Colin Terris.

Expansion

By 1976, the reorganisation of the company and the new departments were working. Demand exceeded output, with the Wick factory producing hollow ware and engraved ranges, and Oban producing paperweights. The Board decided to open a third, custom-built factory at Inveralmond in Perth in 1979. Perth was chosen as it was a historic city at the 'centre' of Scotland that attracted many tourists. It was also reputedly a 'city of 90s', being 90 minutes away from 90% of the population of Scotland in all directions. Like the factory and shop at Oban, the Perth factory would act as a major visitor attraction and sales venue.

Built by the Scottish Development Agency, at a cost of £1m, the new factory was 25,000 square feet in size. With a total staff of 170, production volumes across the three factories ballooned, and the reject ratio was reduced to only 7%. By 1980, the enlarged company controlled 70% of the paperweight market, and a healthy proportion of the decorative glass market. Only 10% of the company's output was exported, primarily to the US, but it was felt that this could be extended.

In 1980 Whitefriars, one of the company's major British competitors, closed. The following year, Caithness Glass acquired the name, rights and moulds. The initial idea was to open a small factory under that historic and well known name in, or close to, the City of London. It was felt that not only would glassblowing be a superb, new visitor attraction for the millions of tourists who visited each year, but sales through the factory shop could also prove to be very lucrative.

However, costs proved to be too great, and the idea was abandoned. Some tableware and other moulds were used at Wick and, later, at the King's Lynn factory, but the company never re-released the popular textured designs that Whitefriars had been known for.

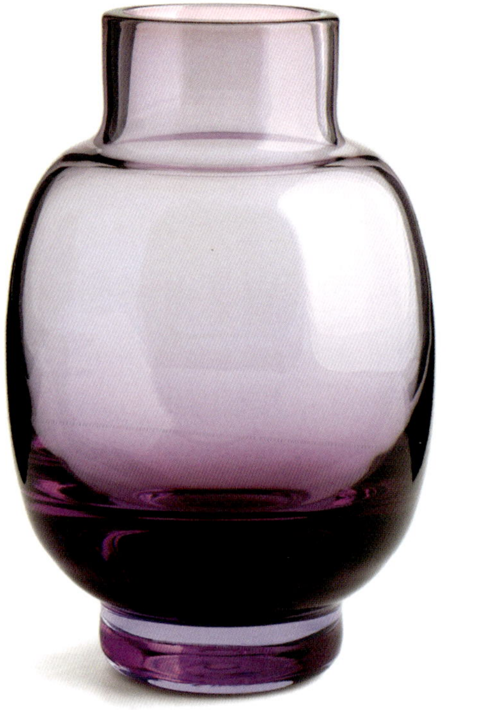

A 1980s Lantern Vase, no.4103, in Amethyst, from the Glenisla range designed by Colin Terris c1982, 6.5in (16.5cm) high. This shape was also used in the Cadenza and Art Nouveau ranges.

The 1980s Onwards

Many designs produced during the decades that followed were typical of the tried and trusted Caithness look. Ranges such as Glenisla (see p.53), Shelligoe (see p.113), Braemore (see p.54), and the vertically ribbed Strathspey added to the continued success of the Stroma range, which still included many of ÓBroin's original designs. Many of the decanters and tableware ranges in Stroma were slowly discontinued from the late 1980s onwards, with the range itself fading away during the 1990s. Dining had become considerably less formal during the 1980s, and displaying the label on a bottle of wine or a spirit became almost as important as the contents, meaning that the use of decanters declined rapidly.

Apart from paperweights, the company's decorative ranges became almost exclusively giftware and souvenirs.
During this period a new aesthetic began to creep in as paperweights began to dominate production. Although the striped design introduced with Oban would still form a major part of production, pattern and decoration moved on and became more complex. Italian glassmaker Franco Toffolo had also joined in 1981, and brought a wealth of experience and new hot-working techniques to the increasingly experienced team. The growth of the important studio glass movement from the late 1960s onwards also led to changes in design.

Refreshed Stripes

By the early 1980s, the Oban range was over a decade old and sales were waning. The new 'Rainbow' colourway was not enough to refresh the range, although it was felt that there was still mileage within the market for striped designs.
In 1985, the design was completely refreshed by applying it to bodies in 'traditional' Caithness Glass colours. The format of the stripes was also modified, and new shapes were introduced. The resulting Spinningdale range (see p.61) revived the market, and was initially successful, but sales soon began to fall against the increasingly popular mottled Rondo range (see p.71).
By the late 1980s, Oban and Spinningdale had made striped designs a recognisable hallmark of Caithness Glass. A further refreshing of the technique occurred in March 1987, when the company expanded by acquiring the King's Lynn Crystal factory in Norfolk, which it ran as 'Caithness Crystal' until 1992. The first batch was melted in May, and the rest of the year was spent developing "*a range of cut crystal, a plain and spiral crystal range and a contemporary coloured crystal range.*" according to the Collectors Newsletter in March 1988.
Although the cut crystal tableware, vases and bowls were disappointingly staid and traditional in style (see p.98), Colin Terris and Alastair MacIntosh did react to fashion with the Flamenco range (see p.63). Existing and newly created moulds had a strong optical spiral effect, with colour being added using Orr's and Ysart's original 'ribbon colour' technique. Such optically moulded designs had proven to be commercially successful for competitor Dartington Glass under designer Frank Thrower, and Caithness Glass undoubtedly hoped to acquire a certain part of that market. Their hopes were justified, and Flamenco went on to become a bestseller, alongside the Rondo range.
Stripes were also incorporated into ranges of tableware, using fashionable period colours such as pink, black and white (see p.62). These too became successful, the rounded Panache in particular. After 1992, production of the most successful ranges was transferred to Wick.

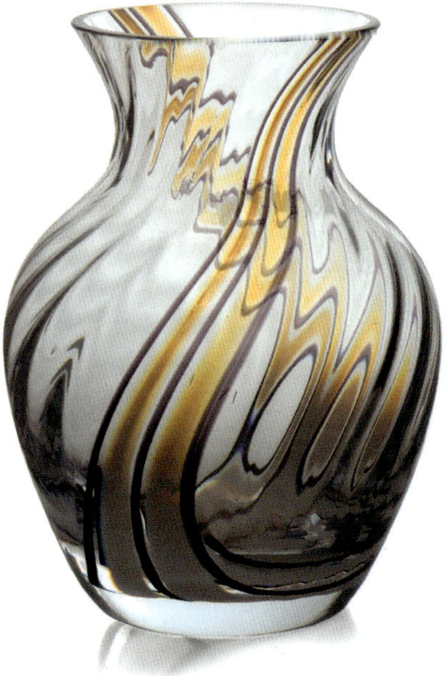

A 1990s-2000s baluster vase from the Flamenco range, designed by Colin Terris from 1987, 5.75in (15cm) high.

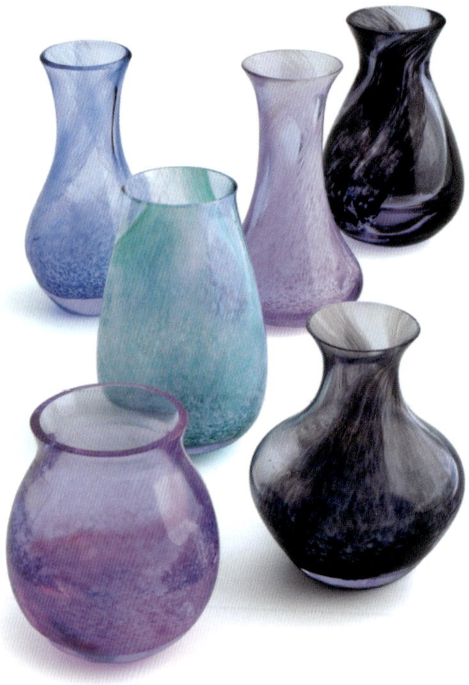

A group of 1980s-2000s mottled vases from the Rondo range, introduced in 1984, tallest 5.5in (14.5cm) high

Combined Techniques

As skills in hot-worked designs grew alongside the growth in the importance of sandblasted designs, it is not surprising that some ranges combined the two techniques. Two early examples include the Floral and Seascapes ranges, both designed by engraver Denis Mann (see p.96) in the early 1980s. During the 1990s, the two techniques were combined a number of times, including for the Waterlily bowls from the Prestige range, and for a range of commemorative bowls produced for the Bank of Scotland (see p.82) in 1995. However, the best and most successful example was the Images range (see p.123). Released in 1994, the range was devised by Alastair MacIntosh and produced at Wick. It comprised simple forms, such as ÓBroin's original Barrel Vase, blown in colourless glass and decorated with a broad, spiralling applied trail. A colourless gather was made first, to eventually form the body. A separate gather was then formed, elongated, and then half of it was rolled over white and coloured chips of different sizes and densities to give a multicoloured mottled effect once they had been melted in the furnace. That was then applied to the colourless gather, which was finally blown into a mould.

The swirl formed the perfect backdrop to sandblasted designs that included animals such as birds, stags and dolphins, and flowers and plants. The Images range proved to be immensely successful almost immediately, and the range of sandblasted designs grew enormously.

The range was also highly popular in North America and Canada, which had become the company's most important export markets. Distributor, retailer and

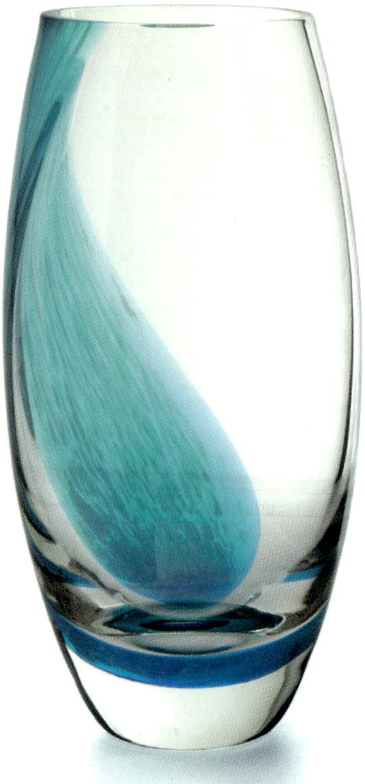

A 1990s–2000s un-decorated Barrel Vase, typically sandblasted with a design as part of the Images range, 8in (20.5cm) high

manufacturer Lenox was a major client, producing its own exclusive sandblasted designs for manufacture in Scotland. Once imported, they would be professionally photographed, aggressively marketed, and sold in large quantities.

Increased Complexity

Successful as these ranges were, the most important change that began during the 1980s, and blossomed during the 1990s and early 2000s, was the development of increasingly complex combinations of techniques and designs. From the 1960s until the early 1980s, Caithness Glass had largely relied on form and colour, with coloured stripes or sandblasted and engraved motifs being the only additional embellishments. By the mid-1980s, this changed dramatically.

Two key developments lay behind this. As the paperweight division grew in importance and success, it seemed logical for the complexities of their designs to be translated into blown giftwares. This was possible as glassmakers had become considerably more experienced. The rise of the studio glass movement from the 1970s also led to a demand for greater visual interest than the pure simplicity of Scandinavian designs. The same was true of tastes in interior design during the 1980s. More decorative designs with bold patterns sold better, particularly those with floral inspired patterns.

The earliest and most important of these innovative complex ranges was Colin Terris' landmark Cadenza design, released in 1986 (see p.74). Cadenza, with its many layers, melted in chips and rods, and applied and pulled heart shapes, was effectively a 'blown out' paperweight. Even the Caithness Collectors Newsletter drew attention to this inspiration by asking in April 1986, "*What happens if you take a paperweight with surface decoration, give it a further coating of clear glass, and blow it?*" However, as the production rate averaged around two pieces per hour, making it expensive to make and thus buy, Cadenza was only produced for a few years. By contrast, the mottled Rondo range (see p.71 & p.117) introduced in 1984 was a great success, and proved to have enormous longevity. Quick and efficient to produce, and inexpensive to buy as a gift or souvenir, the range had wide appeal and began an entire new look for the company, becoming a bestseller. As such, mottled ranges like Rondo would be produced into the 2000s.

Other more complexly decorated ranges that followed Cadenza's lead during the 1980s included Adagio (see p.64), and Springtime (see p.115). Later, Tranquillity (see p.81) and Oriental Lily (see p.80) were

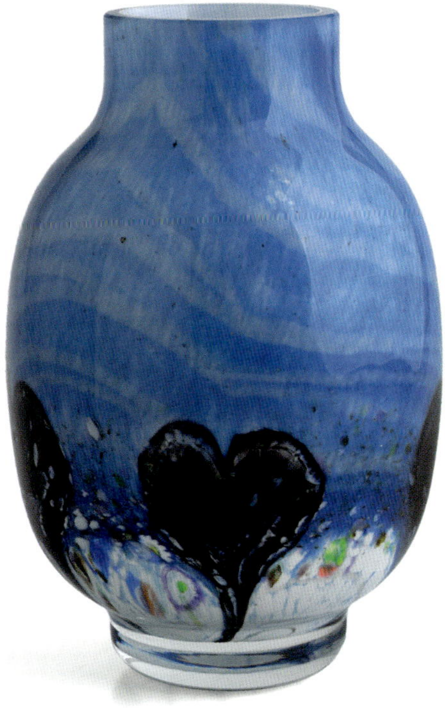

A Lantern Vase, no.4402, in Blue, from the Cadenza range designed by Colin Terris in 1986, 6in (15cm) high. Note that the shape is identical to the Glenisla vase on the previous page, showing how shapes (and moulds) were re-used.

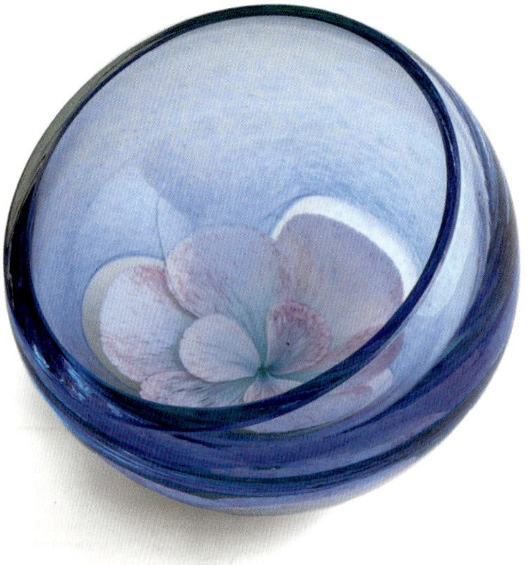

A late 1990s Large Rose Bowl, no.5042, in Blue, from the Tranquillity range designed by Jimmy Manson, Jeneo Lewis and Colin Terris in 1995, using a shape designed by Terris in the 1970s, 4.75in (12cm) diam.

the most successful ranges incorporating techniques based on paperweights. The delicate floral theme and resonant colours caught the imaginations of buyers, despite the comparatively expensive price tags.

The 1990s also saw the traditional and historic technique of casing being used in a different manner to create opaque designs that were more akin to ceramics than glass. An opaque white layer was used under coloured glass applied to give interesting surface effects.

The most successful example of this was Ebony, with its strong Art Nouveau styling (see p.75 & p.125). Less successful, but perhaps more influential was Xanadu (see p.78), which led to a small group of trial and production ranges, such as Salomé (see p.79). This theme was continued by Gordon Hendry in the early 2000s with Touchstone (see p.84).

These designs, and others, were produced by a design team that expanded greatly in number and profile during the 1990s. Under Colin Terris' guidance and leadership, new designers were employed, or found from within the company's talented staff. By the early 2000s, names such as Helen MacDonald, Gordon Hendry, Alastair MacIntosh, Sarah Cable and Sarah Peterson produced designs for engraved, paperweight and hollow ware ranges. As the cult of the designer and personality infiltrated popular culture more deeply, they would be profiled in catalogues, attend events and be promoted as 'names'. This was quite a change from previous decades, where only ÓBroin or Terris were named, but rarely appeared in marketing literature. Undoubtedly, the company was also aware that successors to the ageing Terris would need to be found.

From the late 1990s into the early 2000s, regular design meetings were held where designers' ideas and thoughts were discussed, and new ranges devised. These were collaborative efforts, with each team member contributing to shapes, colours, pricing, and the technical aspects of the production process. Talented glassmakers such as Jimmy Manson would work with a designer to make trials for discussion,

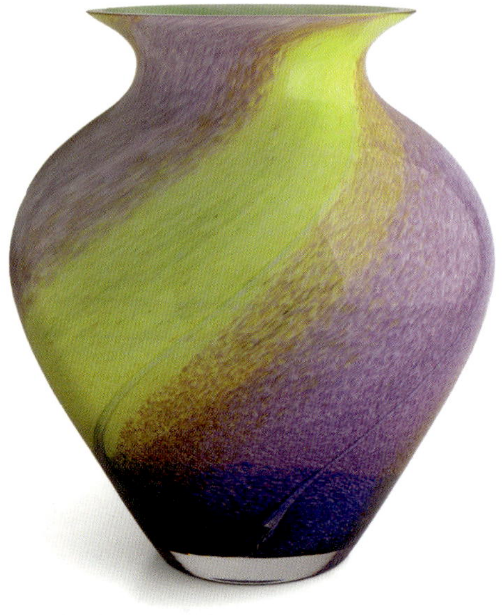

A late 1990s Large Greek Vase, no.7041, in Purple Sunset, from the Caribbean range designed by glassmaker Jimmy Manson and Colin Terris, 9.75in (25cm) high

or submit samples of their own design. Constant revision of past successes and failures also meant that some ranges or well-practised techniques were re-used. This led to the release of a number of ranges that looked similar to other designs. Trends in interiors and fashion also began to play a larger role in the attempt to grow sales and profile. Designers would build 'mood boards' with photographs cut from magazines or newspapers that showed current or developing trends. Themes would be drawn out, and a range based on them would be devised. The best example of this was Helen MacDonald's Alchemy range (see p.77). Many of these were short-lived as fashions began to change increasingly rapidly. There was also a need for at least one new product range for the company to promote annually.

Sometimes ranges were introduced simply to plug a perceived gap in the market, or in the company's offerings, in terms of price level or function. Caribbean was produced in the late 1990s in answer to a request from the marketing and sales department who wanted a range that was large, affordable, practical, and colourful. Jimmy Manson produced the design, and Rob Arrowsmith (a key manager at Royal Doulton, who then owned the company) selected the shape from moulds used at King's Lynn. The range was then discussed and approved by the team.

From the early 1990s until around 2004, the profile of design team members and key glassmakers was pushed further with the release of complex, high end limited edition or limited production ranges. Peaking around 2000, these were grouped in collections under banners such as 'Prestige', 'Studio' and 'Signature'. This had begun in 1990 with the Cameo Plate range (see p.116) designed by Helen MacDonald. Designs such as Poppies (see p.83) by Colin Terris, Peter And The Wolf (see p.85) by Gordon Hendry, Big Cats by Irene Farquhar, Cold Fusion (see p.86) by Alastair MacIntosh, and Tsarina (see p.122) by Franco Toffolo, typically combined numerous techniques and represented a highpoint for the company. Prices ranged from around £150 to £2,000. Sometimes paperweight designs were used again for limited edition hollow ware ranges, as with MacDonald's One Starry Night (see p.69).

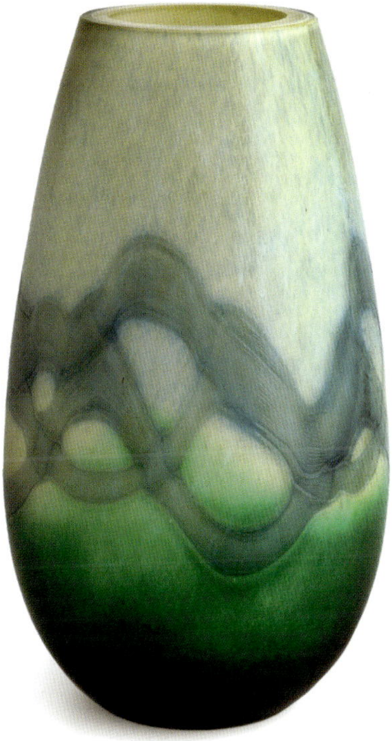

An ovoid vase, probably from a trial range designed in the late 1990s after Xanadu, 7.25in (18.5cm) high. This was probably only made in limited quantities, and sold in factory shops.

Changing Times

Design innovations, a reflection of public tastes, and a strong organisational management ensured that the company survived the difficulties of the recessions of both the early 1980s & 90s. In fact, the company thrived enough between them to change ownership a number of times.

In 1984, the company was bought out by its management with Royal Brierley as a partner. In 1991, it was acquired by Drambuie, before being bought out by the management again after the recession hit. In 1996, the company approached Royal Doulton over a distribution partnership, which led to Doulton adding the company to its expanding portfolio of brands at a cost of £5.5million. However, as inexpensive Chinese and Central European imports flooded the market, and the gift-buying public turned to subjects other than glass, sales tumbled. Problems were exacerbated when the business and requirements from later owners changed during the early 2000s. In 2003, the company made a loss of £1m on sales of £8m, leading to it being sold by the receivers to Edinburgh Crystal in April 2004. In late 2004, the Wick factory closed, followed by the Perth factory in late 2007. During this period, some new ranges were bought-in from factories in China and Poland in an attempt to reduce costs. Certain standard production ranges, such as Ebony (see p.75), were also out-sourced to Poland. Other changes also occurred, ending with the company being bought from the receivers in 2006 by Dartington Crystal, its current owners. In 2008, the company was relocated to a small factory in Crieff, with Sarah Peterson as the last remaining key designer, and products being focused on paperweights.

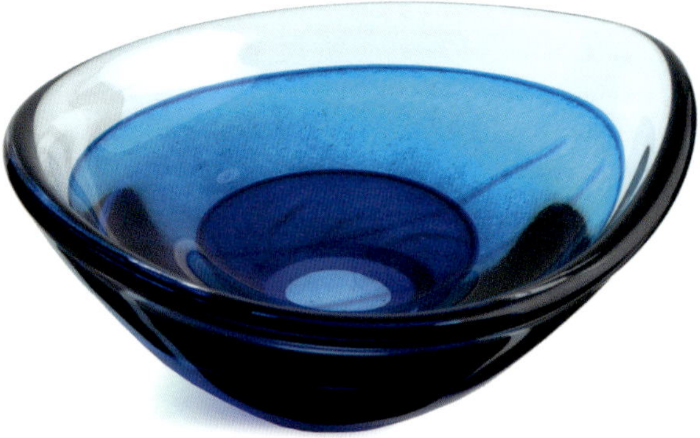

A mid-late 2000s Rainbow cased bowl, marked 'Caithness Scotland Rainbow', designed by Sarah Peterson, 8.5in (21.5cm) widest

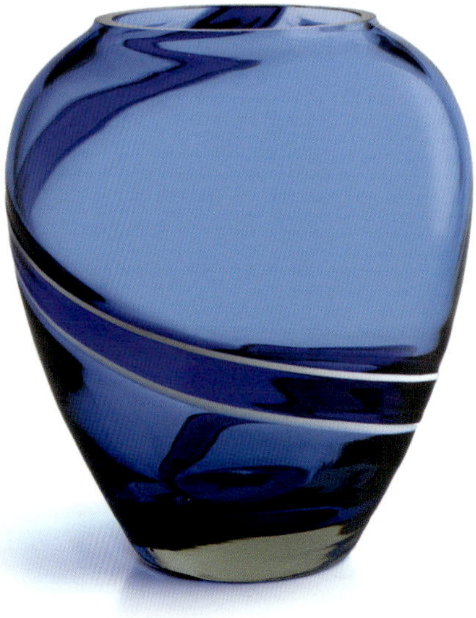

A Chinese blue ovoid vase with an applied cobalt blue and white stripe, the base with CAITHNESS round acid stamp, 8,25in (21cm) high. This was part of a number of ranges made in China or Poland and sold exclusively in the UK under the Caithness brand during the early 2000s.

Into the Future

For over four decades Domhnall ÓBroin's and Robin Sinclair's original aims were fulfilled. Despite its current smaller state, it is heartening that this world class glass company from Scotland, with innovation, creativity and quality at its soul, still survives. So many of its competitors have not. The words written by Robin Sinclair's son, John Thurso, for Domhnall ÓBroin's obituary sum up ÓBroin, but could also be used to describe the company, its employees and its products across those decades. Thurso said that ÓBroin was "*...so passionate about what he was doing. The company was always precarious financially, but his designs were innovative, modern, yet classical. They have stood the test of time and helped to create substantial quality employment. He made a great impression on the country, and left an enduring legacy.*"

Clear Colour

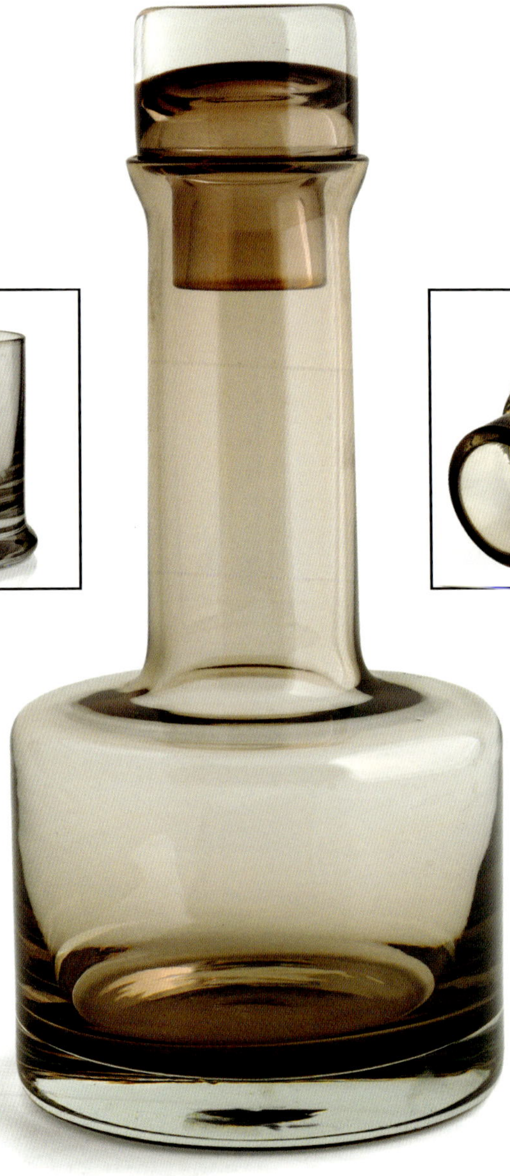

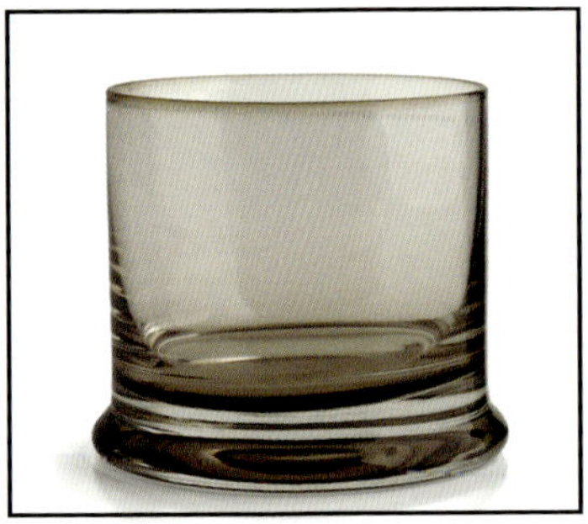

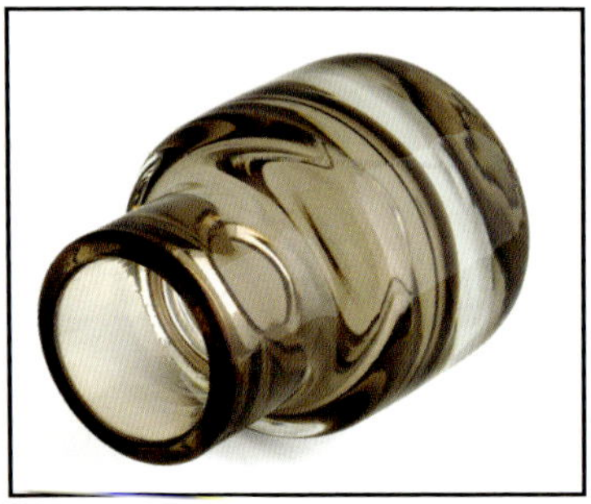

A 1960s-80s Morven decanter, no.4025, in Peat, designed by Domhnall ÓBroin c1964, 10in (25cm) high. The angular form is typical of ÓBroin. The cased stopper is hollow, and is carefully sized to rest perfectly in the curved rim. It was originally sold with slightly tapered cased tumblers no.4025. By c1985, it was also offered with the no.4042 tumbler shown above. The most common colours are Peat or colourless, but it was also made in Soot. No examples are known in Moss, Loch, or Heather, as colours were chosen to ensure the contents (whisky) looked appealing. Despite the angular shoulders meaning that it had to be almost turned over to drain the contents, Morven was very successful and was sold until c1988.

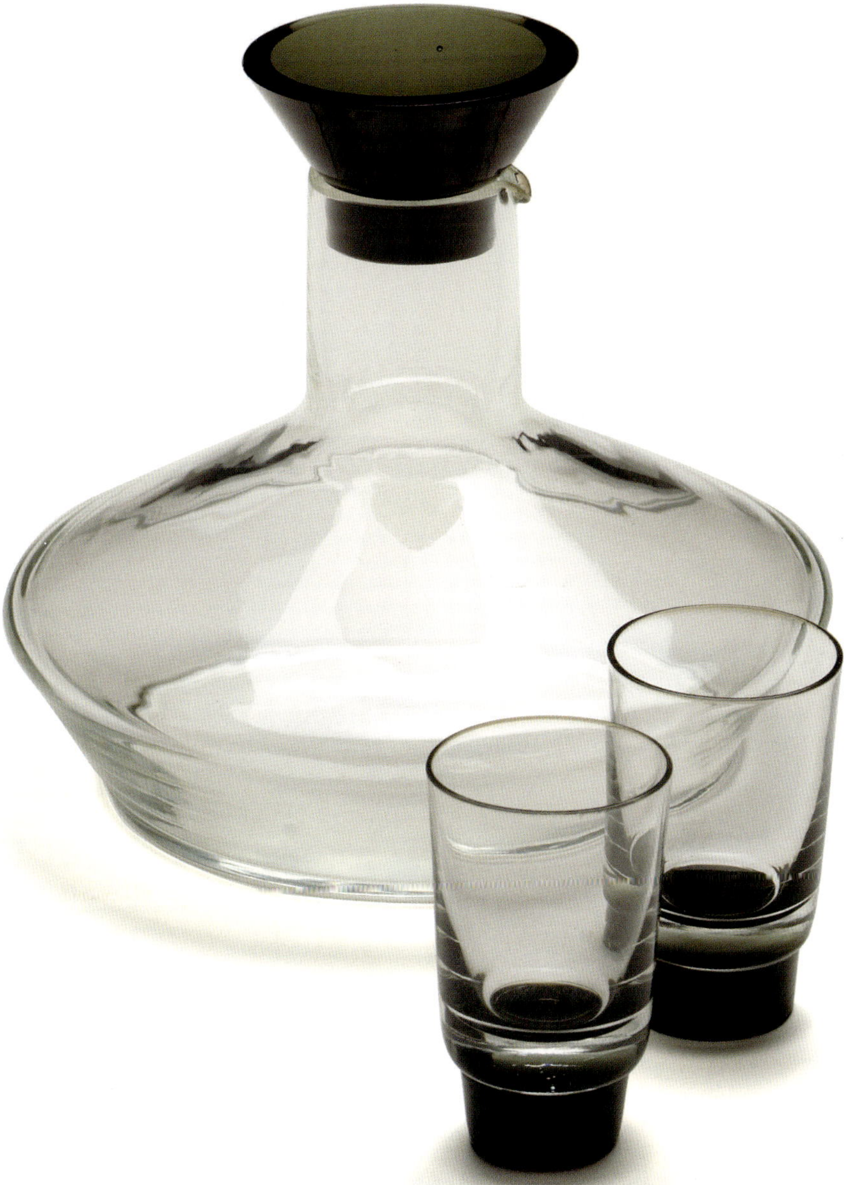

A 1960s Scaraben ships' decanter and two tumblers, with a Soot stopper and feet, designed by Domhnall ÓBroin c1962, decanter 5.75in (14cm) high, glasses 3in (7.5cm) high. Twelve different shapes and sizes of glasses were produced to match this modern, Art Deco styled decanter. Due to the small pouring lip, spirits cannot be stored in Scaraben. Examples engraved by ÓBroin were presented to the Duke of Edinburgh and Chancellor Ludwig Erhard of Germany in 1965. In 1963, the decanter was priced at £2 2s, and a 10oz tumbler was 15s. By comparison, a Whitefriars M121 decanter was priced at £3 3s at the same time. Expensive and requiring skill to produce, Scaraben was discontinued in the mid–1960s, and is very rare today.

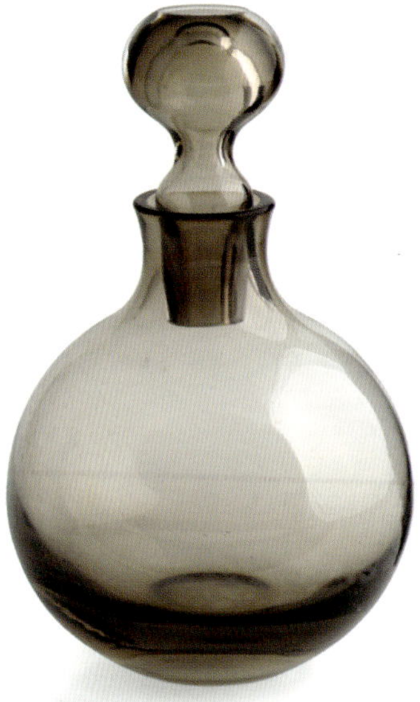

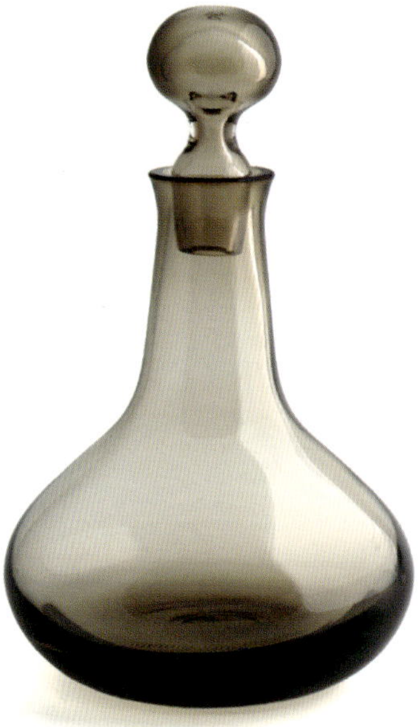

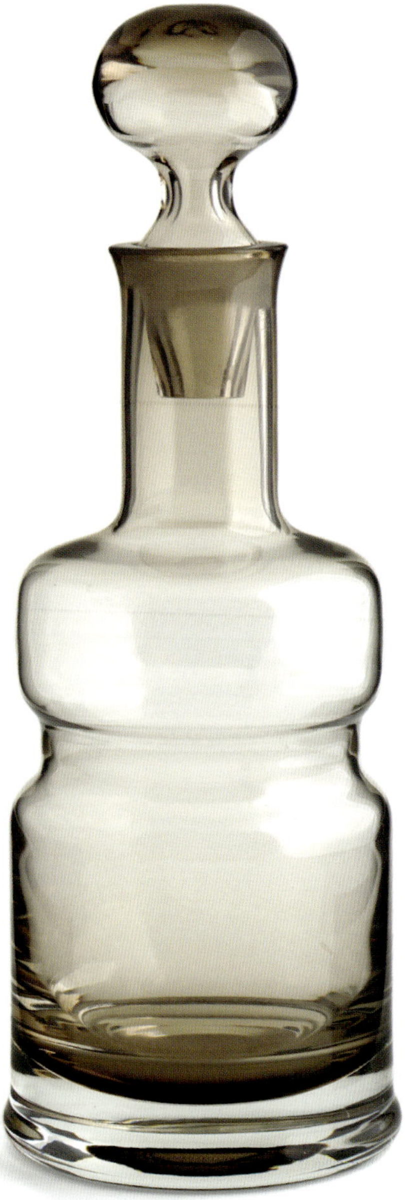

Top left: A no.4080 spherical decanter in Peat, designed by Colin Terris, 8in (20.5cm) high. Introduced in 1977 in Peat only, the hollow stopper has a polished flat top. Bottom left: A 1970s-80s Lybster decanter, no.4042, in Peat, designed by Colin Terris in 1972, 9.5in (24cm) high. Although shape no.4042 is shown in the 1972 catalogue with two rings on the neck, a catalogue from c1985 shows this form, which was discontinued around this time. The removal of the practical rings seems unusual. Right: A 1970s–80s decanter in Peat, designed by Colin Terris, 11in (28cm) high. The waisted body allows the decanter to be gripped safely. The lipped base matches the glass shown with Morven on p.38.

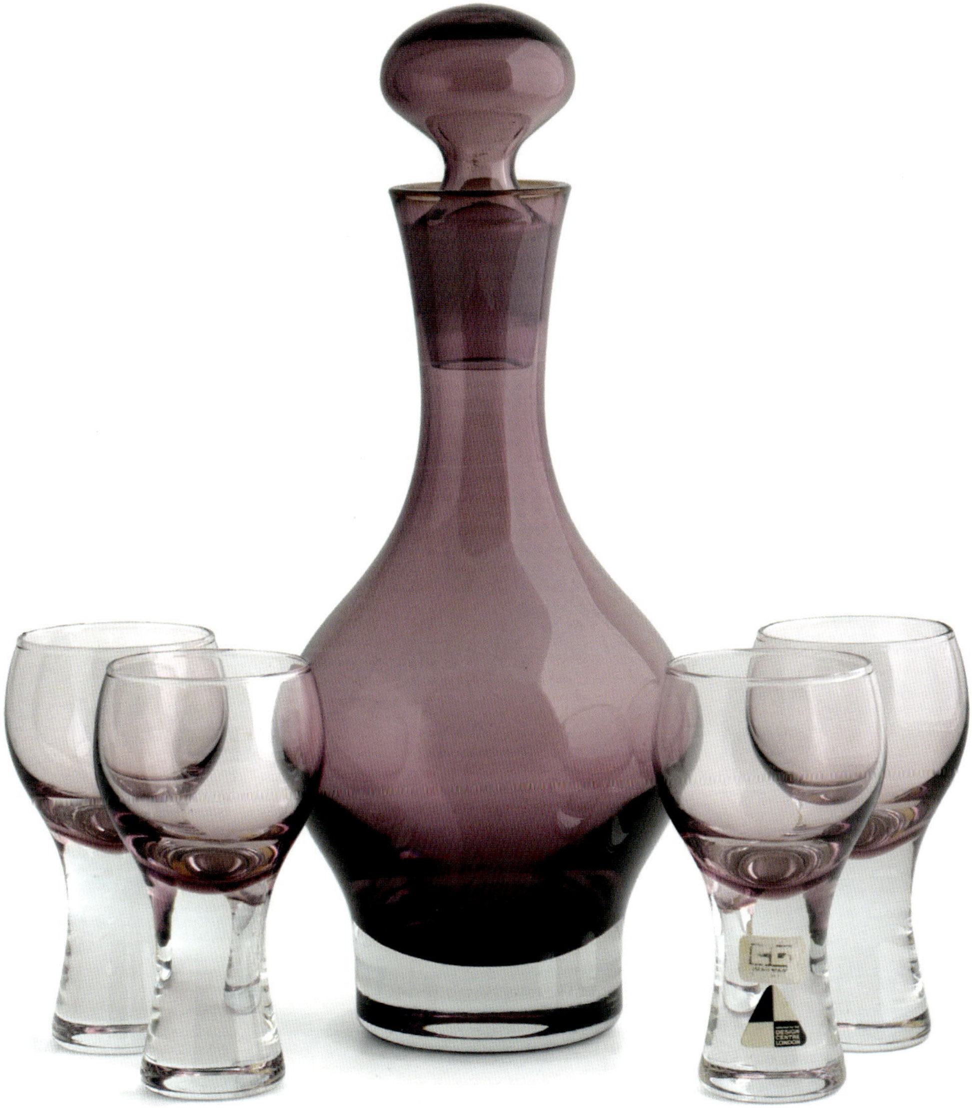

A 1970s-80s Canisbay decanter, no.4060/D, and no.4060/GO goblets, in Heather, designed by Colin Terris in 1972. Decanter 11.25in (29cm) high, glasses 4.5in (11.5cm) high. Introduced in 1973, Terris' first decanter continued the use of hollow stoppers, even though this has a ground seal. Commonly found in Peat or Heather, no examples in Loch or Moss have yet been found. Stems were thick as very few glassmakers at the time could form and apply stems and feet. Four sizes of goblet were made along with a goblet with a wider bowl and shorter stem for beer. The design won Design Council accreditation shortly after its introduction. The Canisbay range was highly successful and was produced until c1988.

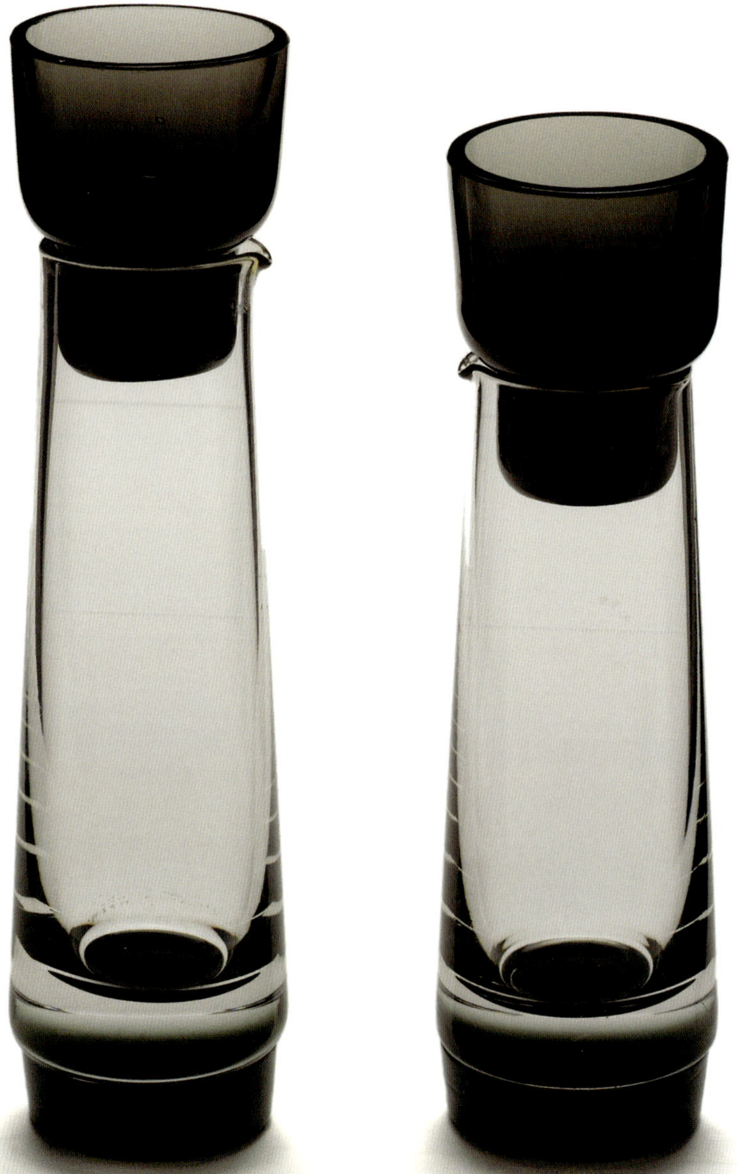

A pair of Scaraben oil and vinegar bottles, with Soot stoppers and feet, designed by Domhnall ÓBroin c1962, tallest 6in (15cm) high. Of avant garde Modernist or almost Art Deco design, the Scaraben range of tableware was described at the time as '*a starkly modern symbol*'. It is not known in any other colourway, although the tones of the Peat stoppers and feet vary. Stoppers may also be in colourless glass. This oil and vinegar set is rarer than the decanter or glasses, as it was less practical and less widely desirable at the time. In 1963, it was available from Ansons of Dover St, London, for £2 14s. During the 1970s, the 'black foot' Scaraben range was chosen for reintroduction, but samples indicated it would be too expensive to produce.

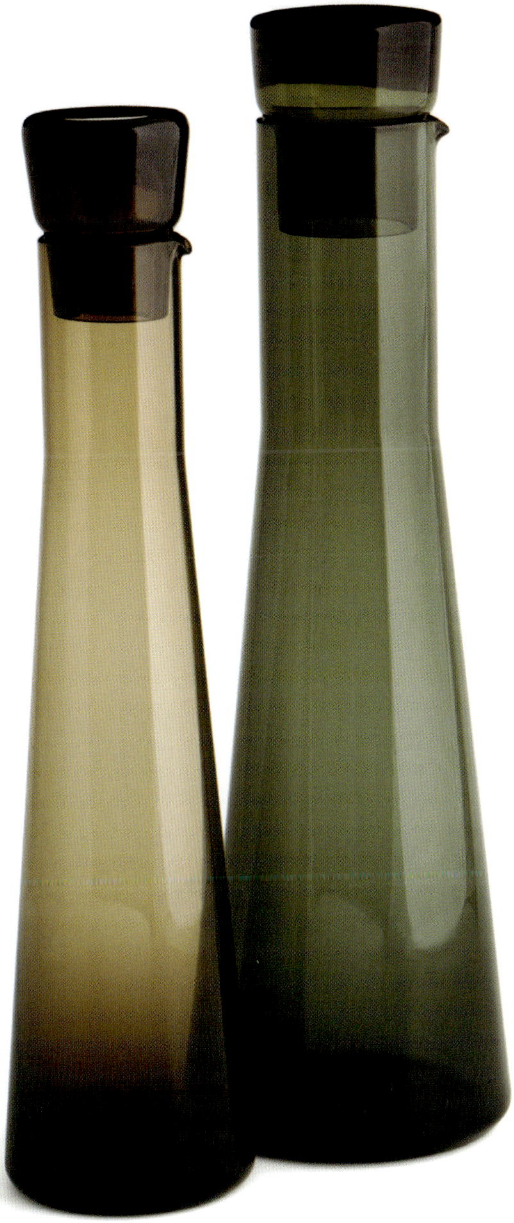

Two Stroma decanters in Peat and Soot, designed by Domhnall ÓBroin c1962, tallest 14in (35.5cm) high. These decanters were accompanied by 6oz or 8oz tumblers like those shown with the Stroma water set on p.45. The set was part of a range of tableware that also included a very popular water set comprising a cylindrical jug with a pinched spout, and matching cylindrical glasses. Only these two colours were offered, along with a colourless version. None are cased. The form is similar to Kaj Franck's ceramic cruet set designed for Finnish company Arabia in 1955. The smaller 18oz decanter cost £1 12s, and the larger 30oz decanter cost £1 19s 6d. Like the Scaraben oil and vinegar set, this set had been discontinued by 1972.

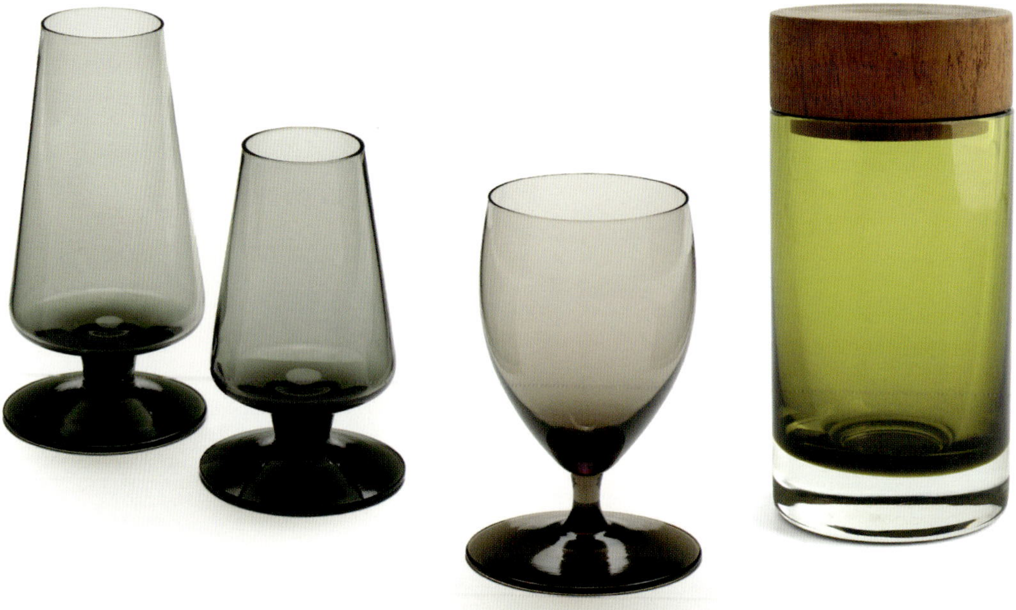

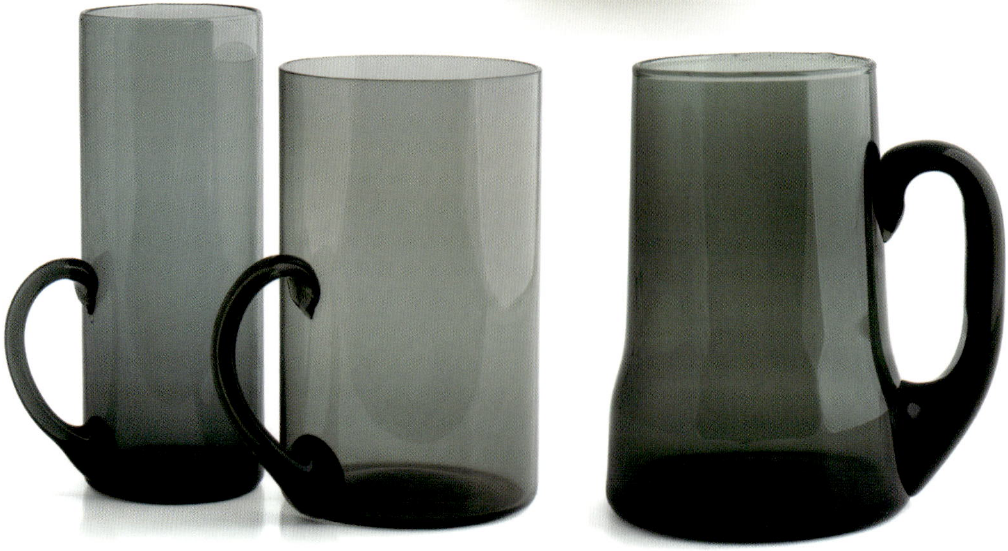

Top row: Three 1960s goblets in Soot or Peat, designed by Domhnall ÓBroin c1962, 5.5in (14cm) high, and 4.75in (12cm) high. Different shapes or sizes of drinking glasses comprised much of the company's initial production. A 1960s storage jar, in Moss, with a teak lid, designed by Domhnall O'Broin c1961, 5in (13cm) high. All four forms had been discontinued by 1972.

Bottom row: Two 1960s tankards, no.4004, in Soot, designed by Domhnall ÓBroin c1961, tallest 6in (15cm) high, and a 1960s-70s tankard, no.4041, in Soot, designed by Charles Orr in 1967. ÓBroin's tankards, discontinued during the 1960s, were also made in Loch, Peat, Moss and Flint. Orr's very popular tankards often bore engraved or sandblasted motifs.

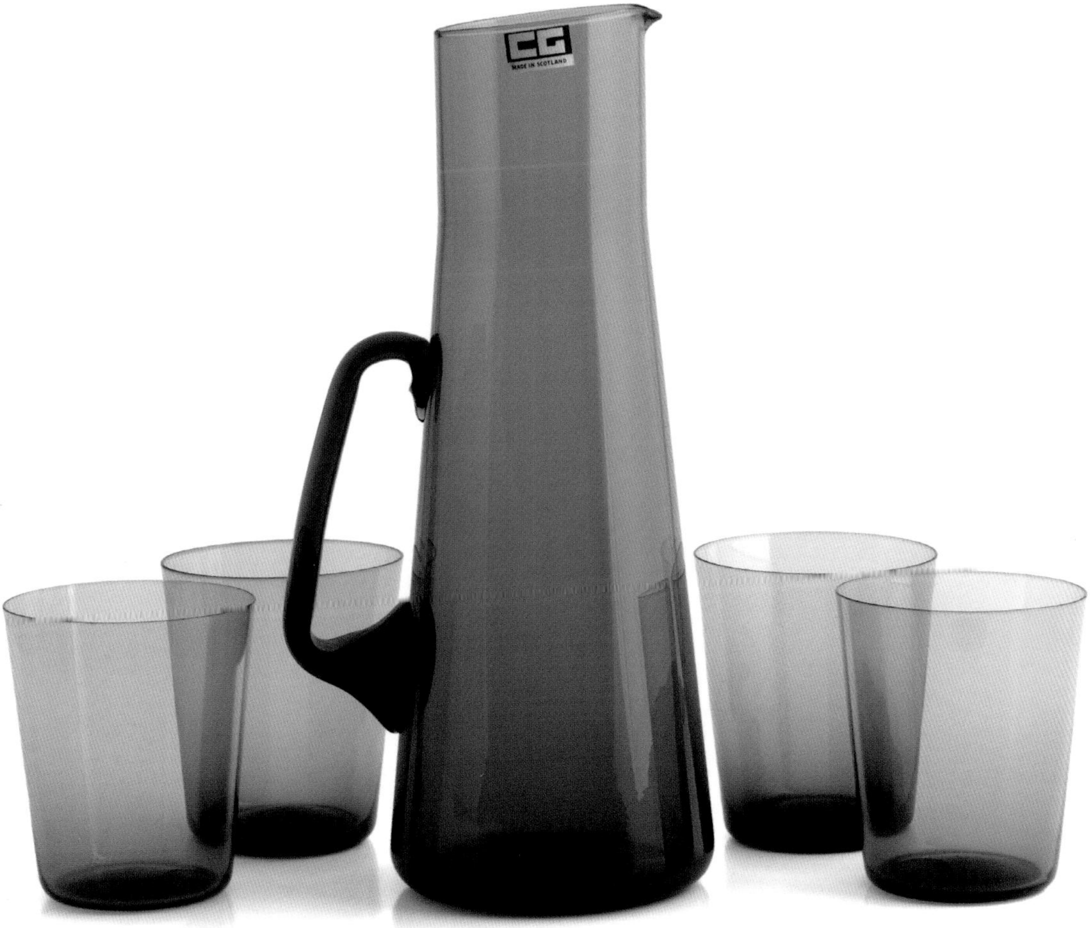

A 1960s-70s Stroma water set, with two pint jug no.4020, and four 8oz tumblers, no.4020, in Soot, designed by Domhnall ÓBroin c1962, jug 10in (25.5cm) high, tumblers 3.3in (8.5cm) high. The jug design recalls both the simplicity and muted colours of Timo Sarpaneva's 'i-line' range of tableware designed in 1956 for Iittala, and the minimal designs of Kaj Franck.

Blown very thinly into moulds, the tumblers recall Franck's 'Purnukka' (Box) tumblers designed for Nuutajärvi Notsjö in 1952, but without the 'kicked-up' base. Note how the angle of the tumblers matches the angle of the taper of the jug perfectly. This jug sold almost as well as a best-selling cylindrical jug with a pinched rim similar to the form of ÓBroin's tankards shown opposite.

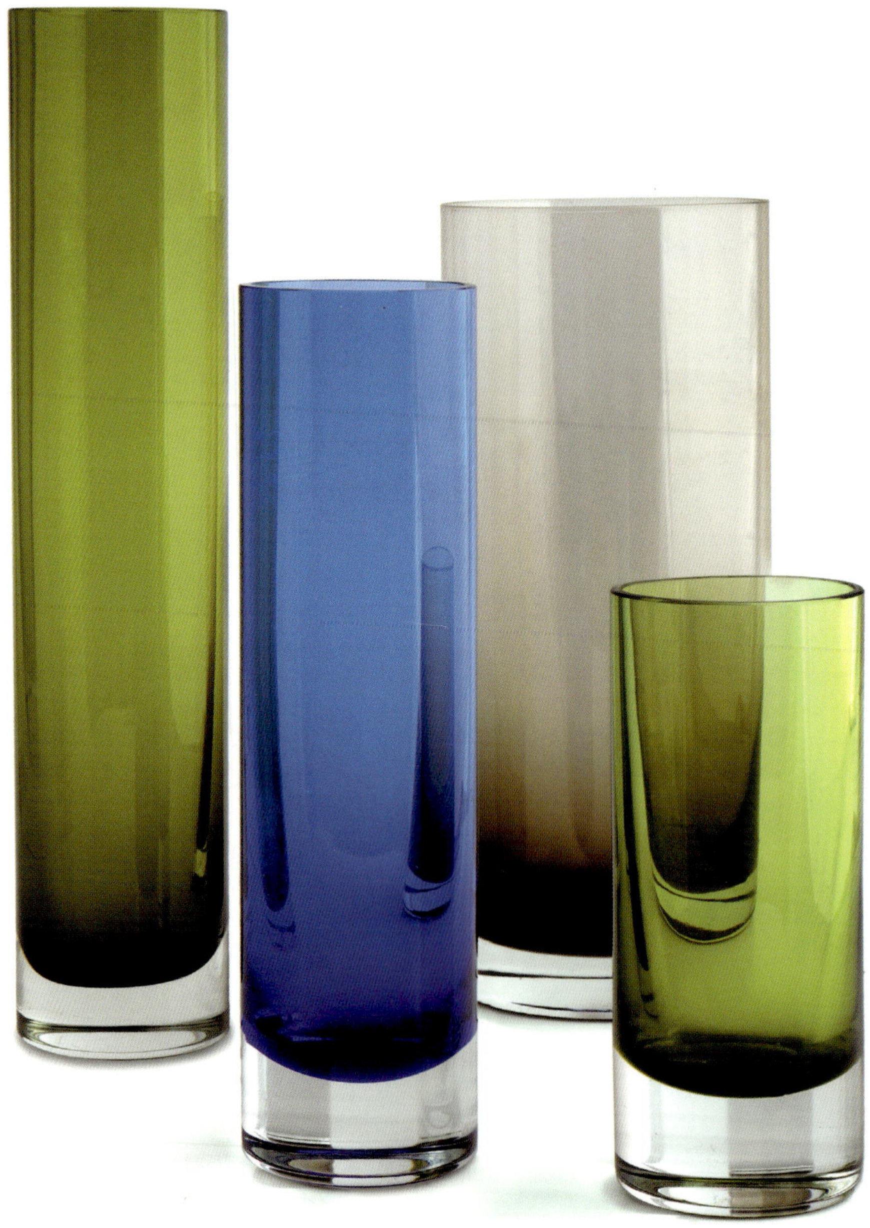

Three 1960s-70s Caithness Cased Vases, no.4002, in Moss and Loch, and a cased vase no.4003 in Peat, all designed by Domhnall ÓBroin c1961, tallest 12in (30.5cm) high, smallest 6in (15cm) high. The 1972 catalogue shows four different sizes for these cylindrical vases. However, as the rims are machine-cut, heights vary widely. The widest and largest form was known in the factory as an 'elephant's leg', and few glassmakers had the strength to form and wield the large gather. They are scarce today. The vibrant colours and simple form would have appeared modern and Scandinavian at the time. A practical and classic form made by many factories, colours identify Caithness examples. The moulds were also used for later ranges.

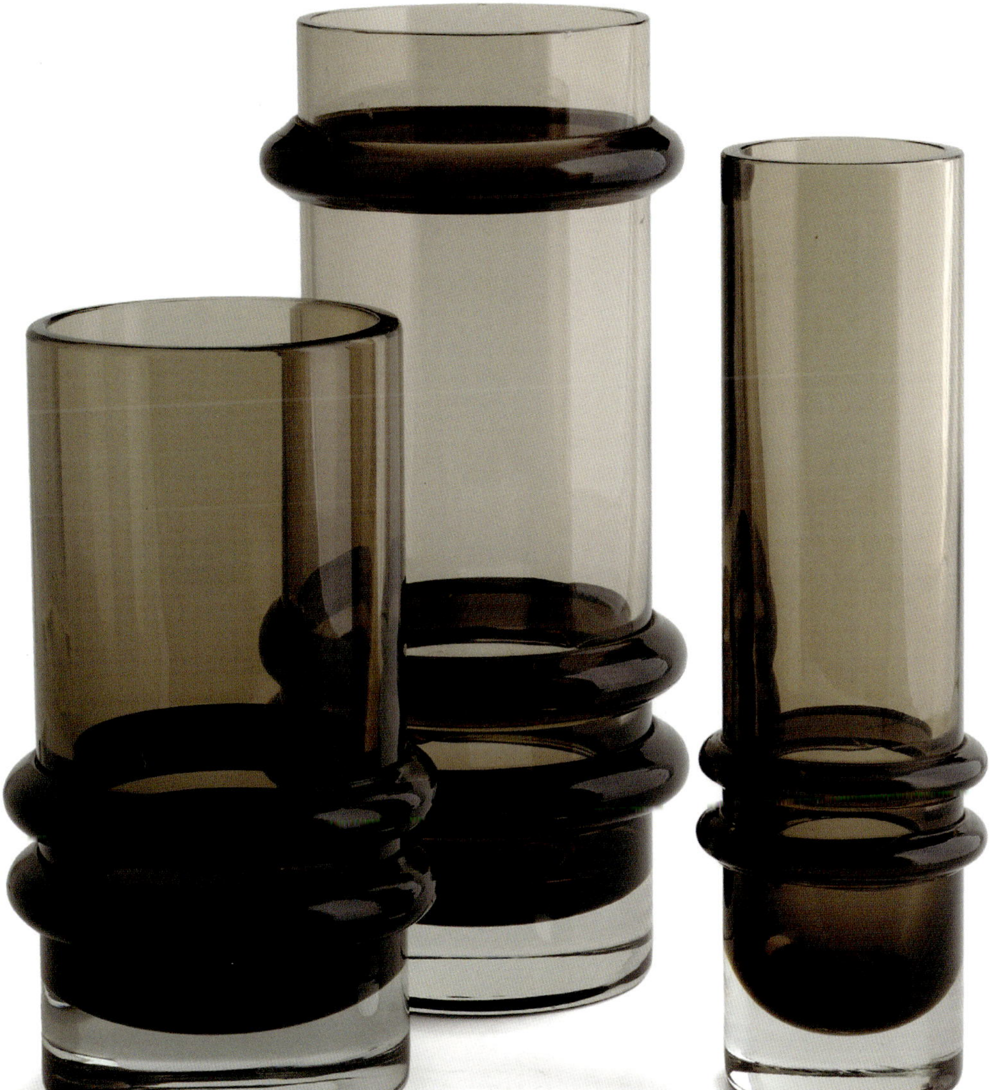

Three 1960s ring vases in Peat, designed by Domhnall ÓBroin c1961, largest 10in (25.5cm) high. ÓBroin's favourite design, these unprecedented vases were made for only a short period of time due to production problems. The rings were trailed on by hand, and then smoothed and rounded with tools, but the technique was difficult and resulted in many seconds. Moulds were the same as for the cylinder vases opposite. They are hard to find today, particularly in large sizes. Examples are usually found in Peat, although very rare examples are in Moss or have contrasting Loch bodies or rings, or colourless rings. ÓBroin converted one into a lampbase during the 1960s. Modern and heavy yet balanced, they resemble part of a machine.

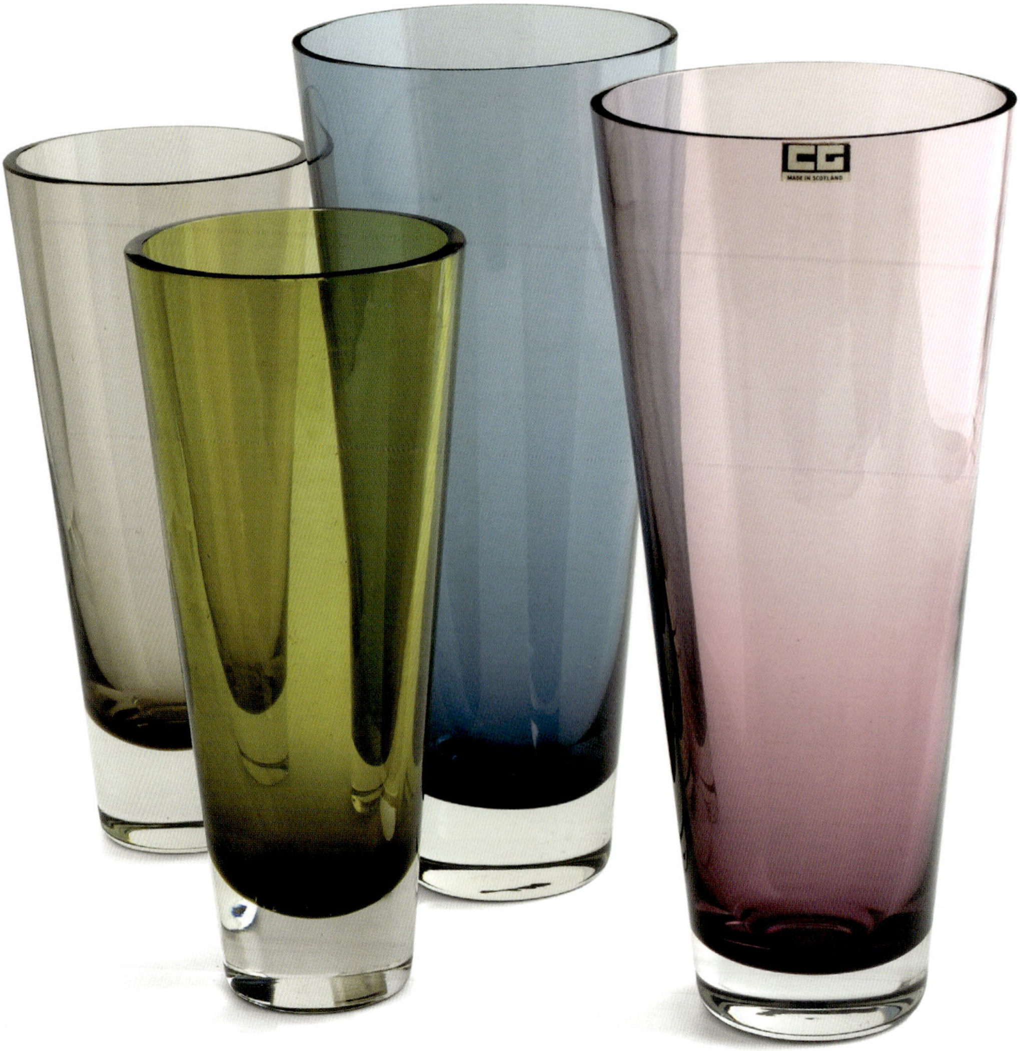

Four 1960s-70s Lochshiel vases, no.4012, in Peat, Moss, Twilight and Heather, designed by Domhnall ÓBroin c1961, tall 11in (28cm) high, small 8in (20cm) high. The numbering indicates that these vases were part of the initial range, and they also appear in early photographs taken by ÓBroin. As with the cylindrical cased vase on the previous page, rims are machine cut, meaning heights can vary even though only two general sizes are known. Called 'Tumbler Vase' in the 1972 catalogue, the form is simple and practical, and they sold well. However, the small diameter base and height may have made them top-heavy when full of water and flowers. Examples can be hard to find today, particularly the large size in bolder tones of Heather.

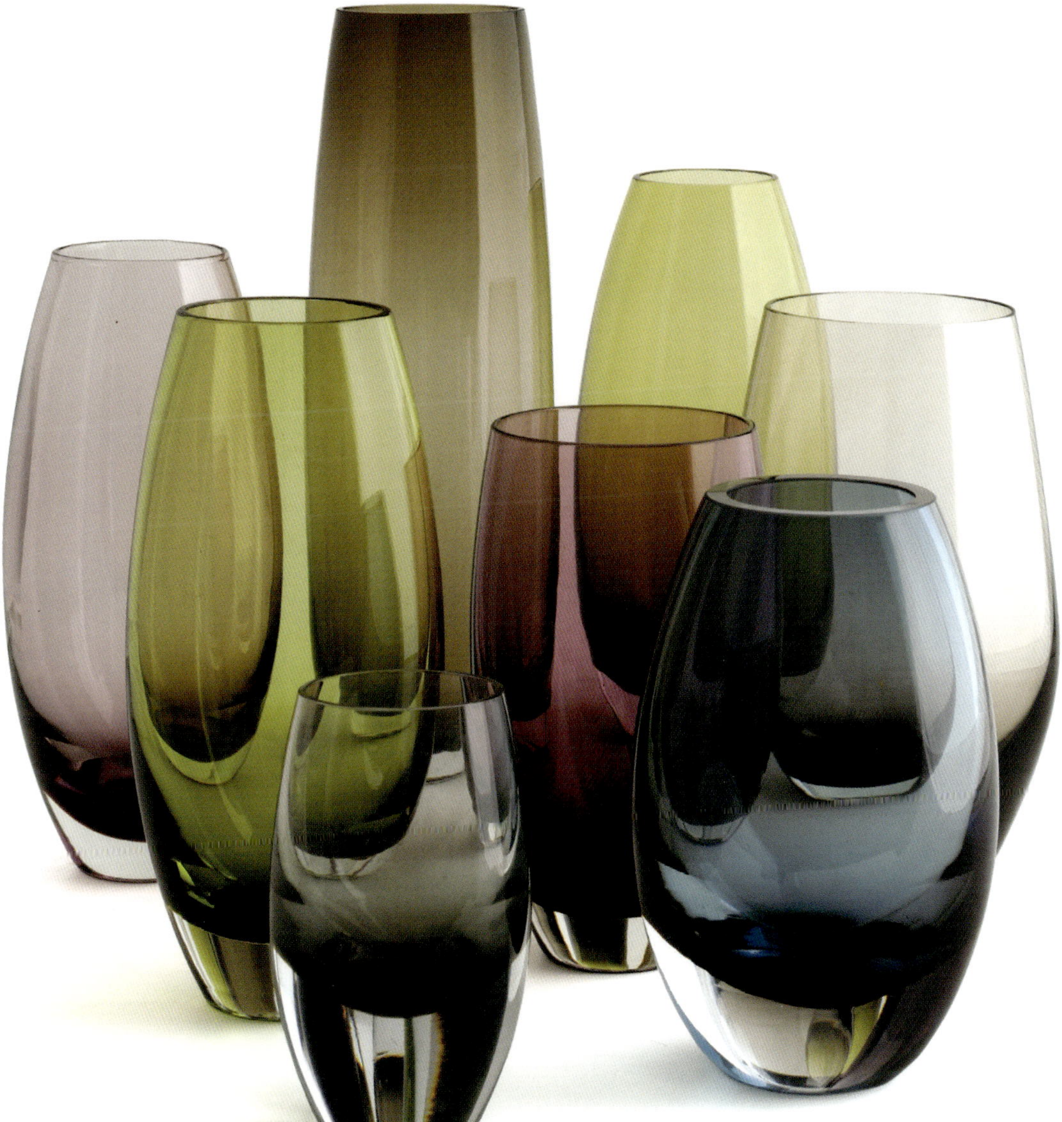

A group of eight 1960s-80s Barrel Vases, no.4019, in Peat, Twilight, Heather, Soot, and Moss, designed by Domhnall ÓBroin c1961, tallest 9in (23cm) high. As with the Cased Vases and Lochshiel vases, rims are machine cut, meaning heights can vary. The 1972 catalogue shows three heights of vases, and one low bowl. Shape no.4023 is very similar, but has different proportions.

This was ÓBroin's most successful and long-lived design, with examples being mass-produced into the 2000s. Most later examples made from the 1970s onwards bear engraved or sandblasted motifs, and many were produced in later colours such as Amethyst or Topaz. This group shows how widely colour tones could vary - stronger tones are more desirable.

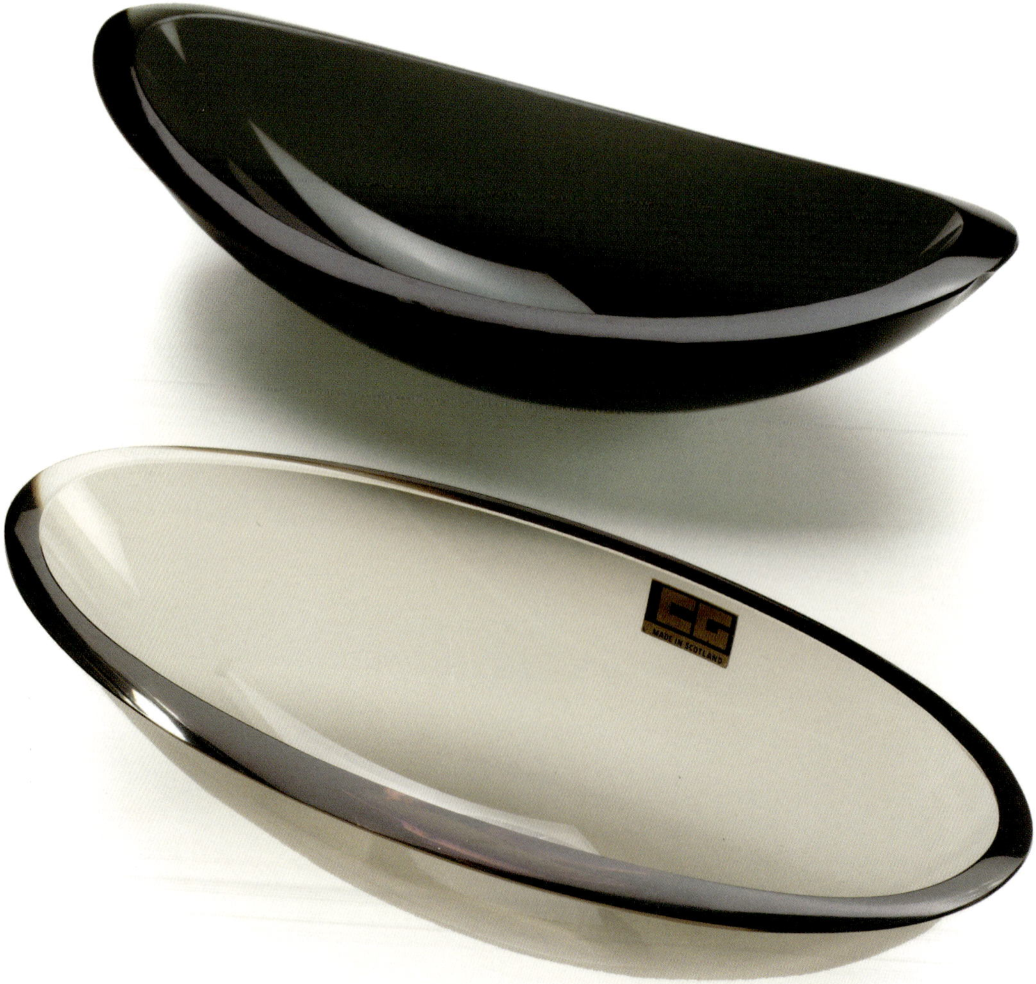

Two 1960s Eclipse bowls in Soot and Peat, designed by Domhnall ÓBroin c1961, 8.25in (21cm) long. The forms and machine-cut rims are similar to the small series of 'studio glass' bowls ÓBroin made while studying at the Edinburgh College of Art, and also recall his 'Boats' design of c1958 (see p.9). They were perhaps also inspired by Gerda Stromberg's austere designs for Sweden's Stombergshyttan factory. They were difficult and time-consuming to form and finish, and were discontinued by 1966. They were formed by cutting three oval shapes from a spun-out disc of glass, with the gentle, even curve of the rims being machine-cut and polished by hand. They are very rare today, especially 'first' quality, flawless examples.

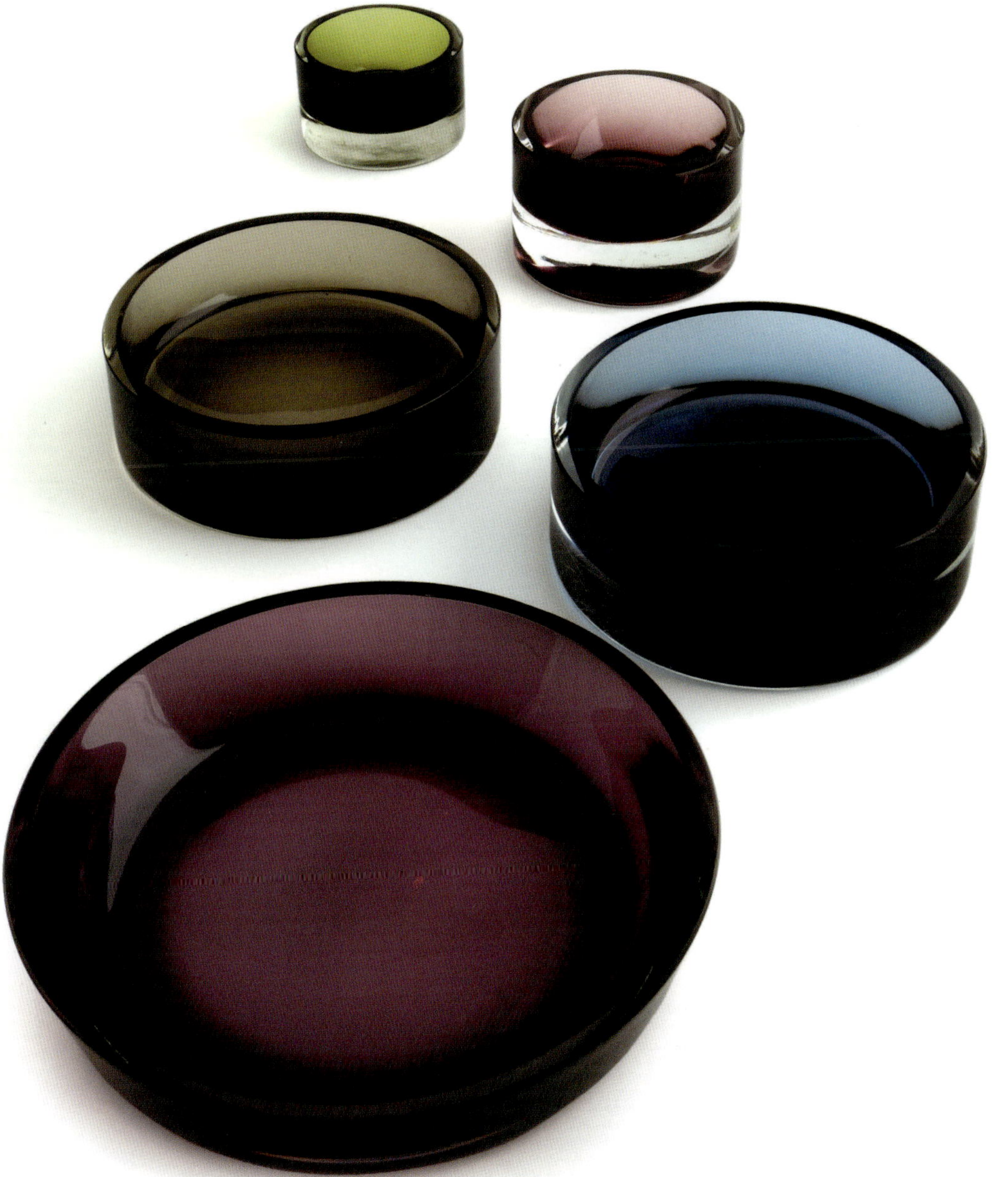

Four 1960s-70s Cased Bowls, no.4006, in Moss, Heather, Peat, and Twilight, and a 1960s-80s large Cased Dish, no.4008, in Heather, designed by Domhnall ÓBroin c1961, dish 8in (20cm) diam, smallest 4in (10cm) diam. The 1972 catalogue shows three sizes of Cased Bowl with straight sides, and two sizes of Cased Dish with tapering sides leading to rounded edges.

A Fruit Bowl (no.4007) version of no.4008, with higher sides, was also produced into the late 1980s. Cased Bowls were usually cut-down second quality Cylinder Vases with flaws such as bubbles in the upper body. A Salad Bowl (no.4009) with a turned-in rim was also offered, as was an uncased tapered footed 'Fruit Bowl' (no.4011). Both are hard to find today.

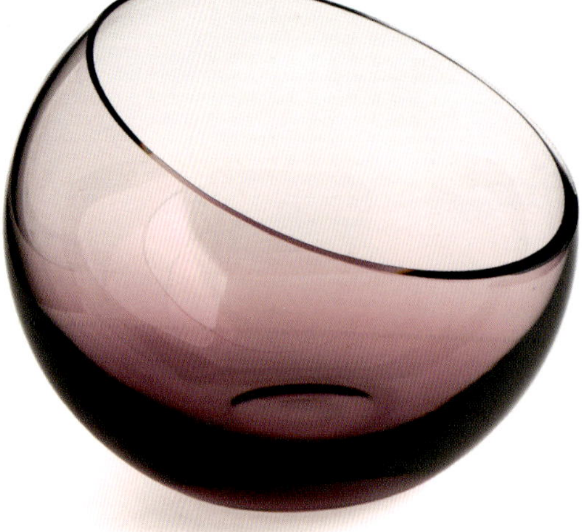

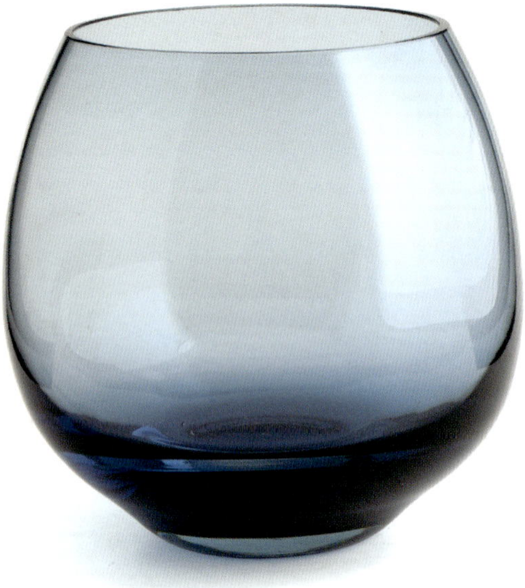

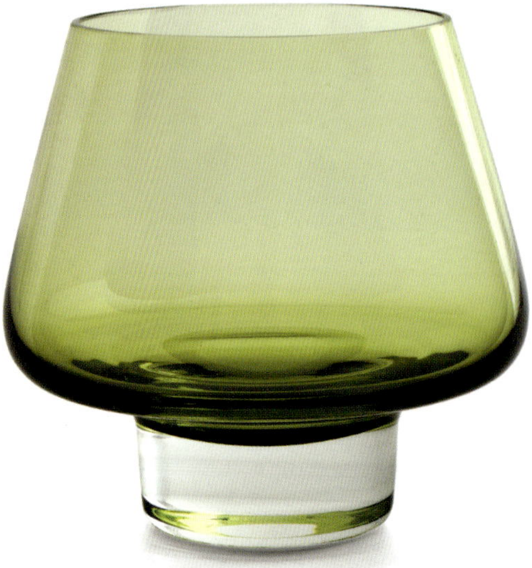

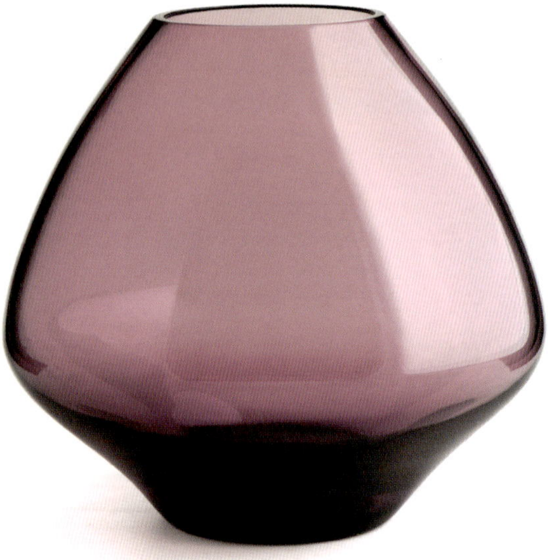

Top left: A 1970s-90s Rose Bowl, no.4071, in Heather, designed by Colin Terris, 4.5in (11.5cm) high. This shape was used in later ranges, including 'Tranquillity'. It was blown in the same mould as the no.4080 decanter on p.40. Bottom left: A 1970s-2000s Flower Bowl, no.4035, in Moss, designed by Denis Mann, 5.25in (135cm) high. Introduced in 1977, this was a smaller version of Mann's 1972 Mastermind bowl. It was produced in large quantities, usually with cut or sandblasted motifs. Top right: A Cased Vase, no.4034, in Loch, designed by Charles Orr c1967, 6.5in (16.5cm) high. Bottom right: A 1970s Cased Vase no.4010, in Heather, designed by Domhnall ÓBroin c1965, 7in (18cm) high. Both vases were discontinued in the 1970s.

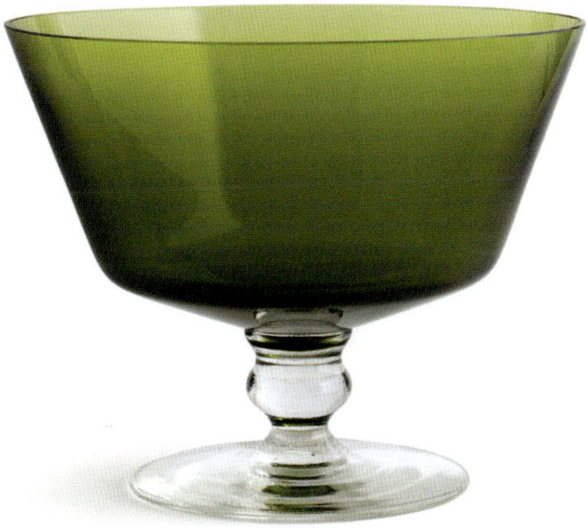

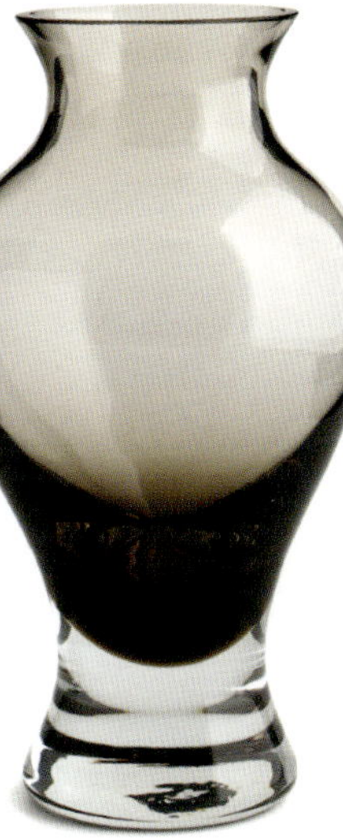

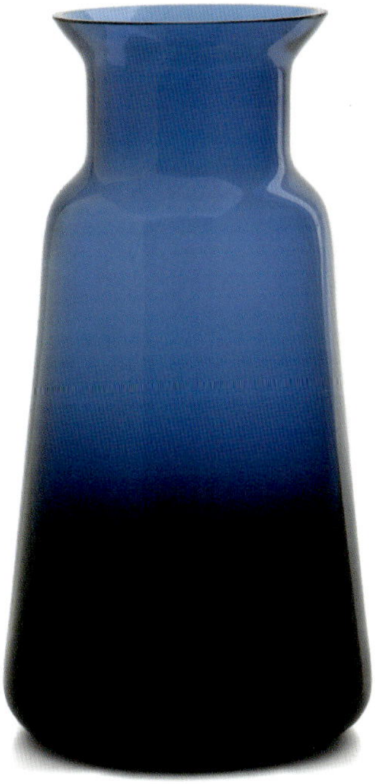

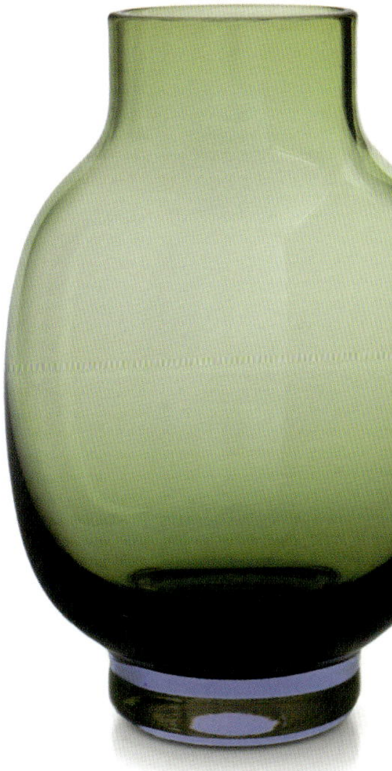

Top left: A 1960s Footed Fruit Bowl, no.4017, in Moss, designed by Domhnall ÓBroin in 1961, 6in (15.5cm) high. The applied stem and foot made this expensive to make. Bottom left: A no.4101 vase, in Loch, designed by Colin Terris c1981, 8in (20.5cm) high. Initially from the Glenisla range, this was re-used for the Art Nouveau collection. Top right: A baluster vase in Peat, designed by Colin Terris c1980, 8in (20.5cm) high. Produced in two sizes, this is often found with sandblasted motifs. Bottom right: A no.4103 vase, in Moss cased with Amethyst, from the Glenisla range, designed by Colin Terris c1981, 6.5in (16.5cm) high. Glenisla comprised single colours in Heather, Peat or Moss, and those also cased in Amethyst.

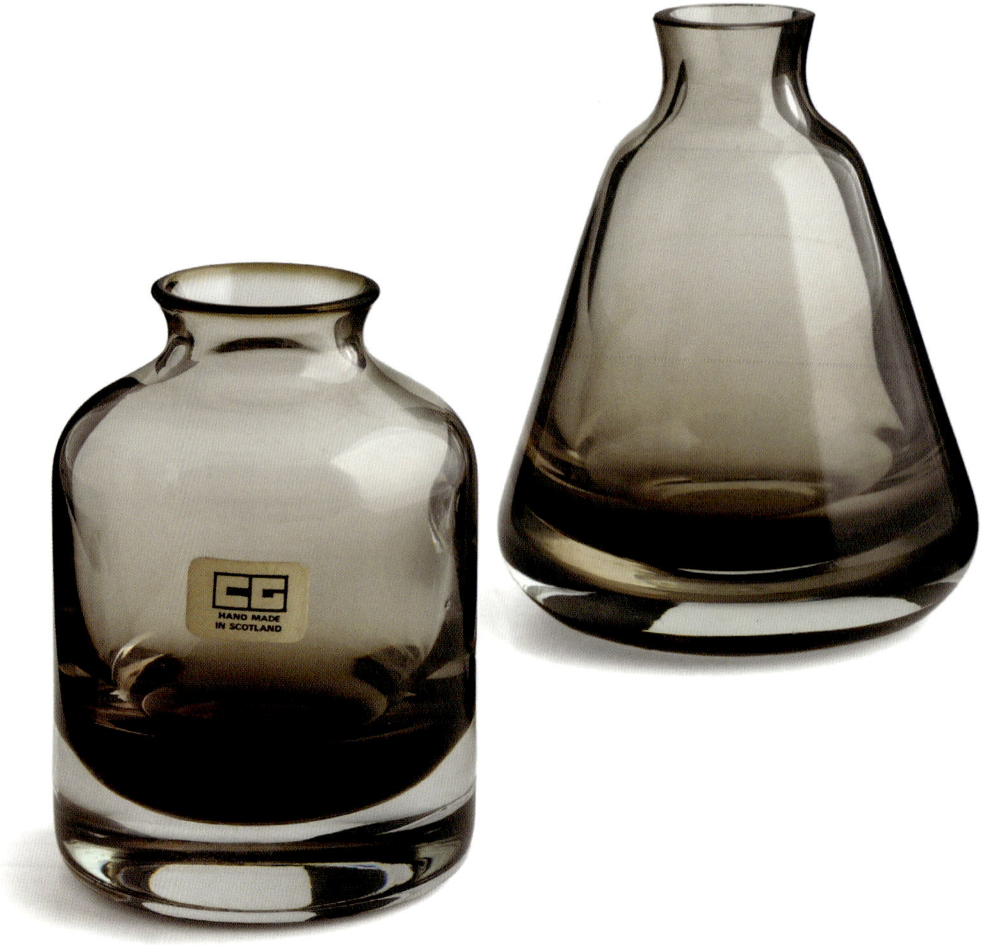

A late 1970s inkwell vase, no.4082, and a conical vase, no.4085, in Peat and from the Braemore range, designed by Colin Terris c1975, left: 4in (10cm) high, right: 4.5in (11.5cm) high. These are the most unusual shapes from this range of six small posy vases with heavily cased bases. The other four shapes can be seen on p.111. Colours comprised Moss, Heather, Peat, Amethyst, and Twilight, and the range had its own specially designed box (see p.107). By 1981, these two shapes had been discontinued, with the rest of the range following c1985. Production costs were marginally less than for larger vases, but the small size meant the price and income were much lower. Despite this, the range was popular and successful.

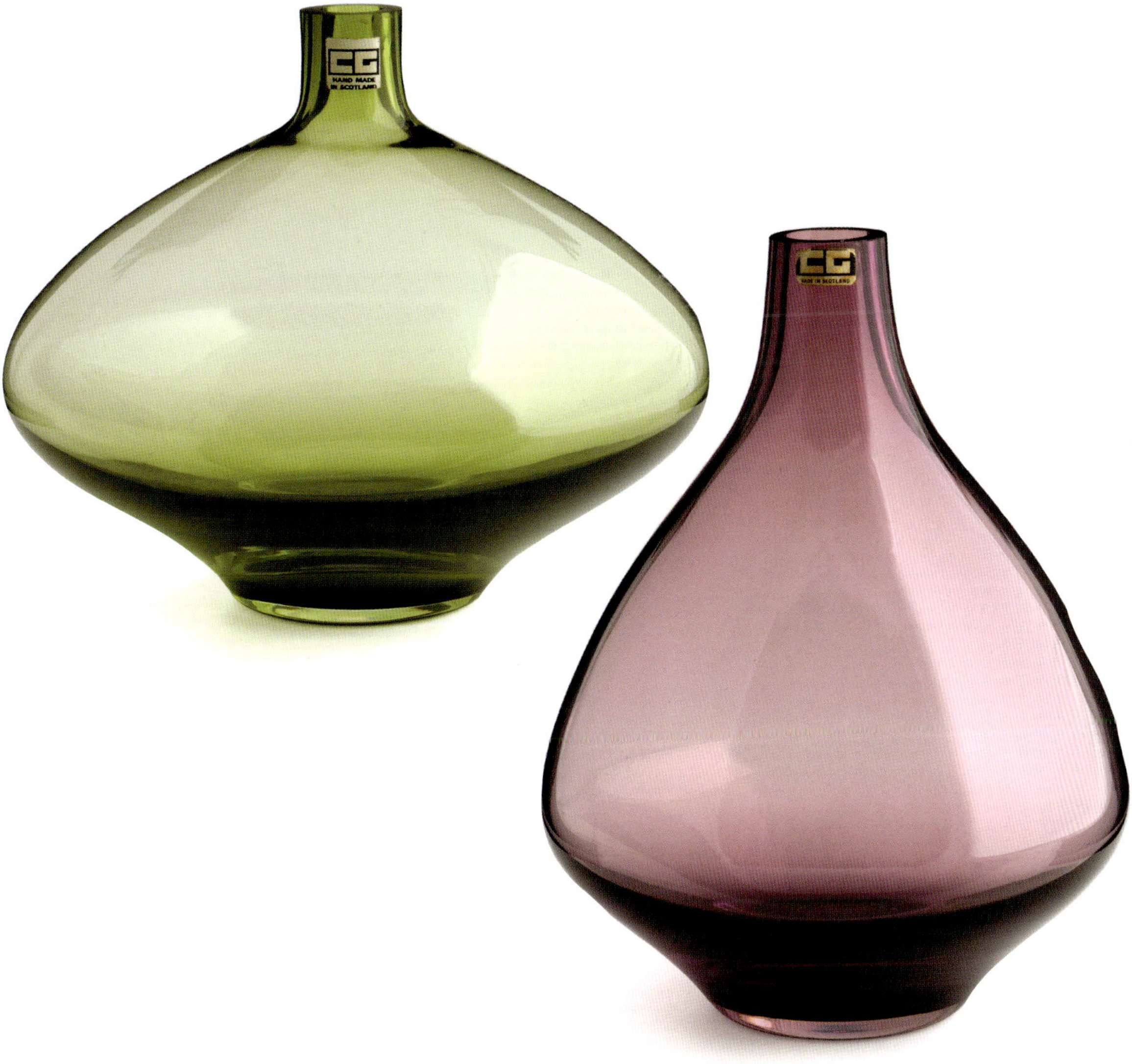

Two 1960s-70s Lamp Bases designed by Domhnall ÓBroin c1962. Left no.4011, in Moss, 7in (19cm) high. Right: no.4010, in Heather, 10in (25.5cm) high. Although their numbering implies that they were designed in the first few years of Caithness, they were first shown in Pottery Gazette in February 1967. They were also not shown in early advertising or photographs taken by ÓBroin, so must have been amongst his last designs put into production. The extravagent, sculptural curves are less austere than many of his other designs. Electrical fittings were glued into the top using Araldite, and they sold well. ÓBroin was a fan of science fiction films and Doctor Who, and the form of no.4011 may have been inspired by UFOs in these films.

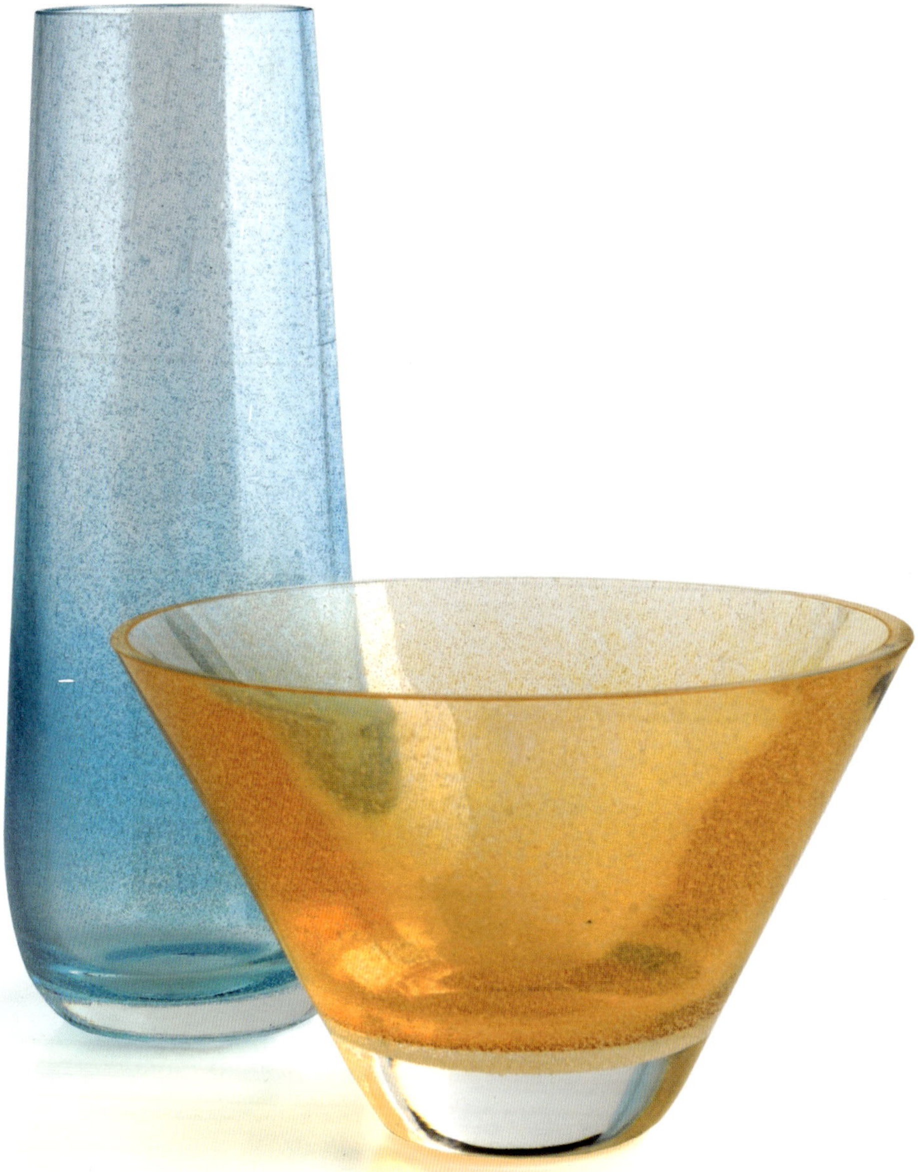

A vase no.8060 in Spearmint, and a candle bowl no.8063 in Papaya, from the Crush range designed by Gordon Hendry in 2001, vase 9in (23cm) high, bowl 4in (10cm) high. Crush comprised three sizes of tapering vase, with this being the largest, and two conical bowls like those used in the Shoreline range (see p.65), with this being the smallest. The range took its name from the sand and powdered colour used between the layers. Intended to be simple and swift to produce and hide flaws, thus yielding more firsts, the sand often caused forms to become mis-shapen and uneven. As it was also tiresome for glassmakers to produce, it was withdrawn after two years. Bowls are rarer as, at £28 and £33, they were more expensive than vases.

Stripes & Mottles

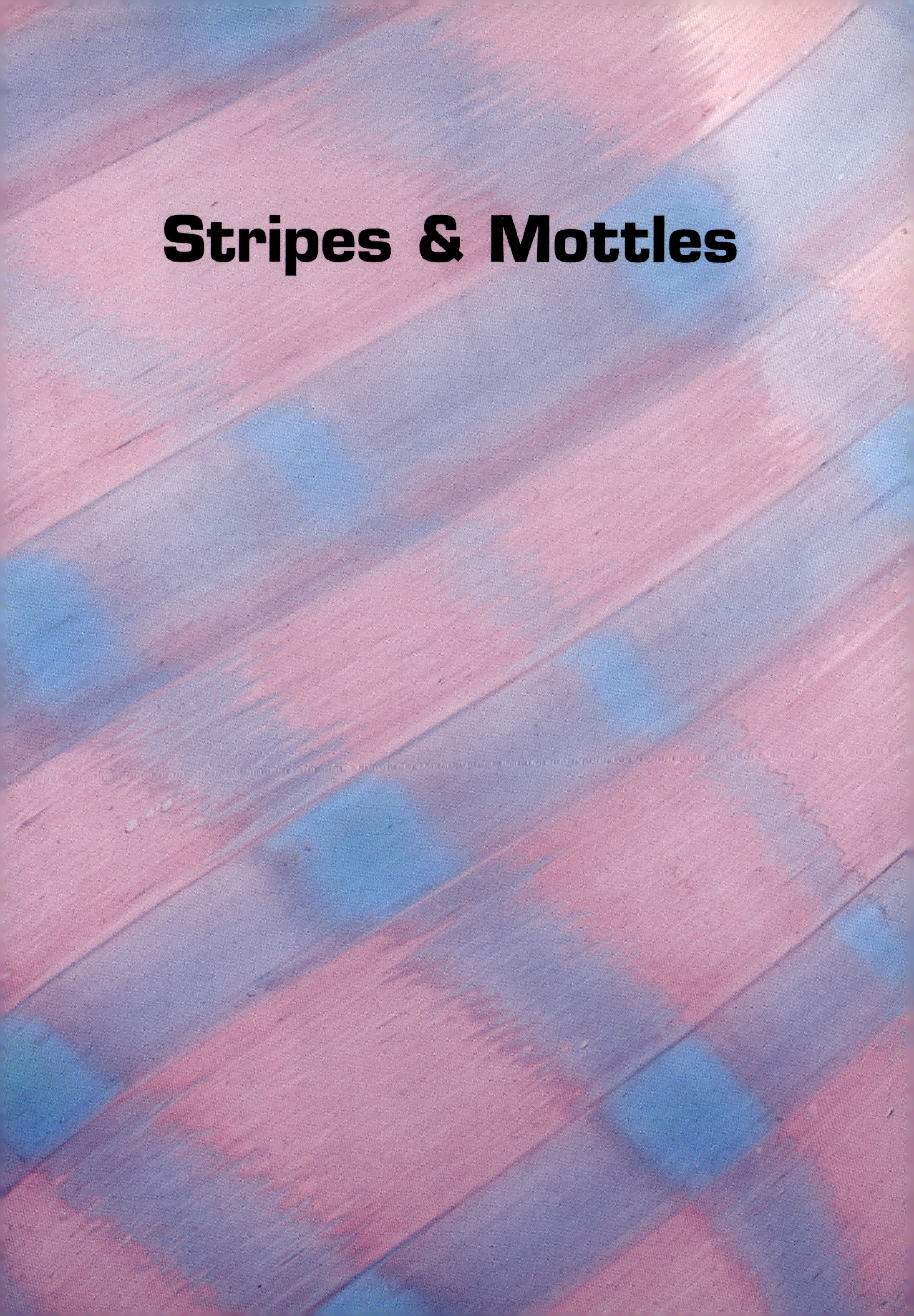

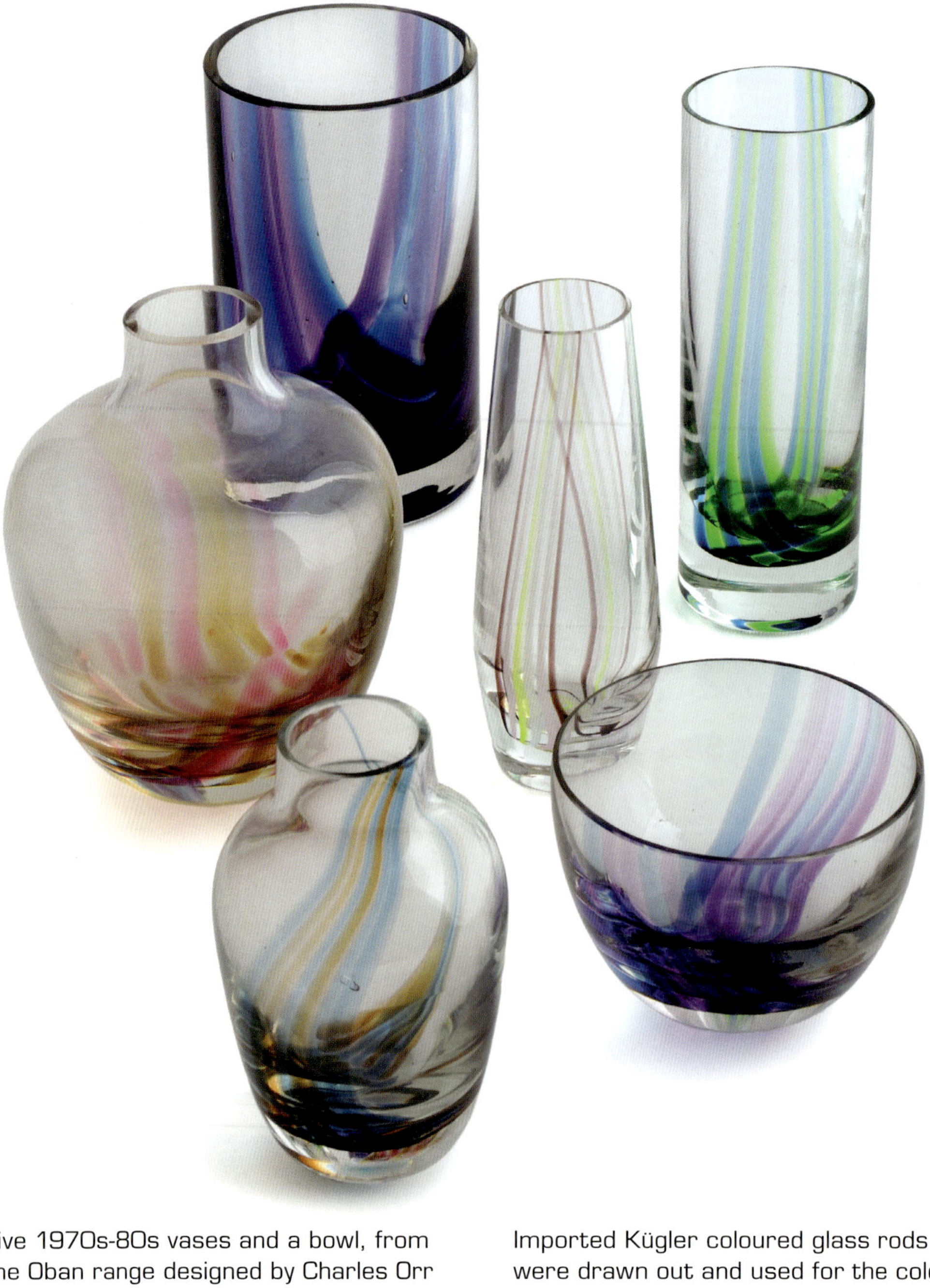

Five 1970s-80s vases and a bowl, from the Oban range designed by Charles Orr and Paul Ysart in 1968, the green and blue striped OG12 vase 6.25in (16cm) high, the pink and yellow striped OG2 vase 5.9in (15cm) high. Oban was a landmark range for the company, changing their hallmark style as it involved surface patterns and introduced stripes as a recurring motif.

Imported Kügler coloured glass rods were drawn out and used for the coloured stripes sandwiched between two layers. Widths vary depending on how the rod was drawn out and how the colour reacted to the body glass. Orr designed a number of new shapes for the range, such as OG2. Green & blue and purple & blue sold better than some of the more insipid colourways.

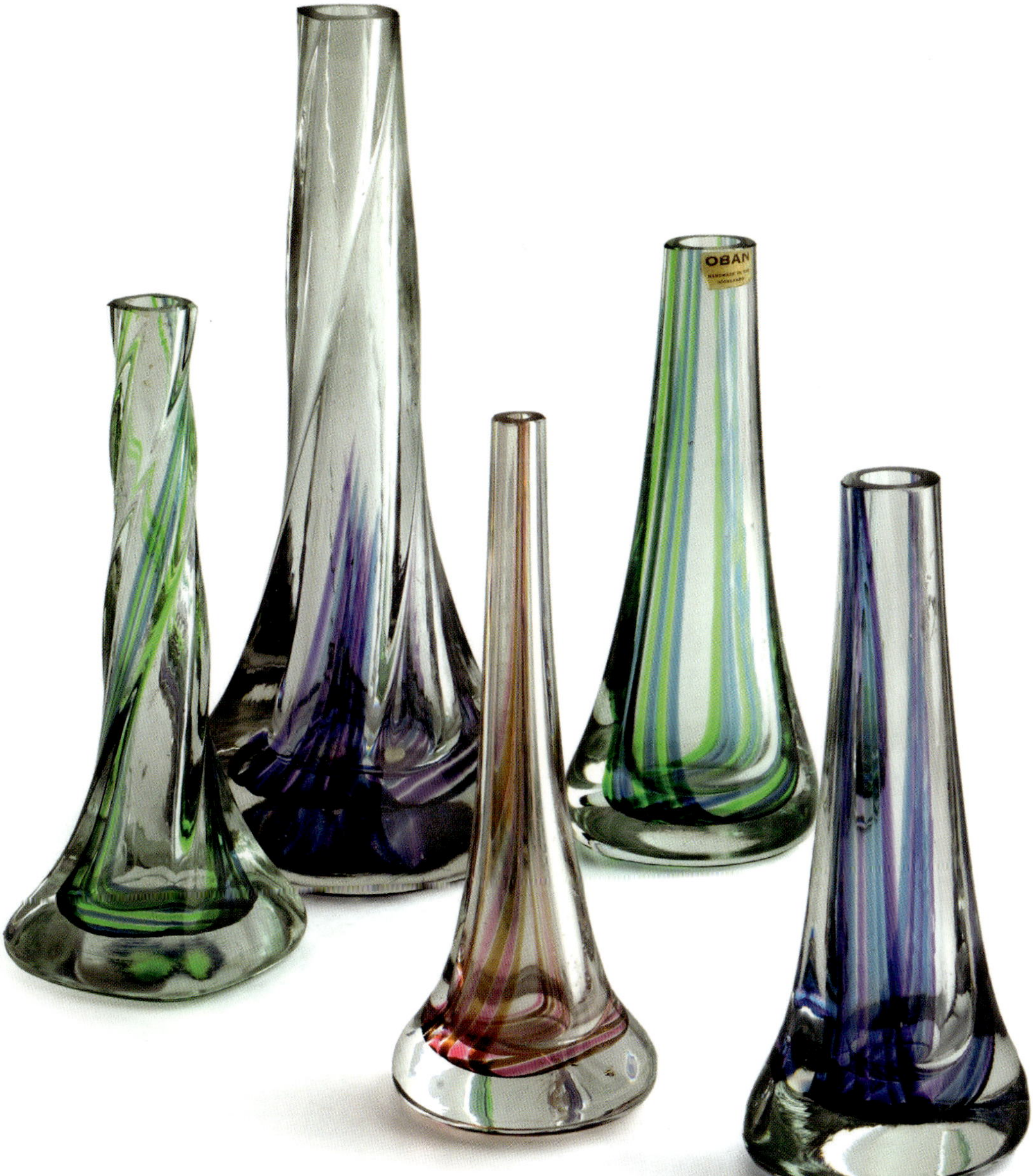

Five 1970s-80s Specimen Vases, no.OG18, from the Oban range, designed by Charles Orr and Peter Fuin in 1969, tallest 10.5in (25cm) high, smallest. These vases with heavy bases were highly successful, and became a hallmark of the Oban range. The form was designed by Peter Fuin and was based on ÓBroin's teardrop specimen vase (see p21). Each side was flattened and rolled slightly on the marver table, the form was then elongated by swinging, and the base was flattened using a pad on the floor. As such, each example is unique in precise form and size. A twist could be added, as on the larger example above. Twisted bodies are comparatively scarce, and some were used as lampbases. In 1981 a standard sized vase cost £8.95.

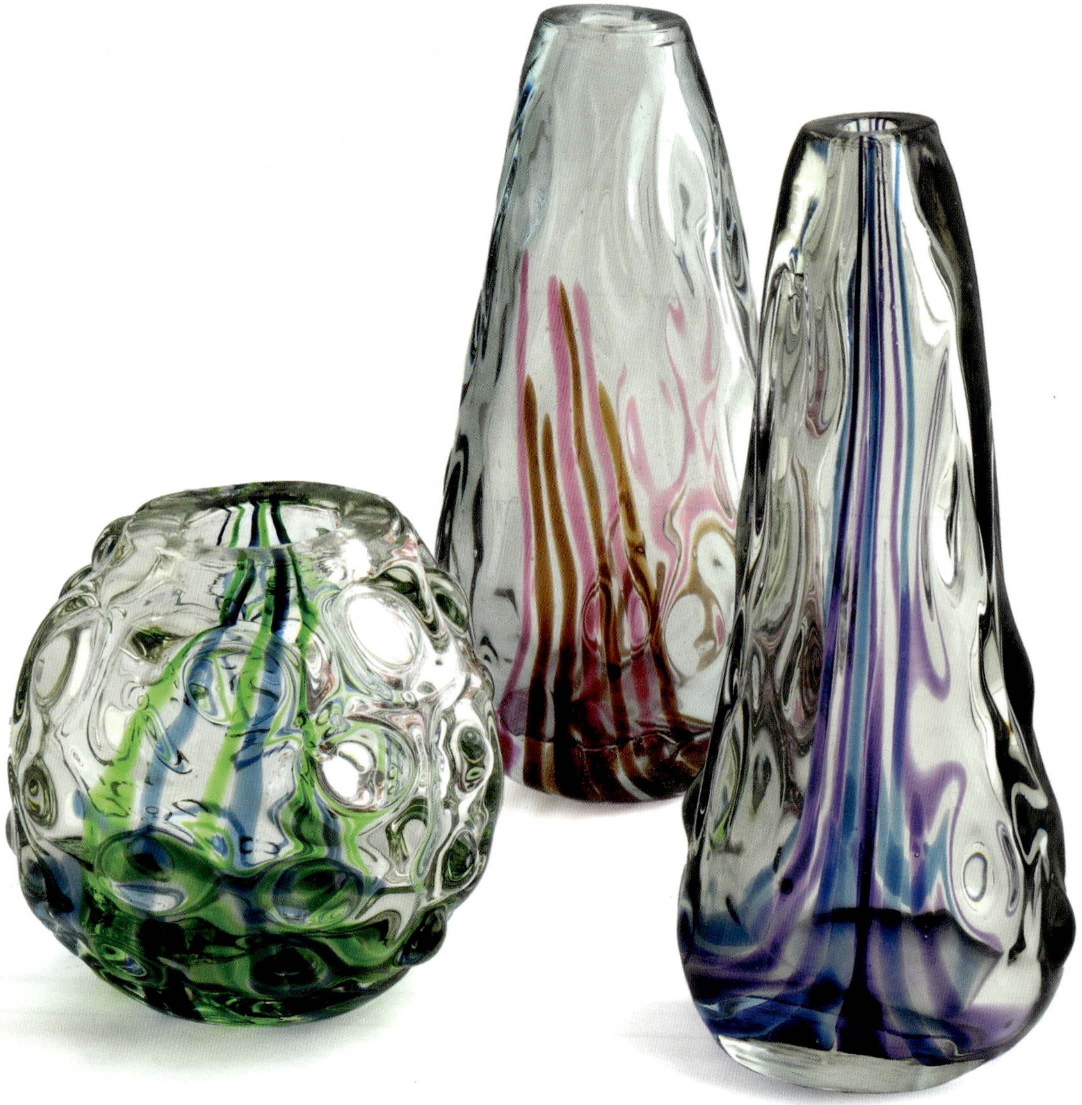

An early 1970s textured spherical vase and two textured lampbases from the Oban range, tallest 9in (23cm) high, vase 5.25in (13cm) high. These knobbly forms are not shown in any catalogue and were not officially part of Charles Orr's Oban range. They may have been an experimental response to popular knobbly ranges made by Whitefriars and Liskeard. The knobbles were added by pressing the end of a pipe into the hot body, which could then be swung-out to elongate it. A small quantity seem to have been made, and the idea may have come from Oban manager Ken Wainwright, who had produced a series of similarly textured glass logs when at the Edinburgh College of Art. The Oban range was replaced by Spinningdale after 1985.

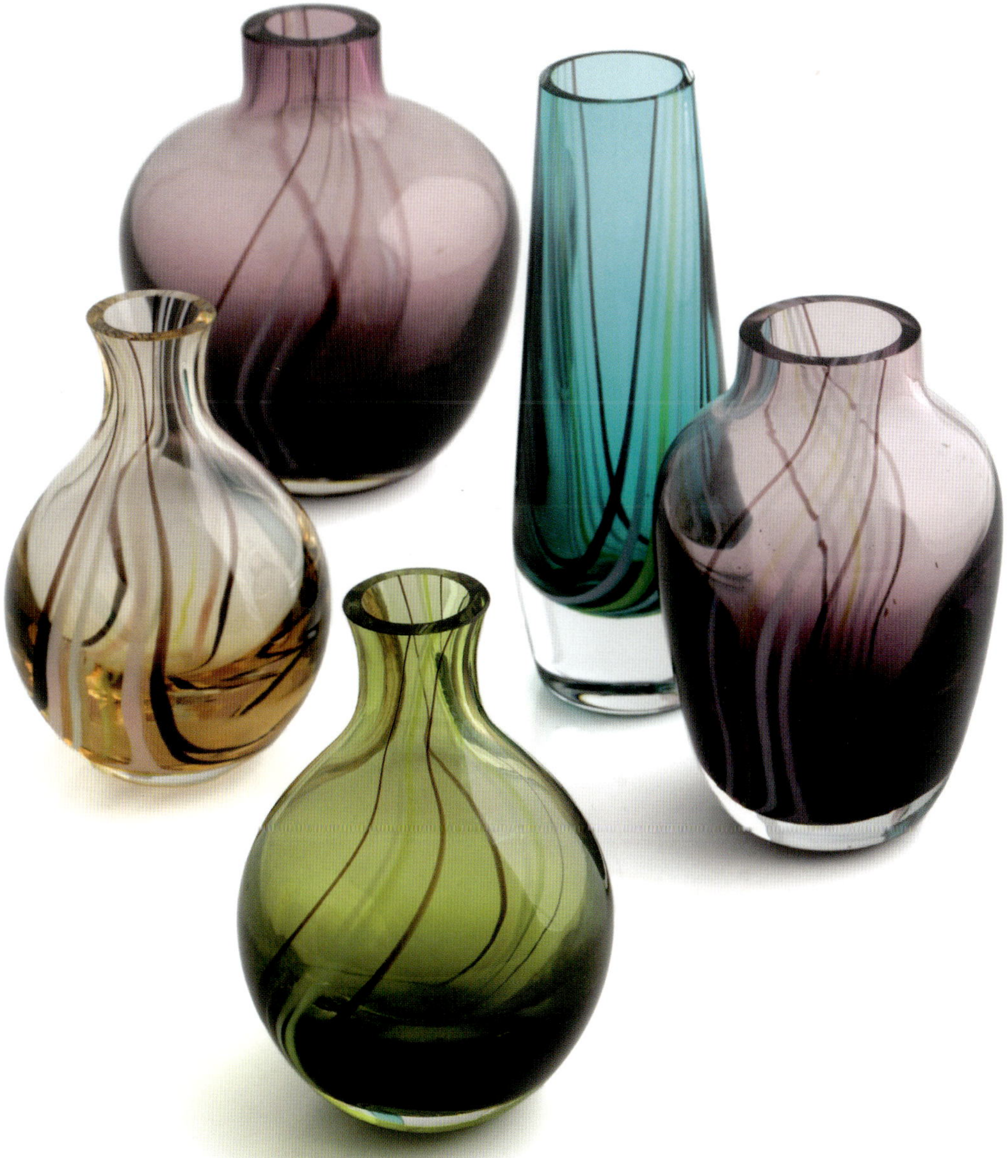

Five 1980s-90s Spinningdale range vases, launched in 1985, the tallest Kingfisher tapered vase no.4300 6in (15cm) high, the smallest Harvest Gold globe vase no.4301 4.75in (12cm) high. A collaborative effort designed with Colin Terris, Spinningdale refreshed Oban's stripes with coloured bodies initially in colourless, Moss or Heather. Other colours came later, such as Kingfisher and Harvest Gold in 1989. The colours and layout of the stripes also differed to Oban. Some shapes were from other ranges, such as the Heather OG2 Oban vase at the top of the group. In 1986, this form was the most expensive piece along with a waisted, flared vase, each priced at £10.95. The range does not appear in catalogues after 1991.

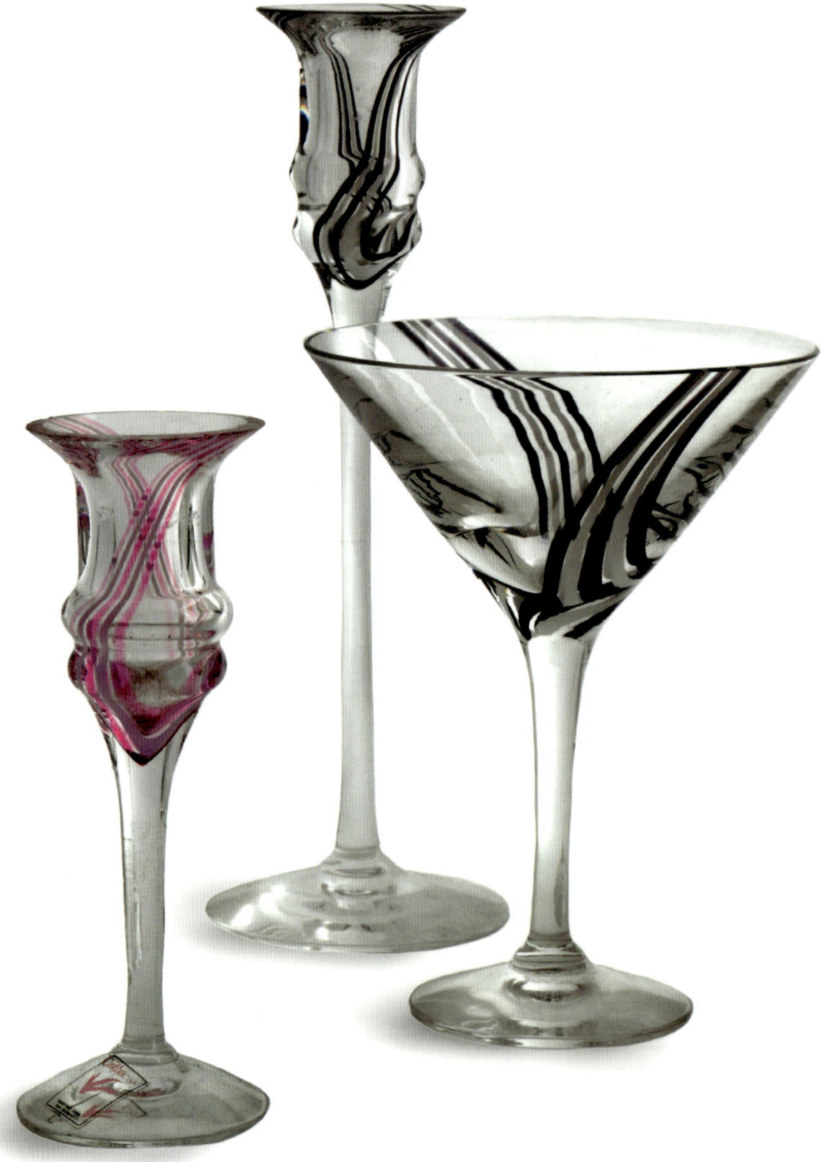

Two Caithness Crystal Lynn Candlesticks and a Cocktail Glass from a range designed by Colin Terris and Alastair MacIntosh in 1987, tallest 8.5in (21.5cm) high. This range of tableware with coloured stripes on unribbed colourless bodies was initially made at King's Lynn. It included bowls (inc. no.4071), candleholders, two carafes, and a jug. A range of conical drinking glasses and a decanter was called Charisma, and a similar, very popular, set with rounded forms was called Panache. Initial colours were Midnight (black & white), Dawn (pink & ruby) and Twilight (blue & pink). Sunrise and other colours were added later, and the most popular colourway was Dawn. Some forms were new, and some were from existing moulds at King's Lynn.

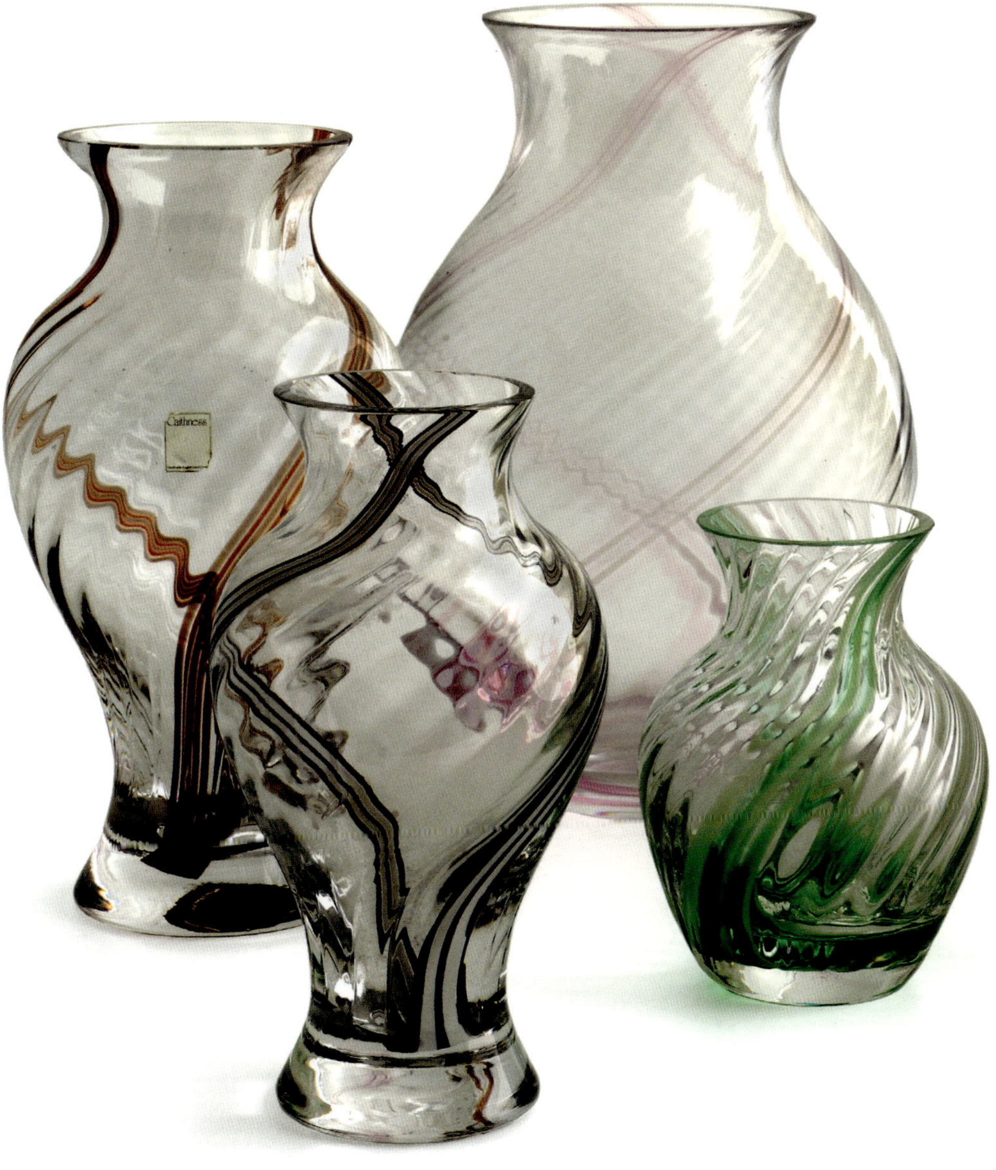

Two Chinese Vases, a small Posy Vase and another vase from the Flamenco range, designed by Colin Terris from 1987, the largest 9.5in (24cm) high. The Flamenco range combined the swirling stripes by then associated with Caithness with spirally ribbed bodies. It was initially produced at King's Lynn Crystal, using existing moulds, although some later shapes were new.

As Dartington had found, optically moulded designs were fashionable and economical to produce as slight flaws were hidden. The range comprised practical baluster vases and low bowls with stripes in a wide variety of colours. In 2002 prices ranged from £9.50 for a small Waisted Vase to £32 for a large bowl. The highly successful range was produced and sold until c2005.

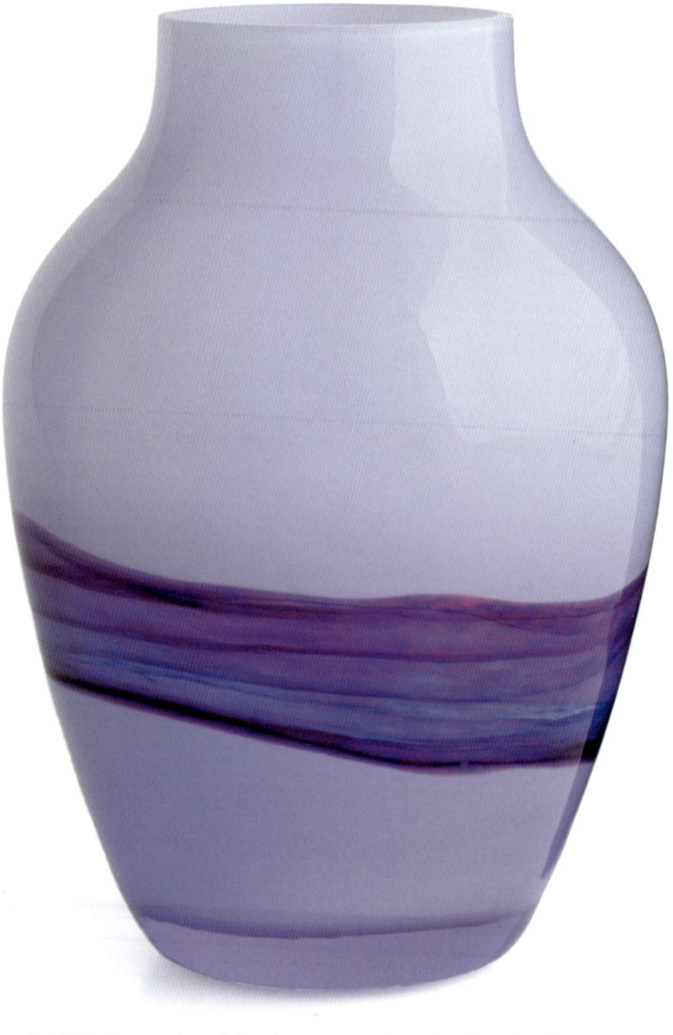

An Urn Vase, no.4453, from the Adagio range, designed by Margot Thomson in 1988, 6in (15cm) high. Launched in the 1989 catalogue, the Adagio range was marketed as "*Delicate veils in pastel tints flowing gently around each classic shape*". The range comprised this form and a Bottle Vase, both taken from the Oban range, a colourless footed Lantern Vase similar to that in Terris' Glenisla range (see p.53), two bowls, and a flattened globe vase. With a white core and an outer colourless casing, the band was in either purple and blue, or pink and cream. Costly to produce and expensive when sold, the range was not popular and was produced for less than 18 months. Examples are hard to find today, particularly in bowl forms.

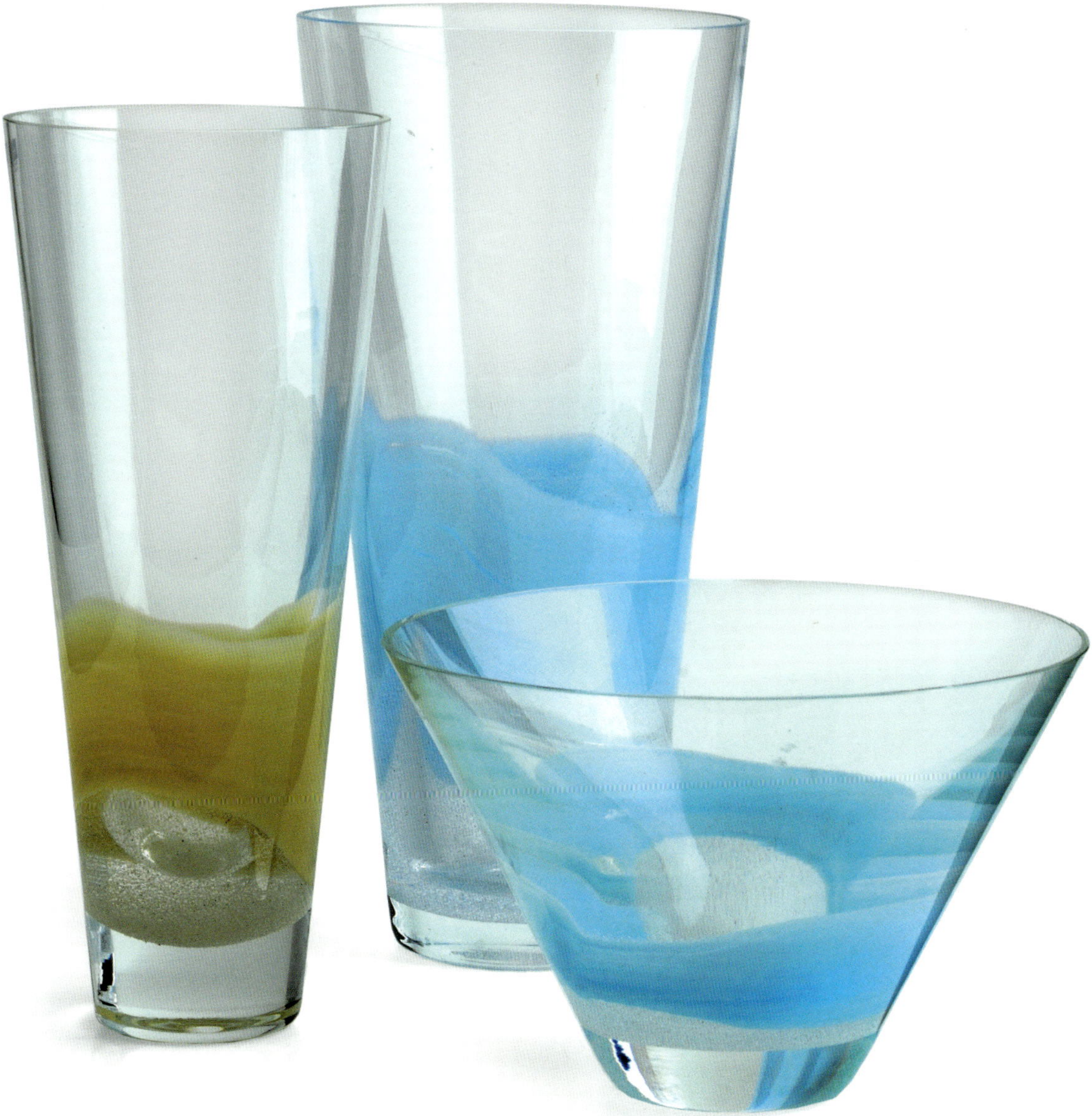

Two Bouquet Vases, no.8040 and no.8041 (smaller) and a Candle Bowl, no.8043, from the Shoreline range, designed by Gordon Hendry in 2000, tallest 10in (25.5cm) high. Launched in 2001, the wave-like band was made in Warm Sand (creamy yellow), Sea Grass (green) and Sky Blue (blue). Like Crush (see p.56), the bases also contained sand. Although the sand did not cause production problems here, the opaque band colours did, and often picked up dust or hairs, or shifted too far up or down the body when blown into moulds. The shapes comprised these two conical vases, (using Lochshiel vase moulds), two sizes of a new conical bowl, a paperweight–like clock, and a paperweight. Like Crush, Shoreline was only made for around two years.

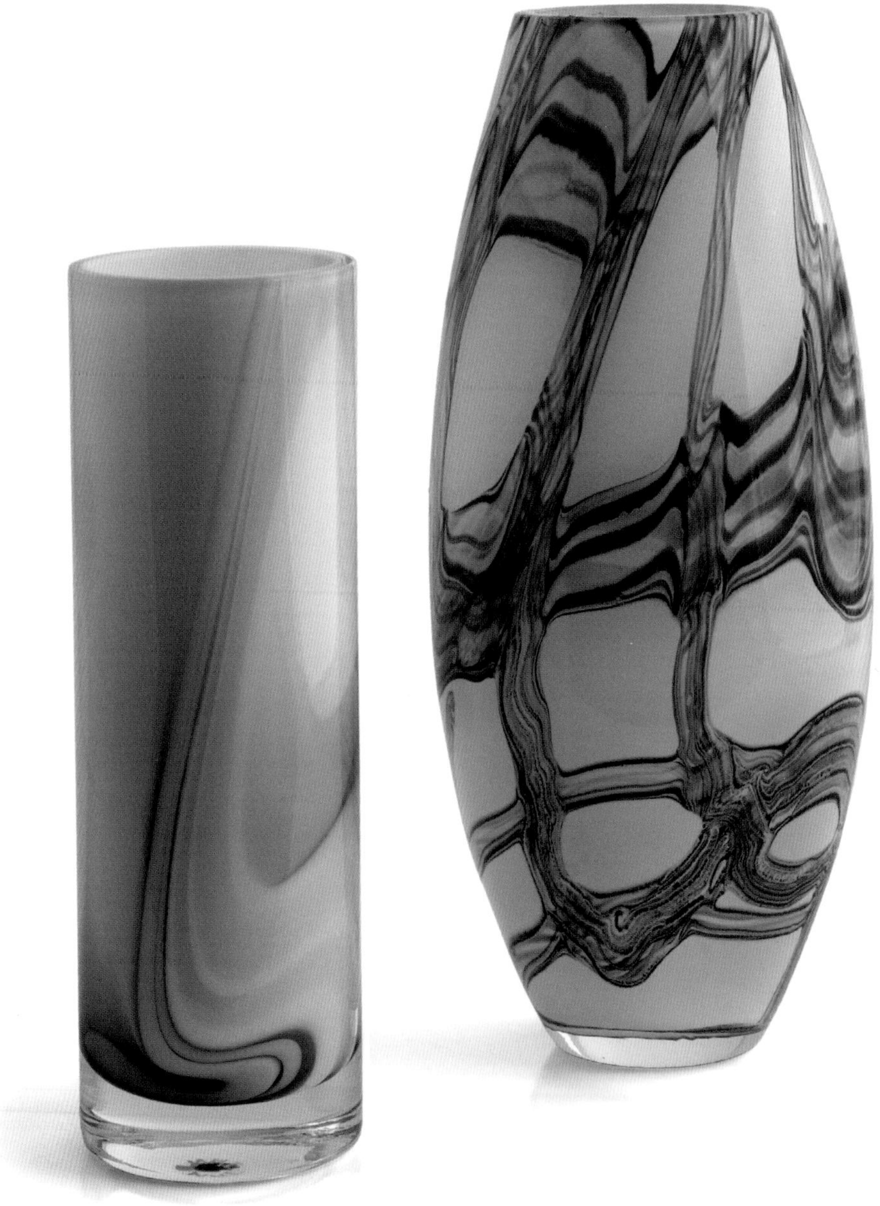

Left: A Small Vase, no.8460, in Smoke, from the Silk range, designed by Gordon Hendry in 2003, 7.5in (19cm) high.
Silk was made from 2003–04 in Smoke (the Soot colour), or in Heather, on white. After being dipped in colour, the gather was twisted to form the swirls before casing. Two sizes of cylinder vase, and a (rare) bowl with a turned-in rim were made.

Right: A large Teardrop Vase, no.8030, in Ivory, from the Marble range designed by Gordon Hendry in 2001, 9.25in (23.5cm) high. Produced from 2001–02, the random criss-cross pattern of the applied trails on each piece is unique. The range comprised two sizes of vase, two rounded bowls, a paperweight and a spherical clock. The Ivory colourway was reversed for Jet.

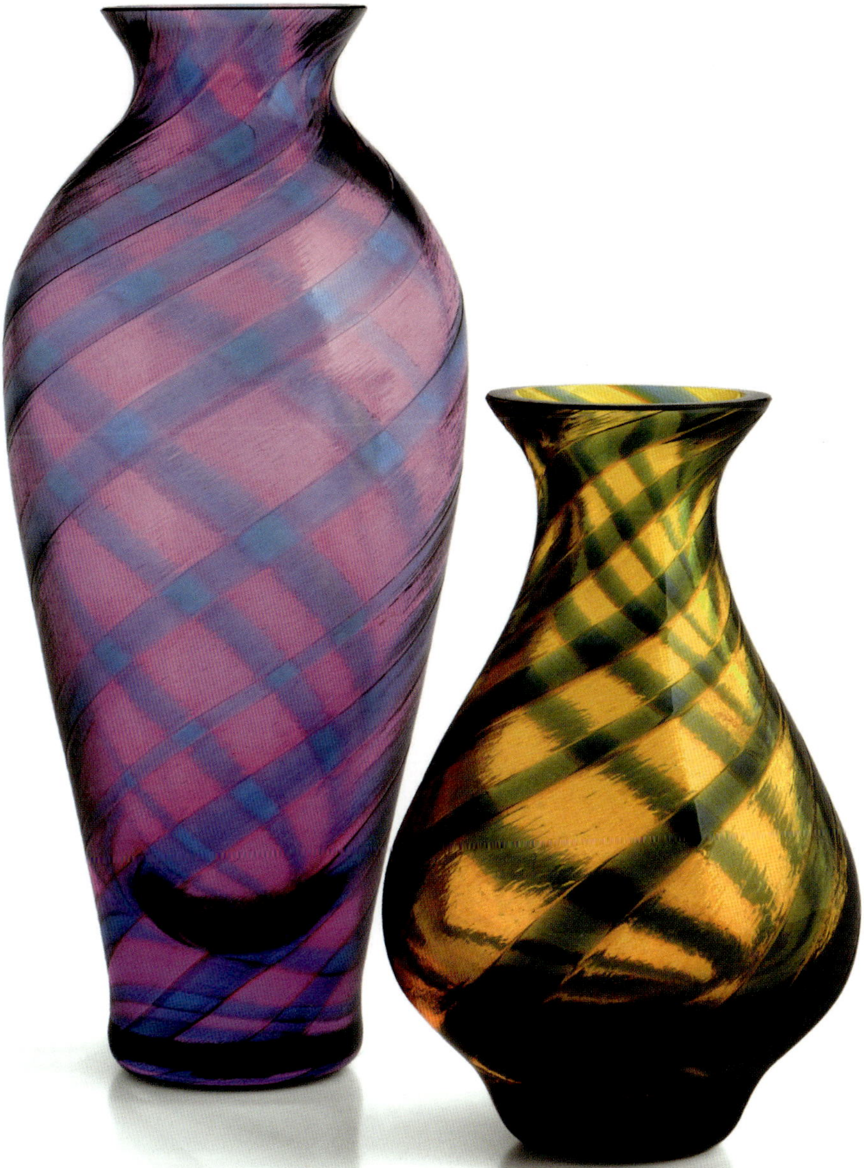

A Tall Vase, no.6400, in Ruby, and an Urn Vase, no.6404, in Topaz, from the Tartan Twist range designed by Alastair MacIntosh in 1995, large 8.5in (22cm) high, small 5.75in (14.5cm) high. This patriotic range was launched in early 1996 in Emerald, Ruby or Topaz colourways. In 1997, Topaz was replaced by Blue, and the entire range, was withdrawn at the end of 1998. Made at Wick, six vase shapes were offered, ranging in height from 4.3in (11cm) to 8.5in (22cm) high, and priced from £16–20. Trails were overlaid and moulded into a coloured body in a spiralling pattern to create a lattice effect that is heightened by a slightly spirally textured surface. A paperweight-like clock and a paperweight were added in late 1996. Blue is rarer.

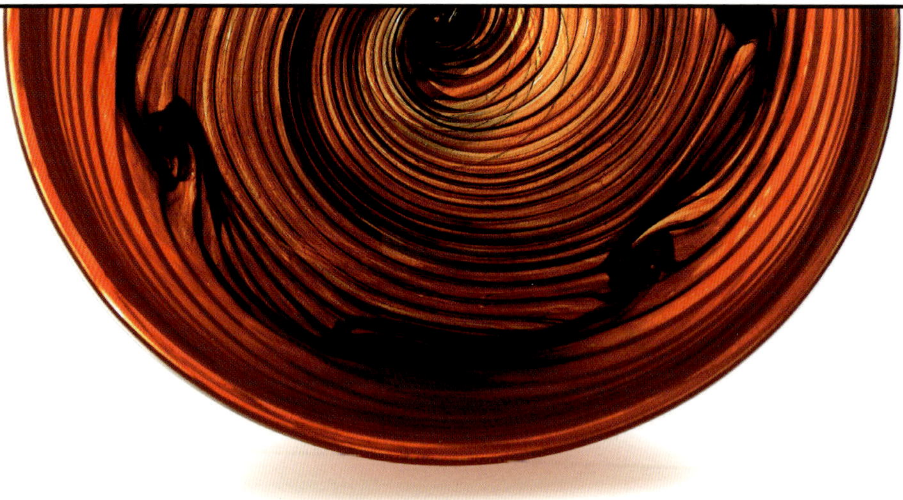

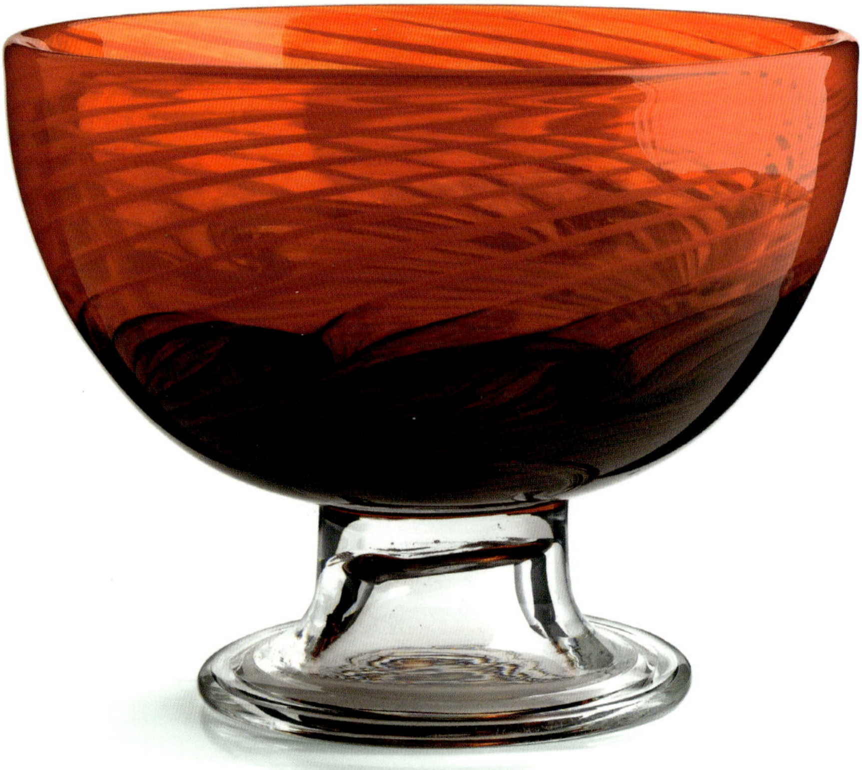

A footed bowl from the Samarkand range, designed by Colin Terris with Franco Toffolo, in late 1993, the foot engraved 'Samarkand Caithness Scotland', 6in (15.5cm) high. Made and sold in 1994 only, the Samarkand range almost harks back to certain Monart patterns, with its swirls pulled into spirals with a tool. The range comprised a bottle vase, a bowl, a plate, an urn vase, and this bowl, in this vibrant colourway only. All examples graduated to darker tones towards the base, bordered by pulled spirals that echoed the spiralling threads around the body. The bowl shown here was almost certainly made by Toffolo. All shapes were priced at £99, and the range did not sell well, particularly in bowl forms, making it comparatively rare today.

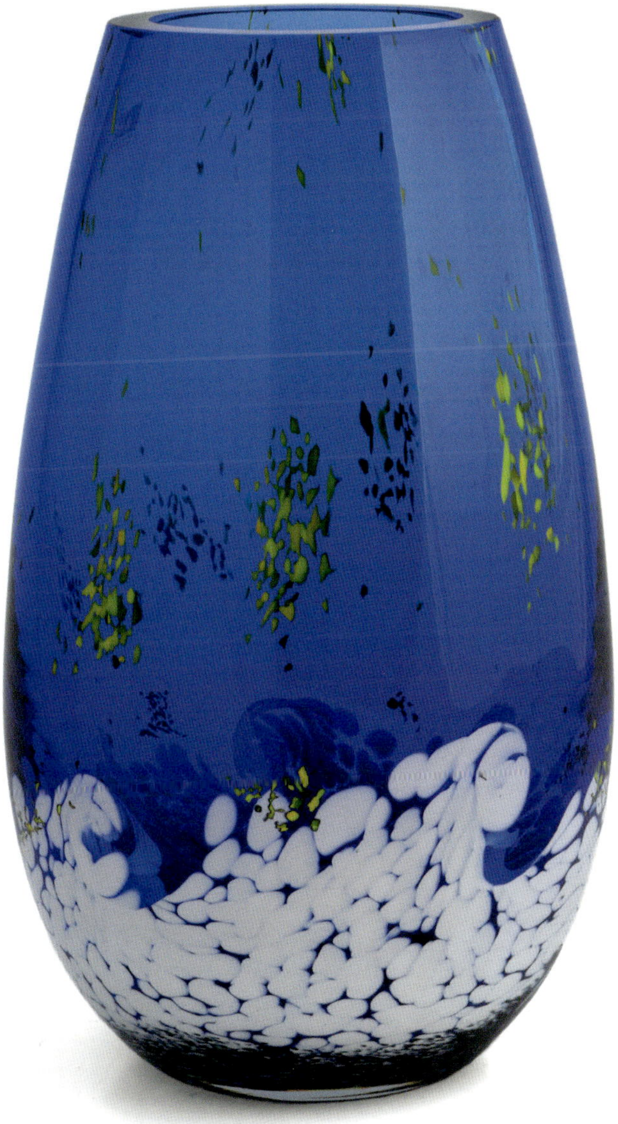

A One Starry Night vase, no.LO1022, from the Van Gogh Inspirations range, designed by Helen MacDonald in 2001, with acid etched mark to base and machine-cut rim, 7.5in (19cm) high. This design was limited to 500 examples, and retailed at £90. It was part of a range of six different limited edition designs based on Van Gogh's paintings that was offered in 2002 only.

Edition sizes ranged from 200-500 examples, with the most expensive being £195 for Golden Sunflower. The series was devised as Caithness Glass had designed and made a number of special paperweights for the Art Institute of Chicago for a number of years. Many of the resulting designs were then extended to vases or bowls, often in limited editions.

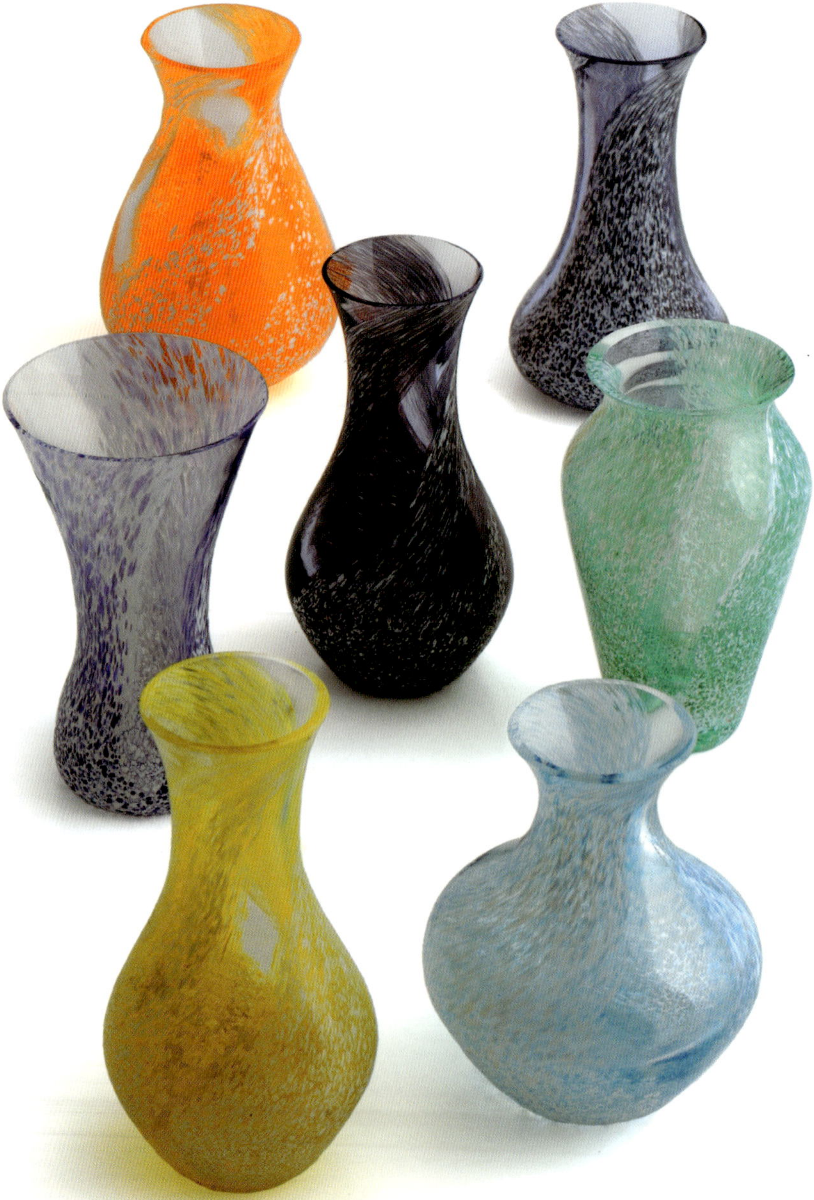

Seven vases from the Allegro range, devised by Jimmy Manson and John Ross with Colin Terris, in 1999, 4in (10cm) to 5in (12.5cm) high. The Allegro range was devised in order to to refresh the highly popular Rondo range, but also to reduce the cost of Rondo to fill a price bracket in the gift market. The outer casing of glass was removed, leaving the powdered enamels on the exterior, but this made the range look and feel of lower and 'cheaper' quality. As a result, although sales were strong, it did not sell as well as Rondo, and was withdrawn in 2004. Many different shapes were used over the years, and colours included Pearl, Berry, Lilac and Sable. Other attempts to replicate Rondo's success included Bolero and Whispers.

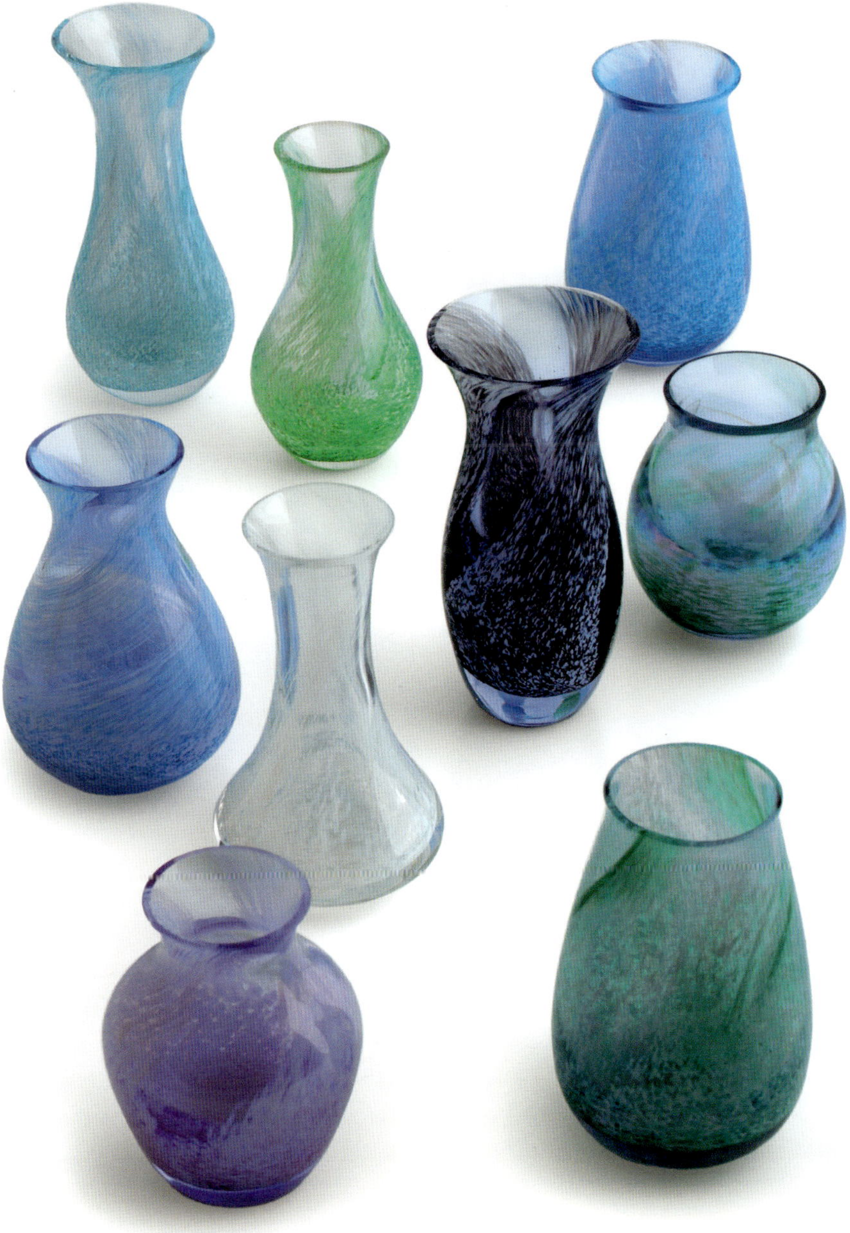

Nine vases from the Rondo range, devised by Jimmy Manson and John Ross with Colin Terris in 1984, 3.5in (9cm) to 5.75in (14.5cm) high. Rondo was the company's most prolifically produced and successful later range, and was sold into the 2000s. Aimed at the gift market, the pleasing and unchallenging design had wide appeal and comprised small perfume bottles and posy vases. A colourless gather was rolled in coloured enamels, twisted and then cased before being moulded. Fast and economical to produce, the yield of first quality pieces was very high. A vast number of shapes were used over the years, some also being used within similar ranges such as Allegro, Pastorale and Bolero. The many colours used included Sable, Jade, and Azure.

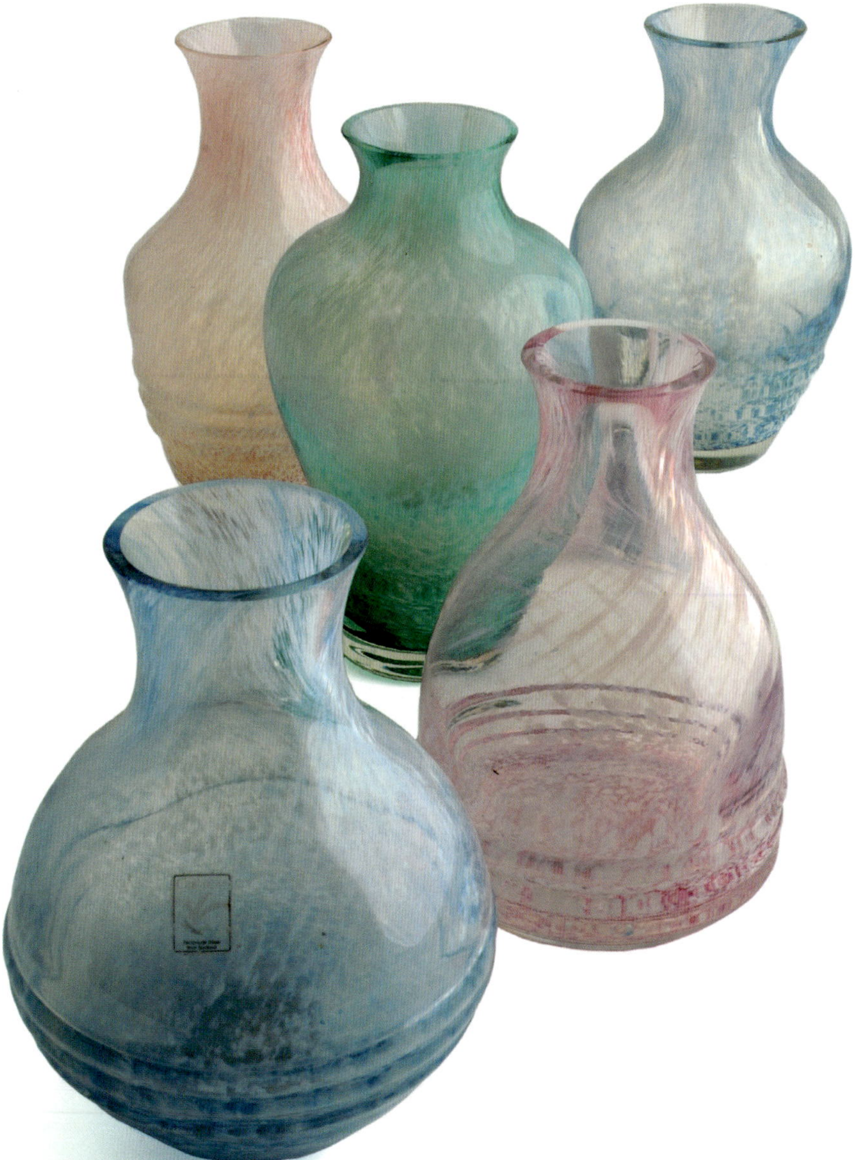

Five vases from the Concerto range, designed by Colin Terris in 1991, with some shapes designed by Alastair MacIntosh, tallest 7in (18cm) high. Launched in 1991, Concerto was made in the same way as the popular Rondo range, but was larger in size and had a band of three moulded rings. The initial range comprised five shapes in Pink, Blue, and Jade. Shapes included the pink Iris Vase above, the blue Rose Vase at the back of the group, and the pink Poppy Vase at the back left. In 1992, the green Tulip vase and blue Dahlia Vase above replaced unsuccessful shapes, such as the Iris Vase. The range was discontinued in 1993 and replaced by Bolero, effectively a larger version of Rondo with some different shapes. Despite this, sales were strong.

Complex Decoration

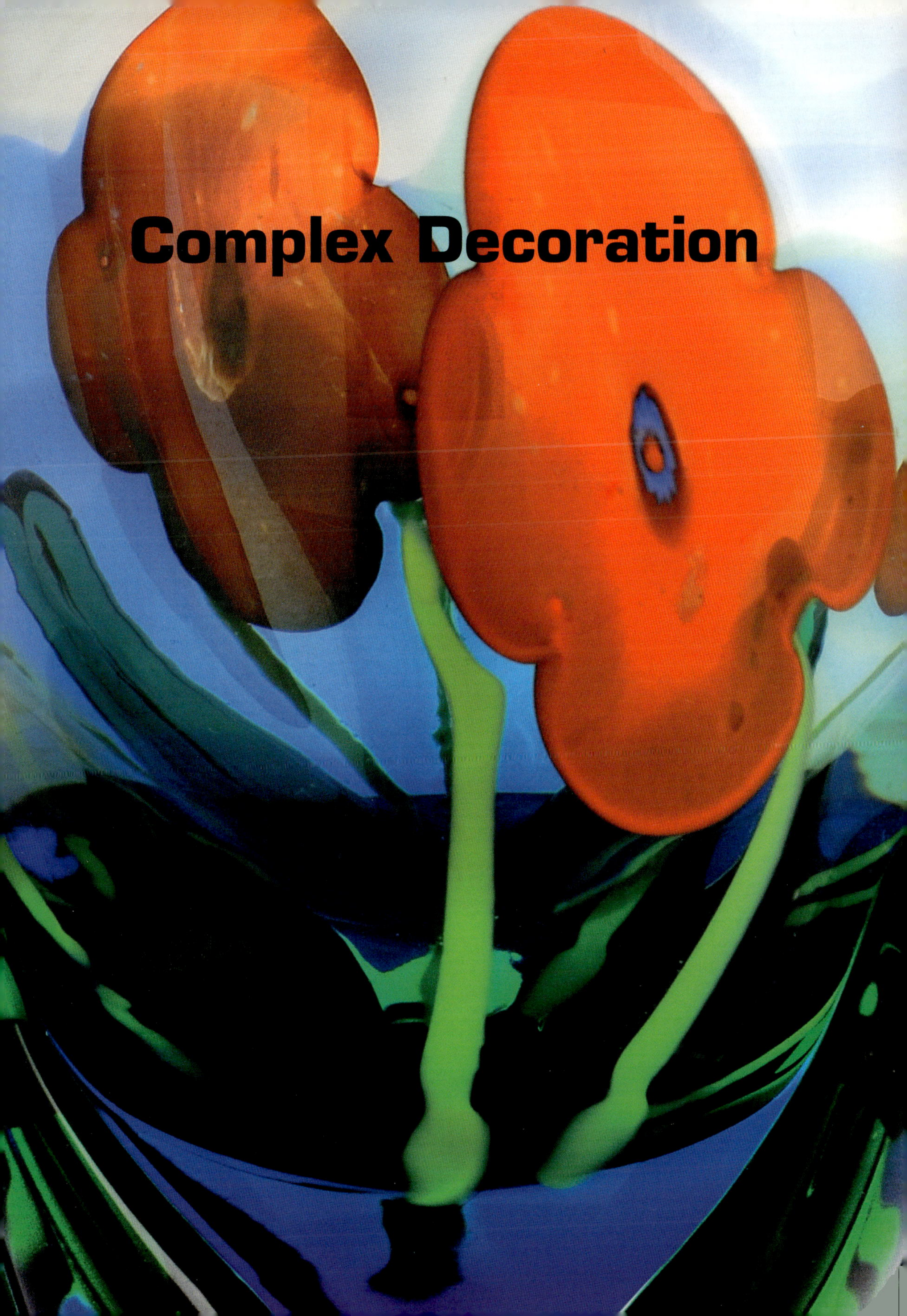

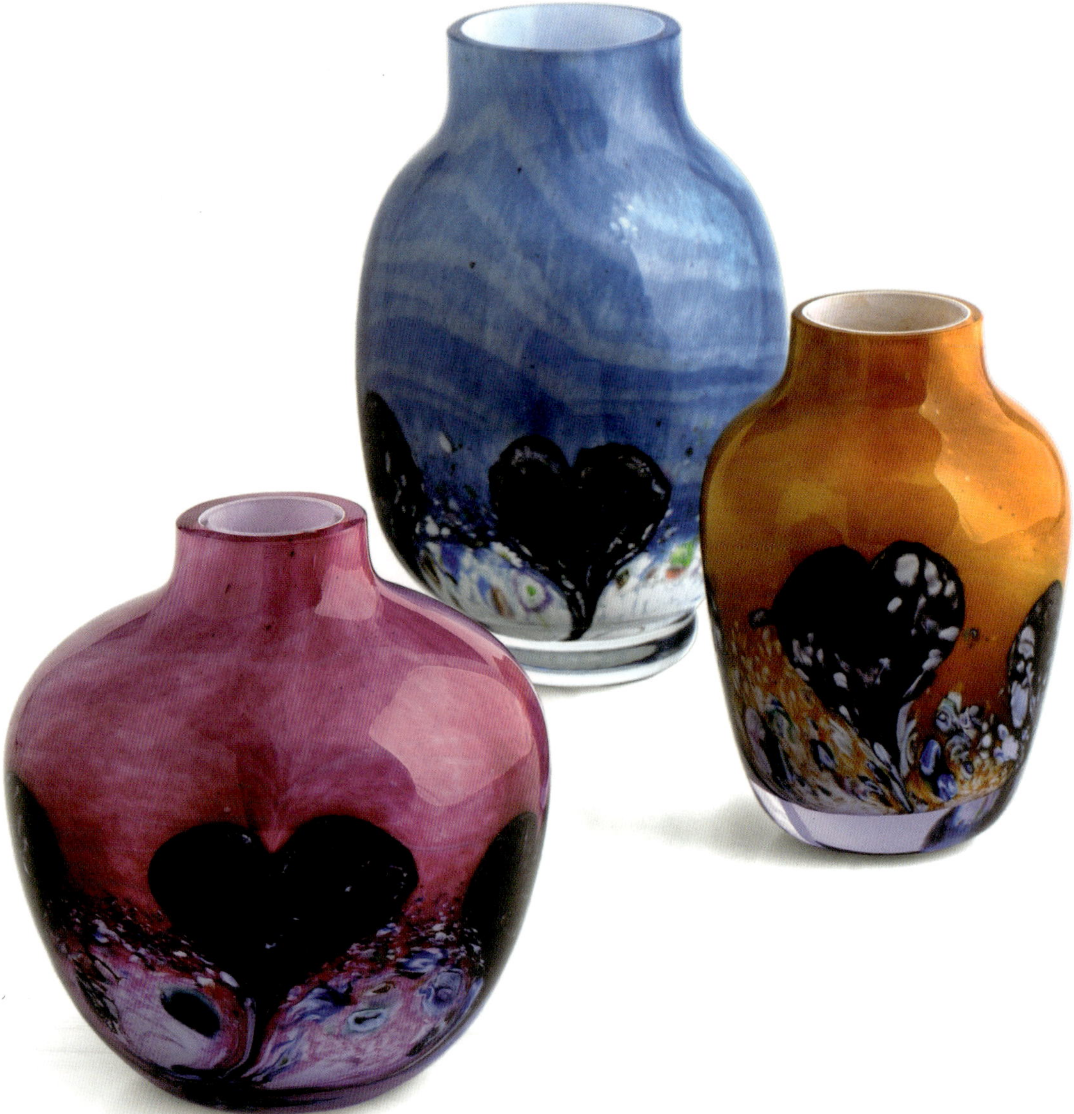

Three Cadenza range vases, designed by Colin Terris in 1986, largest 6in (15cm) high. Cadenza was the first complex hot-worked hollow ware range produced. It was inspired by paperweights, and was made using similar techniques. A colourless gather was rolled in white, then in the intended colour. This was then overlaid with millefiori and coloured glass chips. Fine colourless rods were then rolled on. A separate dark violet gather was dripped on and pulled into a heart shape before it was cased and moulded. Colours comprised Blue, Emerald, Ruby and Topaz, and some shapes were from the Oban and Glenisla ranges. Time-consuming to produce, and ranging in price from £25–50, the range was replaced in 1989 by Adagio (see p.64).

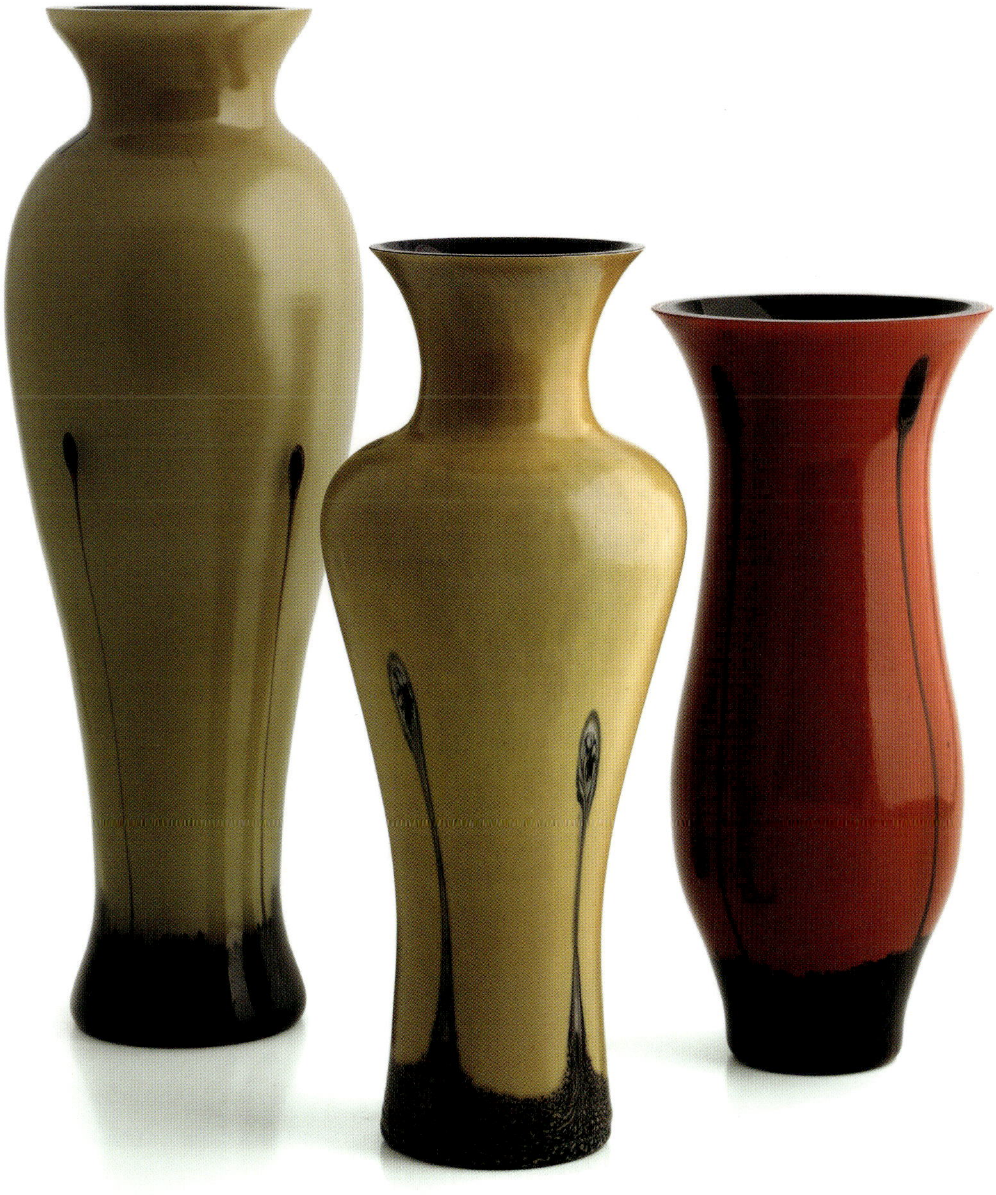

Three vases from the Ebony range, designed by Colin Terris, Phil Chaplain, Gordon Hendry, Alastair MacIntosh, Jimmy Manson, and John Ross in 1996, largest 12in (30.5cm) high. A collaborative design effort, this Art Nouveau inspired range was launched with six shapes in beige (Sand). Two more shapes were added in 2000, and the red Flame was made from 2001. It was made by rolling a colourless gather in dark purple powdered enamels, followed by white, and then red or beige. Before being blown into a mould, the base was rolled in dark chips which were melted and pulled up into the body. A strong seller with prices ranging from £30-48, it was produced until 2004. The flatter Sand tone on the left is indicative of pieces made in Poland c2003.

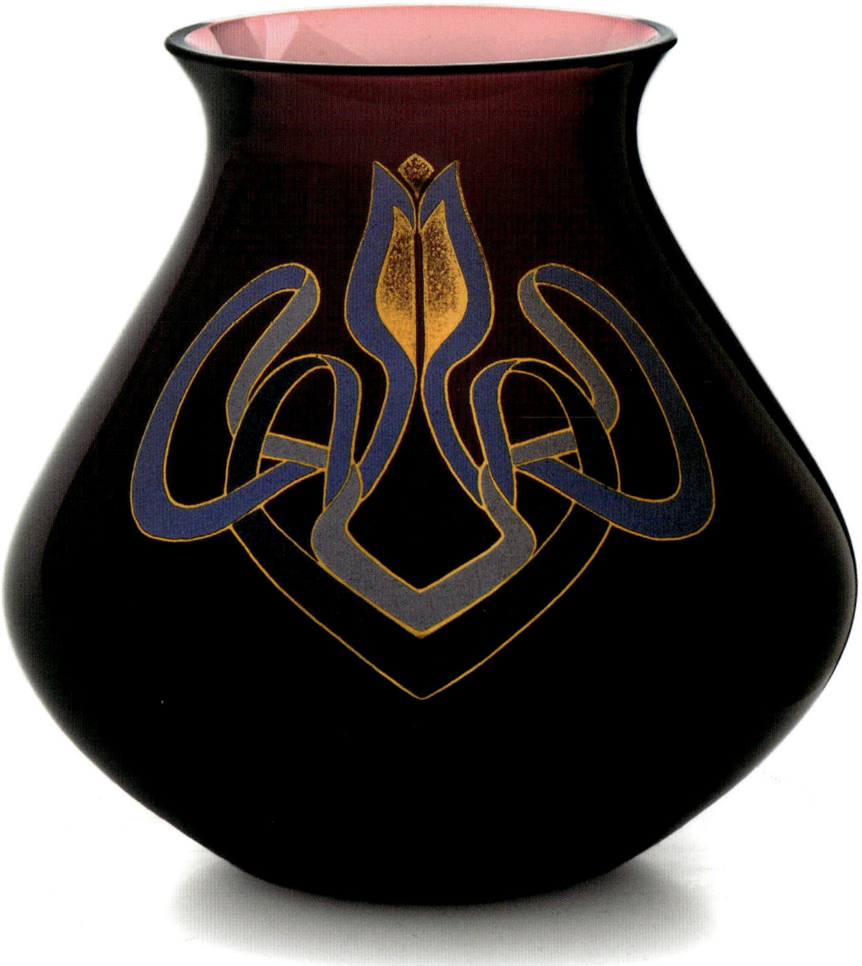

A Bulb Vase, no.5202, from the Art Deco range designed by Margot Thomson in 1992, 4in (10cm) high. The origins of this range lie in the more correctly named Art Nouveau range, designed by Colin Terris and sold c1981-82. Both bore transfer designs of stylised foliate and floral motifs, which were in 22ct gold on Terris' original range. Thomson added more detail and colour for her revival. Both ranges were short-lived as they needed a dedicated furnace to fix the transfer, which proved costly and inconvenient. The range comprised five vase shapes in Twilight Blue, Heather (above), and Harvest Gold. Art Nouveau comprised seven shapes, some taken from the 1980s Glenisla range, in four colours including Moss and Soot.

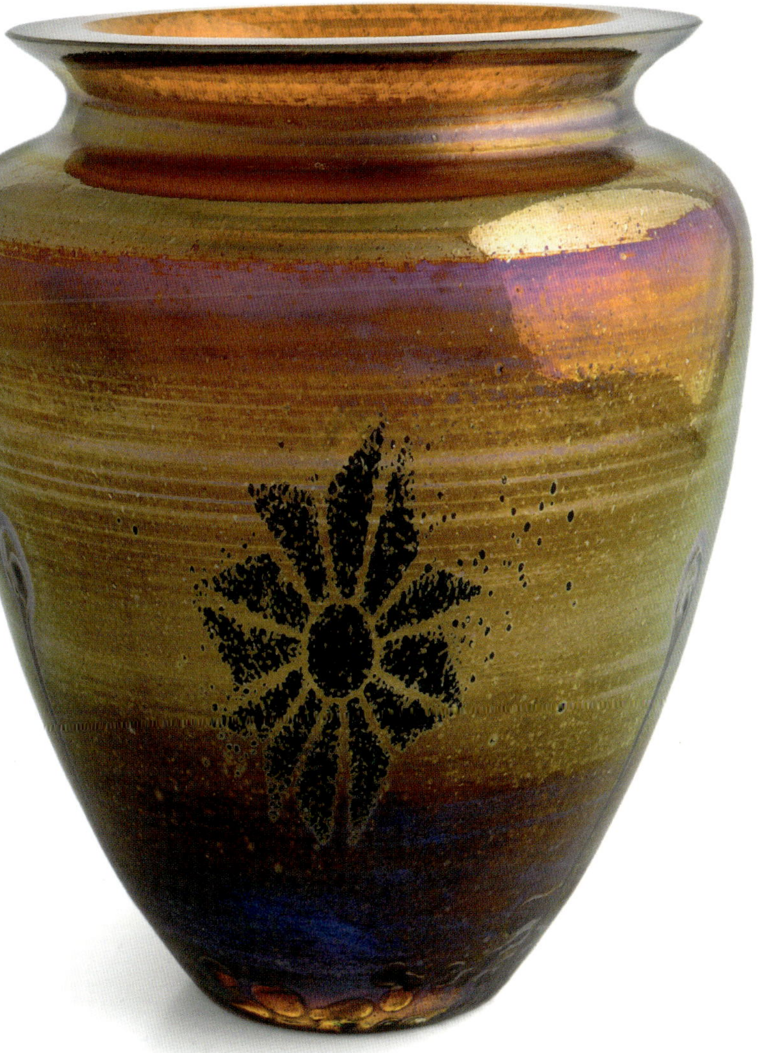

A Large Bouquet Vase, no.8120, in Gold, from the Alchemy range designed by Helen MacDonald in 2002, 8in (20.5cm) high. Launched in Summer 2002, the Alchemy range was developed from a 'mood board' covering period fashions and trends. Themes included Medieval works, turning metal into gold, fur, King Arthur's court, African tribal art, and ethnic looks. Forms were inspired by Classical examples, and comprised three vases and two sizes of bowl. Colours were Gold and the blue Pewter, and the iridescence was created using a flame torch on sensitive powdered enamels. The sunburst, swirl and zig zag motifs were added using a graphite mould containing powdered glass. Made until 2003, it was expensive, but popular.

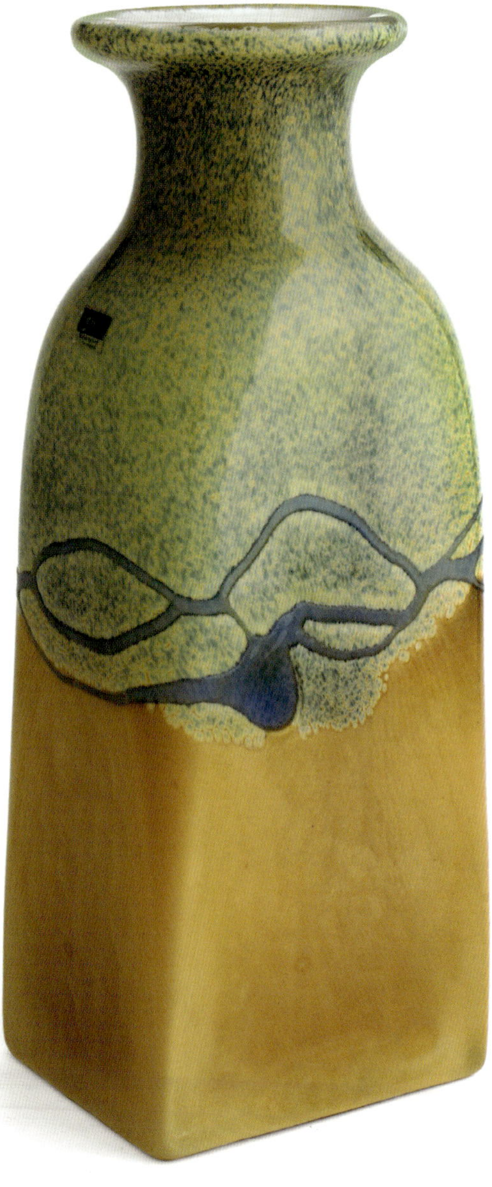

A Rectangular Vase, no.5021, in Moonstone, from the Xanadu range designed by Colin Terris in 1996, 10in (25.5cm) high. Unlike most Caithness ranges, Xanadu had a hand-finished rim. As such, it was reversed onto a pontil rod, adding an extra step to production. Three vase shapes with hexagonal, triangular or rectangular cross sections were produced in Aquamarine, Flame, Indigo, and Moonstone colourways. The angular, mould blown lower bodies contrasted against the curving, hand-finished tops. The range did not sell well, although stronger colours were more popular, and it was deemed expensive at £45. Involving many layers, it was also time-consuming to make, so was withdrawn after two years.

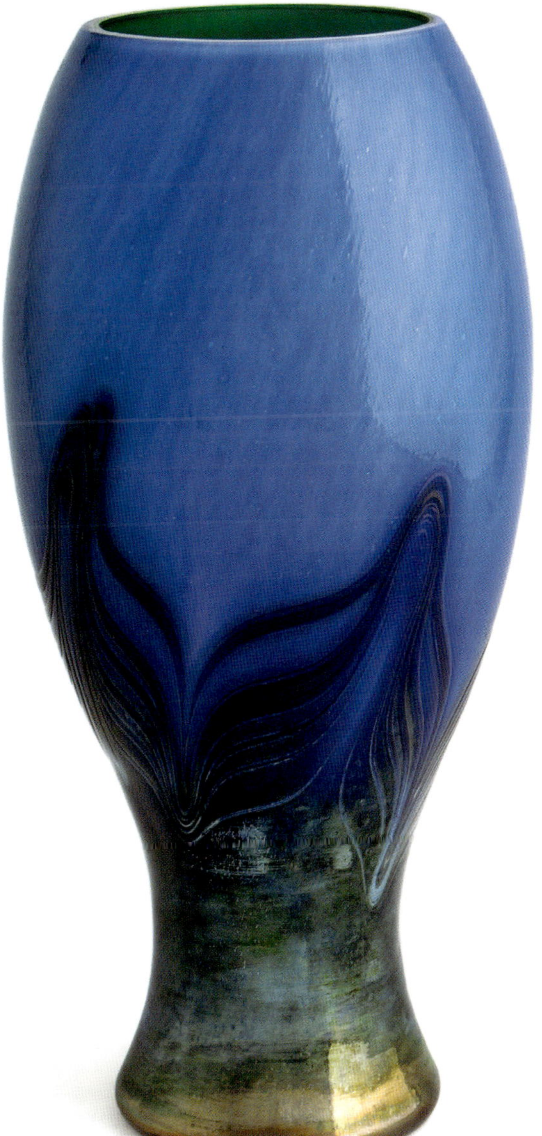

A Medium Bouquet Vase, no.7551, from the Salomé range designed by Phil Chaplain in 1997, 9in (23cm) high. Launched in 1998, Salomé was derived from Xanadu and inspired by Art Nouveau glass, which had also been the inspiration of the successful Ebony range. A green core was rolled in layers of white and then blue powdered enamels, which were melted into the surface. An iridescent trail was applied and combed into a feather pattern. The piece was then moulded, cooled, and lightly fumed in metallic oxides. The range comprised two sizes of this vase, two tall vases with flared rims, and two sizes of footed bowl. Prices ranged from £45–55 for vases, to £90 for the large bowl. Salomé was only sold from 1998–99.

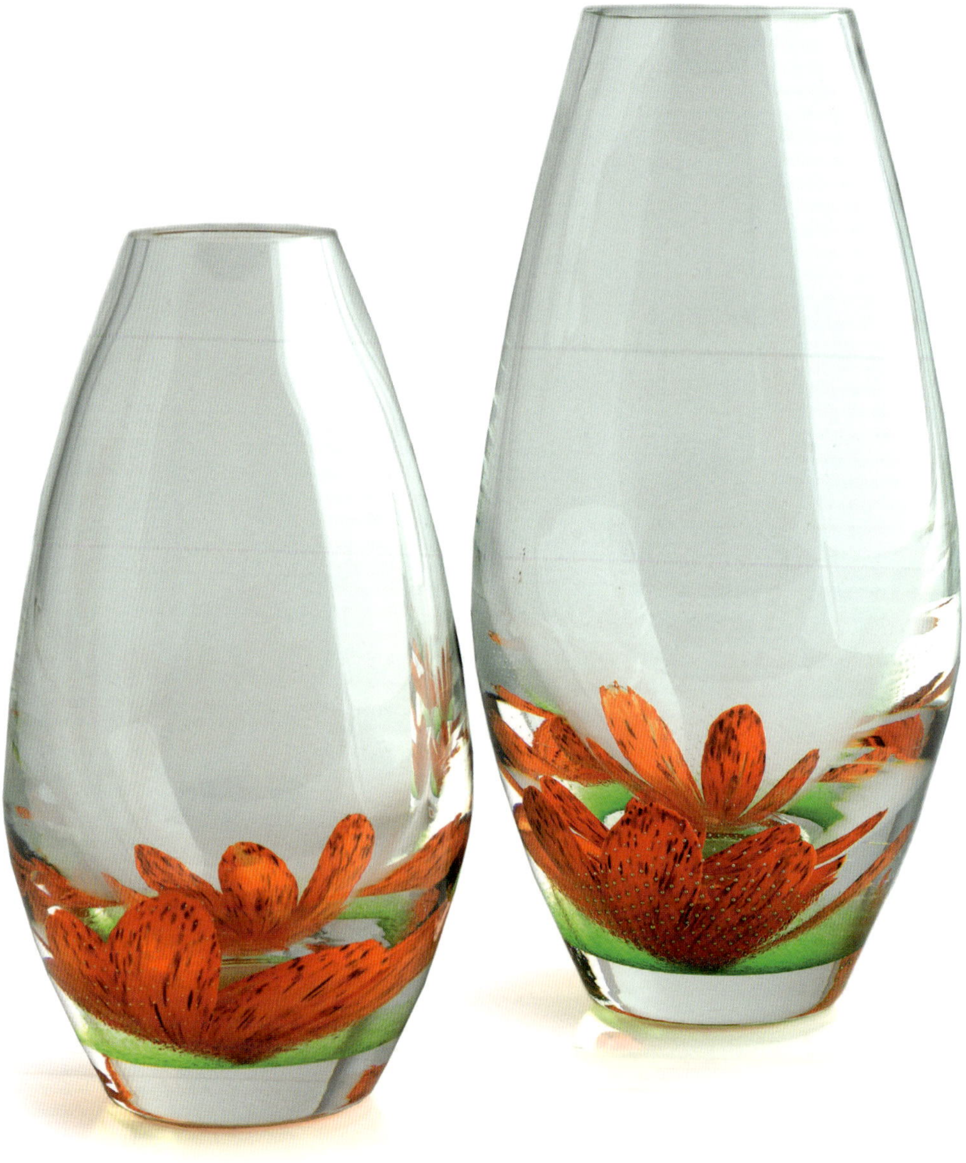

Two Teardrop Vases, no.8070 (large) and no.8071 (medium), in Tiger, from the Oriental Lily range designed by Gordon Hendry in 2001, 9in (23cm) high and 7in (18cm) high. Launched in Summer 2001, this range was developed from Tranquillity, which it superseded. Shapes comprised these two vases (£45 & £55) and a Sweet Dish bowl (£39) in either Tiger or Pearl colourways. It was made using the same techniques as Tranquillity, but also contained a net of bubbles. The dramatic red of Tiger sold better than Pearl, but not as well as Tranquillity, so the range was withdrawn by 2003. The teardrop vase form was used frequently by Hendry, and harks back to ÓBroin's best-selling Barrel Vases designed in the early 1960s.

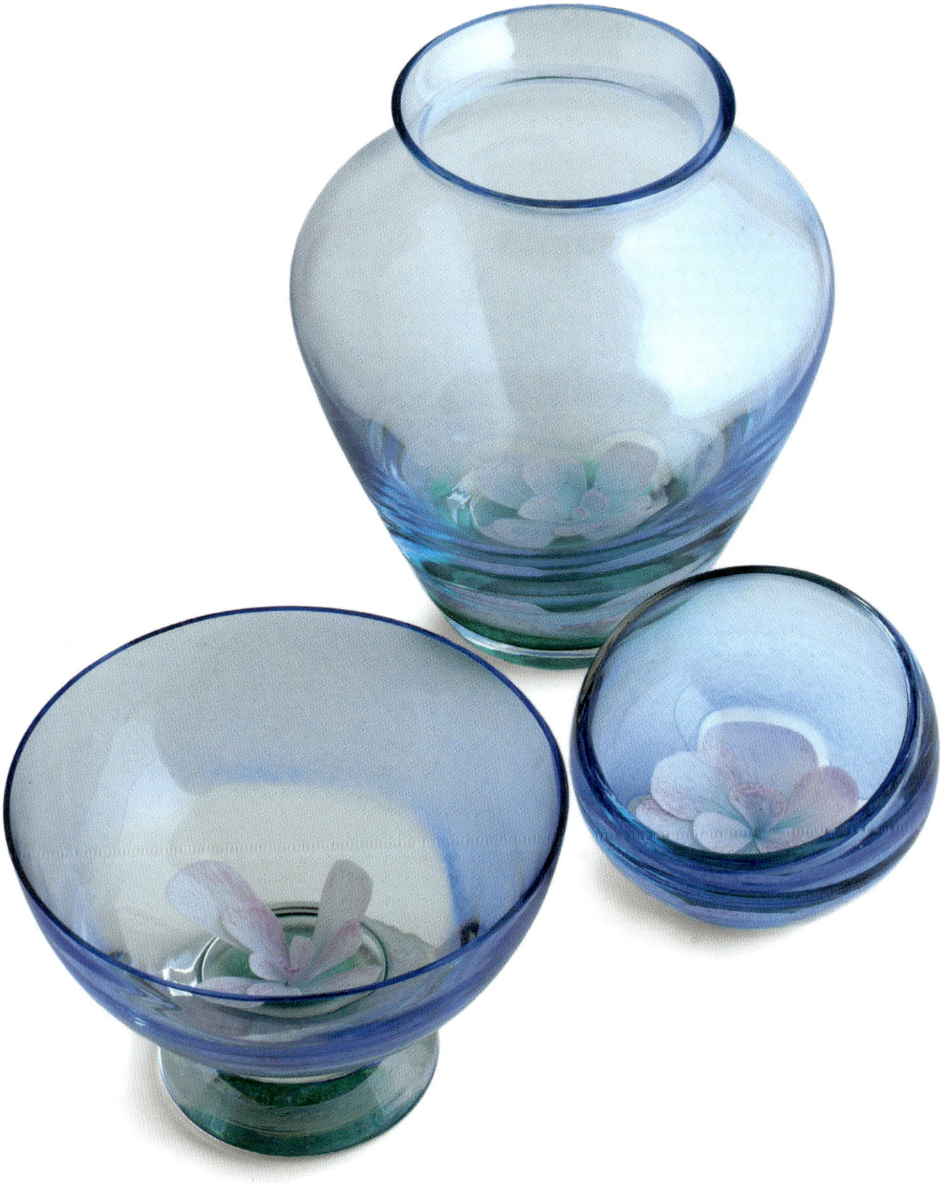

A Vase no.5044, a Medium Bowl no.5041, and a Medium Rose Bowl no.5043, in Blue, from the Tranquillity range devised by Jimmy Manson and Jeneo Lewis with Colin Terris in 1995, vase 9in (23cm) high. Tranquillity was launched in January 1996, with two sizes of bowl and rose bowl, and the vase shown here. Colours comprised Blue, Green, and Pink. Following forerunners like Cadenza, the complex three-dimensional internal flower motif was derived from paperweight manufacture by Wick based glassmakers Lewis and Manson. The footed bowl was made with a mould from King's Lynn. The range was popular, particularly in Blue, and sold well. At £77, the vase was withdrawn in 2000, and the range was discontinued in 2001.

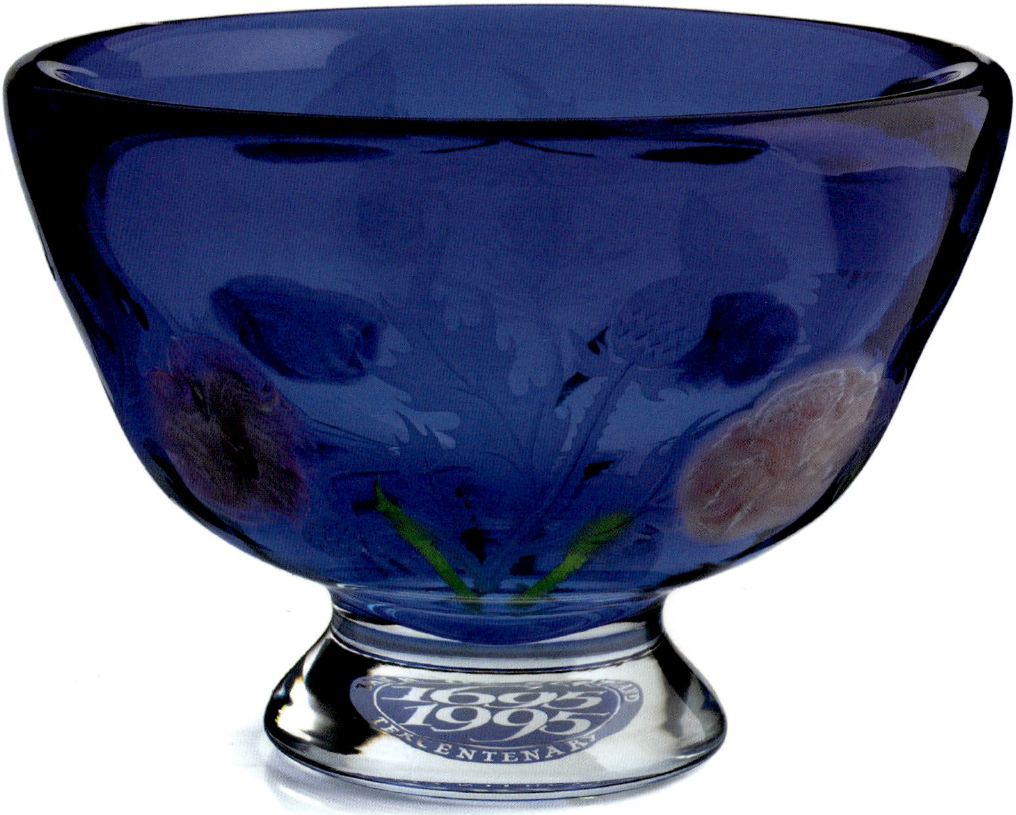

A Bank of Scotland Tercentenary footed bowl, with a sandblasted commemorative decal to the base of the foot, devised by Jimmy Manson, John Ross, and Franco Toffolo with Colin Terris in 1995, 6in (15cm) high. Produced as a commemorative for special staff members of the bank, around 200 of these hand-finished bowls were made. The design combined the flowers from Terris' Springtime range of 1987, (see p.115) with deeply sandblasted thistles, echoing Helen MacDonald's similar combination in her 1991 Summer Meadow range (see p.118). The commission was won in a competition, and the success and the income were important for the Wick factory at the time. Each bowl was contained in a fabric lined, fitted card box.

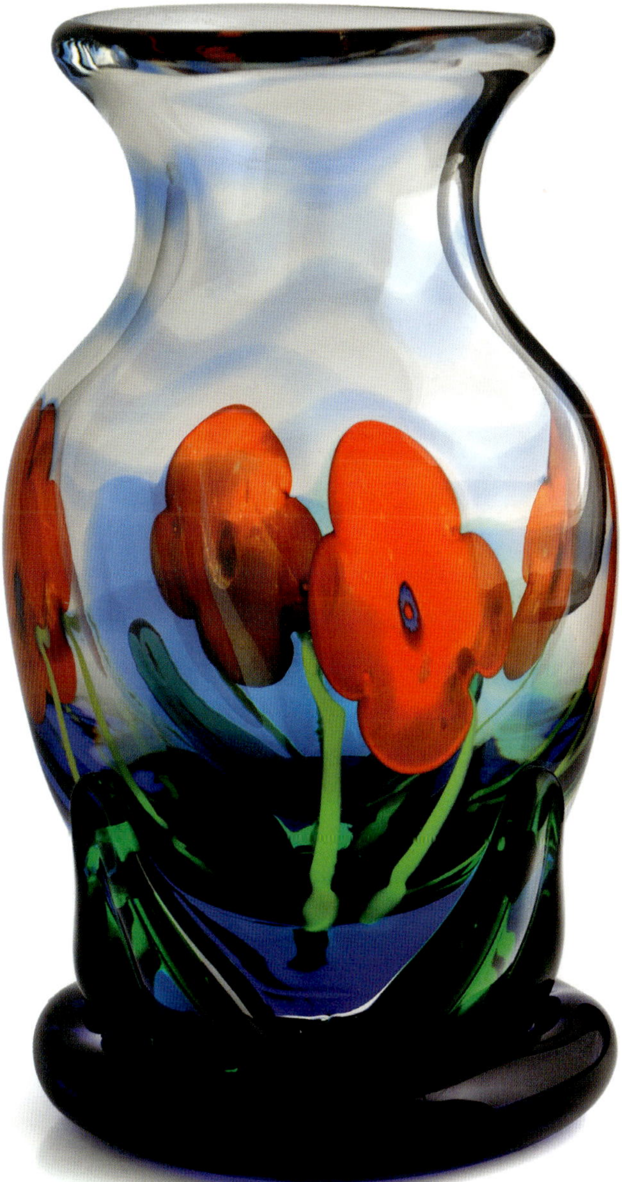

A Roman Vase, no.6667, from The Poppy Collection in the Prestige series, designed by Colin Terris in 1998, 8in (20.5cm) high. Launched in 1999 as part of the new Studio Collection, shapes comprised a torpedo vase, a similar shape with a flared rim, a rounded bowl, a similar bowl with a flared rim, a tapering bowl with an oval rim, and this vase (see p.122). Trials were made by Franco Toffolo, and he may also have made many of the pieces sold. The range was not limited, but pieces were expensive at £200–250, and only a couple of hundred examples may have been made. Complex to make and including many hot-worked elements, each piece was made and finished entirely by hand. The range was discontinued at the end of 2000.

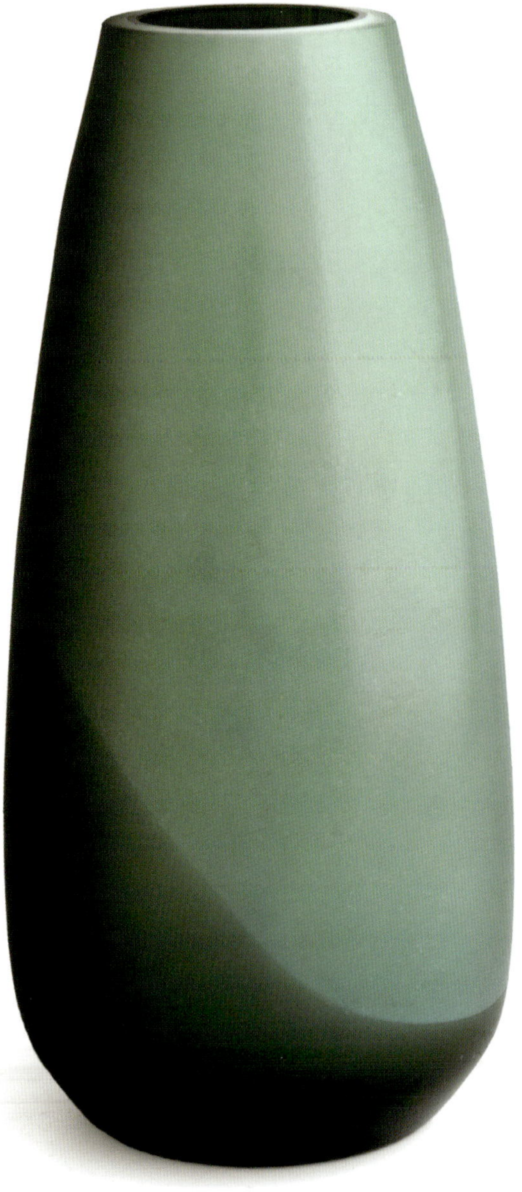

A Teardrop Vase, no.8083, in Smoke, from the Touchstone range designed by Gordon Hendry in 2002, 8in (20.5cm) high. This range was made in Smoke or Ivory, a combination of yellow and grey. Resembling ceramic, the intention was to show subtle differences in texture and colour on simple forms. A gather of Soot glass was cased in crystal, then rolled in white enamel, then cased in colourless glass again before being rolled in yellow or green powder to leave a velvety texture. After being mould blown, the gather was then partially dipped at an angle in Soot, giving a shiny area. Sizes were limited by the furnace aperture, and comprised four rounded vases and a bowl. Priced from £36–42, Touchstone was only produced during 2002.

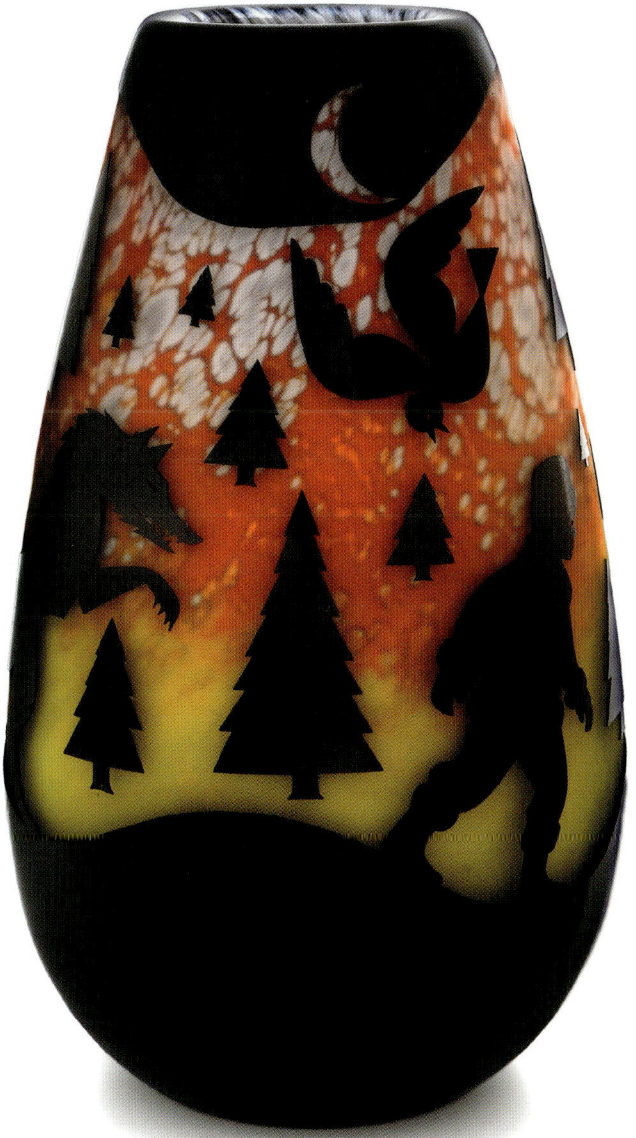

A Peter & The Wolf vase, no.CT838, designed by Gordon Hendry in 2003, from the Signature Collection, the base with engraved title and signature, 9in (23cm) high. Inspired by Sergei Prokofiev's tale of 1936, the look and colours of the design were inspired by silhouettes and the work of illustrator Jan Pienkowski which Hendry had admired when studying graphic design. A complex mottled and orange and yellow body was handblown and cased in dark grey. The surface was then masked off with tape and the motifs were traced on. The tape around the motifs was then cut away and the exposed grey was sandblasted away, leaving the design. At £235, it was the most expensive vase sold at the time, and comparatively few sold.

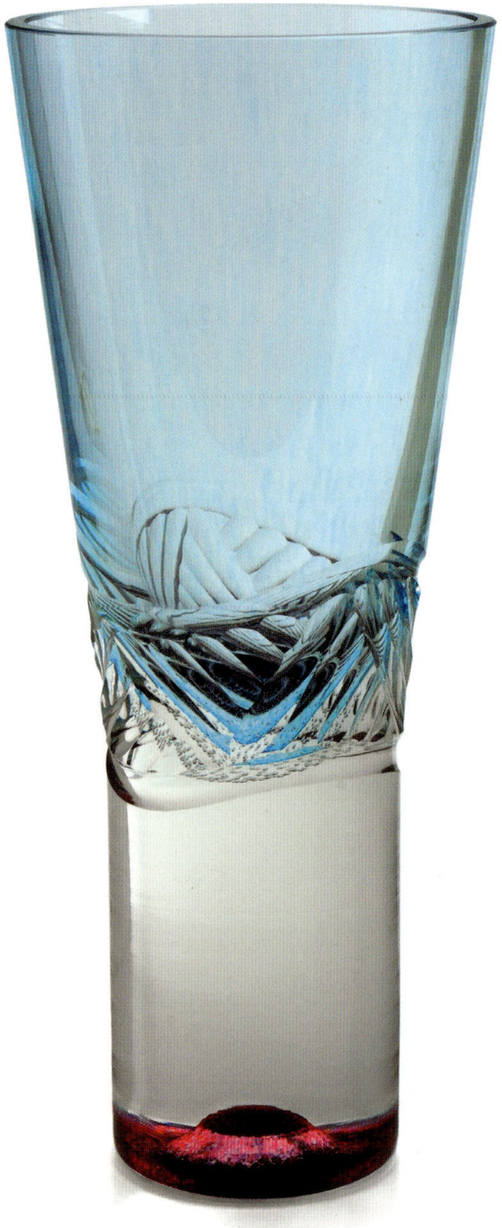

A Cold Fusion Trumpet Vase, no.8105, designed by Alastair MacIntosh in 2002, from the Signature range, signed on the base, 12in (30.5cm) high. Launched as part of the new Signature collection in Summer 2002, this design was intended to be modern and glassy, incorporating hot-worked and cold-worked techniques on a simple form. The coloured base reflected in a network of bubbles halfway up the body, and accentuated by being kicked-up, was a recurring theme in MacIntosh's work. Each piece was cut by Jim Concannon, although MacIntosh had used this modern style of cutting before at his studio in Falkirk. Outer space was a strong inspiration for MacIntosh. Costing £150, these vases were withdrawn during 2003.

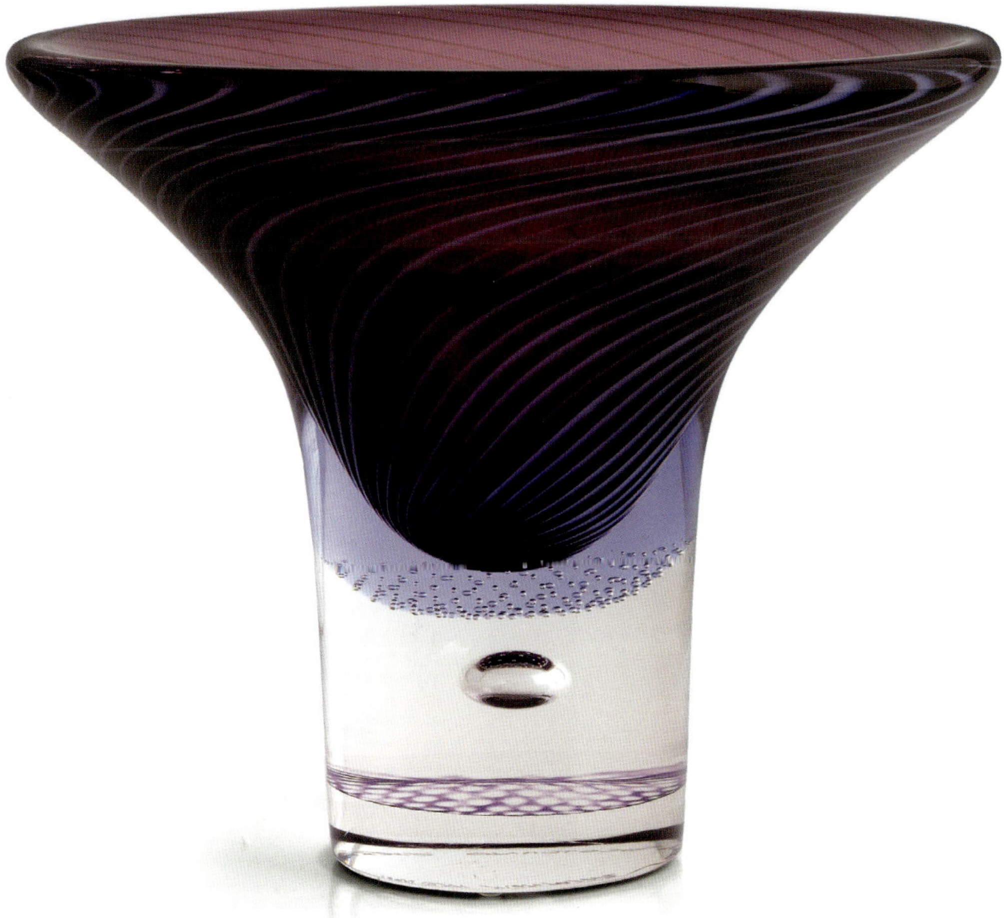

A Cyclone bowl, no.8103, designed by Alastair MacIntosh in 2002, from the Signature range, 7.5in (19cm) high. The Cyclone bowl was launched alongside the Cold Fusion vase, and was also available in one shape only. Challenging to make, the bowl employs MacIntosh's favoured vetro a fili technique to create the effect of a trapped bubble pulled down below a swirling vortex. The simple, glassy form and visual weight were inspired by postwar Czech glass which Ken Wainwright, the glassmaker at Edinburgh College of Art, had admired while MacIntosh studied with him. The example shown here was not produced by MacIntosh – the intended design had a wider bowl and a shorter foot, and the intended colour was lighter.

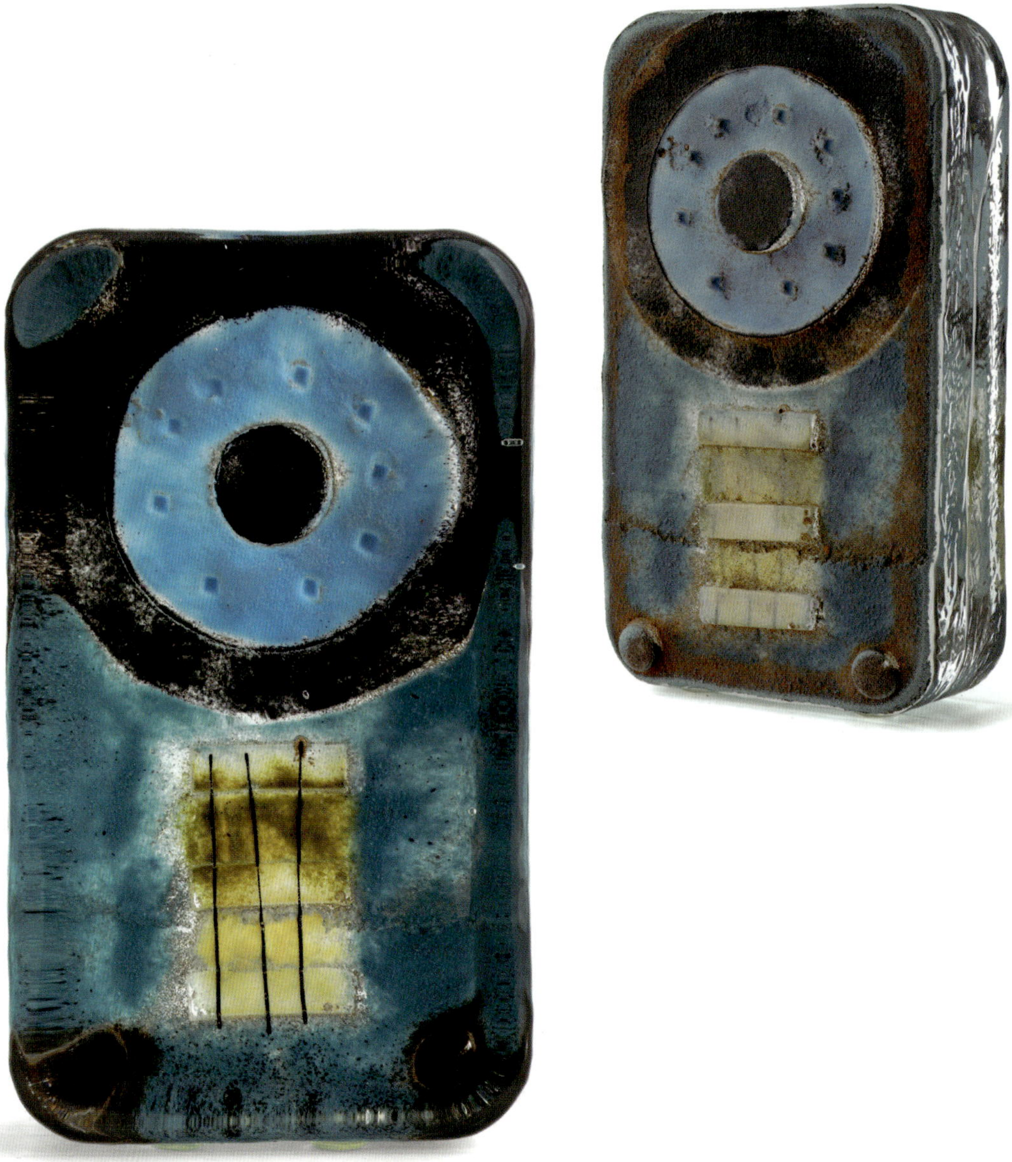

A 'Clockwork' sandcast, UO3123, designed by Sarah Peterson in 2003, 7.75in (20cm) high. Peterson's series of sandcast glass sculptural blocks was first seen in a 2002 catalogue, and was developed after she attended a course in sandcasting under Bertil Vallien at North Lands Creative Glass at Lybster in 2002. The series has included both unique examples, limited editions, and designs produced in unlimited numbers. Appearing like 3D abstract art, some have cog-like sides giving them the air of a piece of machinery. Marketed under the 'Sarah P Collection', differentiating it from more traditional Caithness glassware, the range has sold well. 2011 saw the launch of a range of natural themed designs, including African animals, boats, and beach houses.

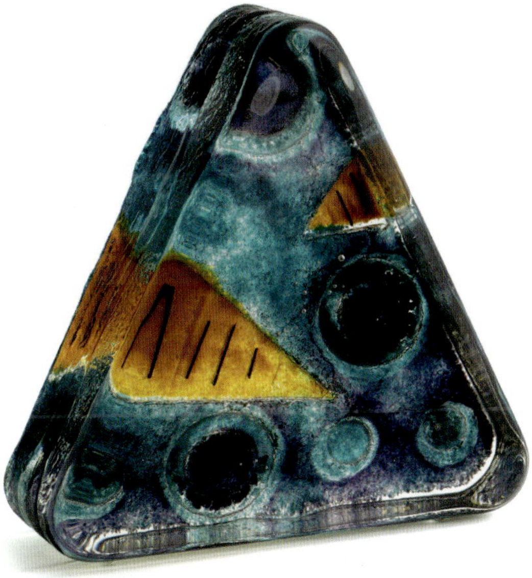

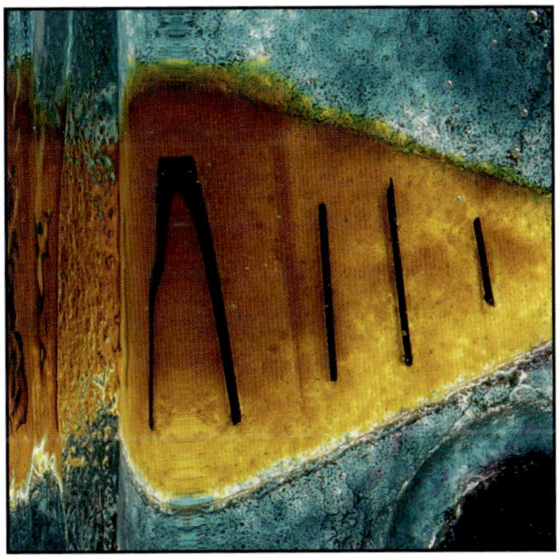

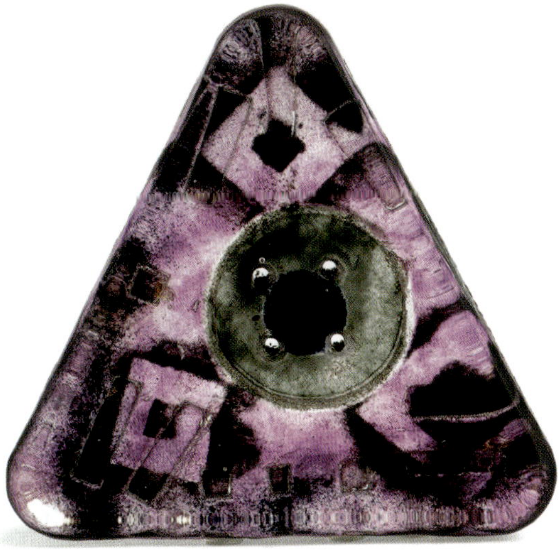

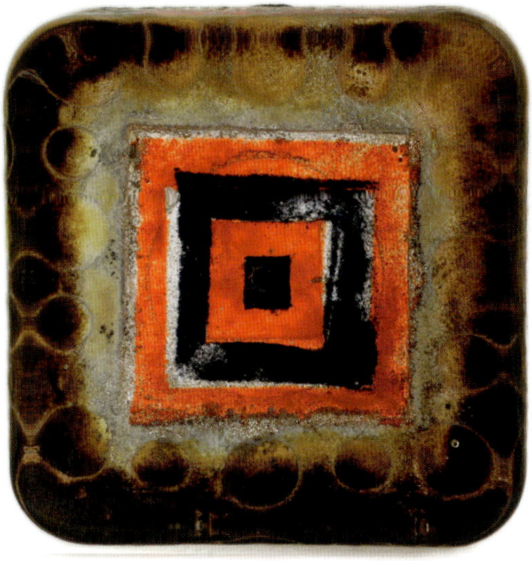

Three sandcast sculptures, designed by Sarah Peterson, top left: 'Beached' c2003, 7.5in (19cm) high; bottom left: 'Trio', 2003, 6.75in (17.5cm) high; bottom right: 'High Voltage', 5.25in (13.5cm) high. Inspired by contemporary trends and tastes in colours and shapes, Peterson first sketches a design. This is then transferred to a bed of casting sand in a graphite frame, using tools and precut shapes to impress the pattern into the sand. Powdered coloured enamels are sprinkled into the design, and molten glass is poured on, bonding to the enamels. The sand 'mould' gives the back of each piece a rough finish. As each piece requires a new bed of sand, each piece is unique in colour and precise pattern, even if it is from an unlimited design.

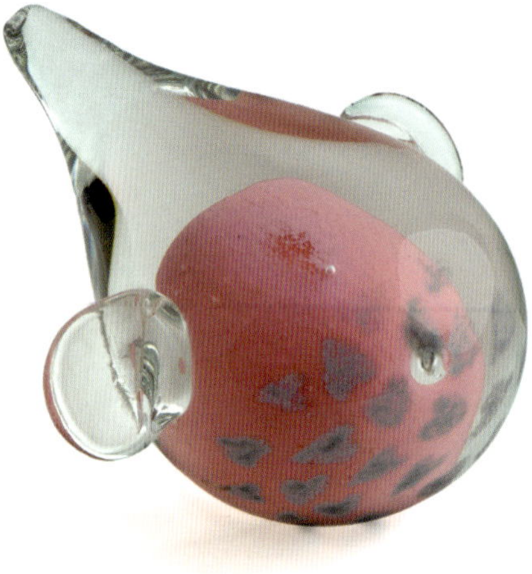

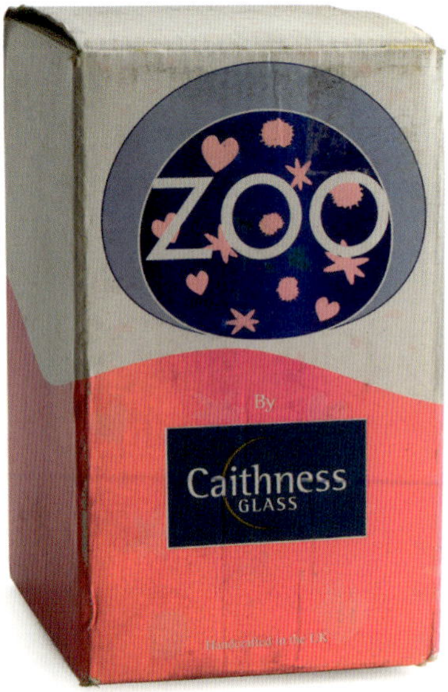

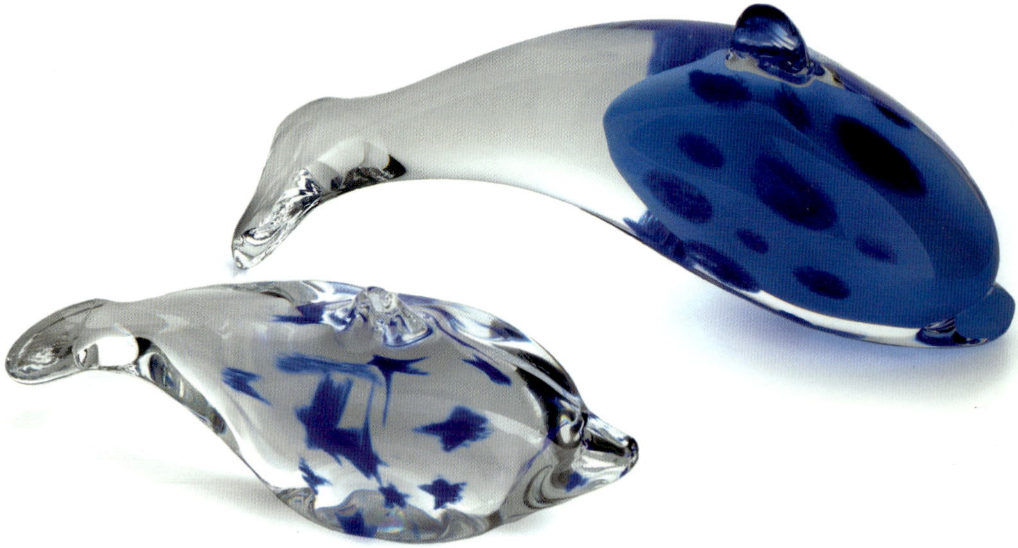

Three animals from the Zoo range, designed by Sarah Peterson in 2002, top left: Trumpet The Elephant, 2.75in (7cm) high; centre: Splash the Dolphin, 7in (18cm) long; bottom: Splish the Dolphin, 5in (13cm) long, with sandblasted marks to base. Zoo (see p.124) was designed in response to a request for a range of animal figurines. The result was a more sculptural, modern and fun look, that captures the essence of the animal. Each contains shaped motifs added by rolling the core over powdered enamel in a graphite mould. From the range of twelve costing from £25-35, Shuffle the Penguin was the most popular, and Tikka the Chicken the least popular. Contained in a special box (above), the range sold well until c2004.

Cut, Engraved & Sandblasted

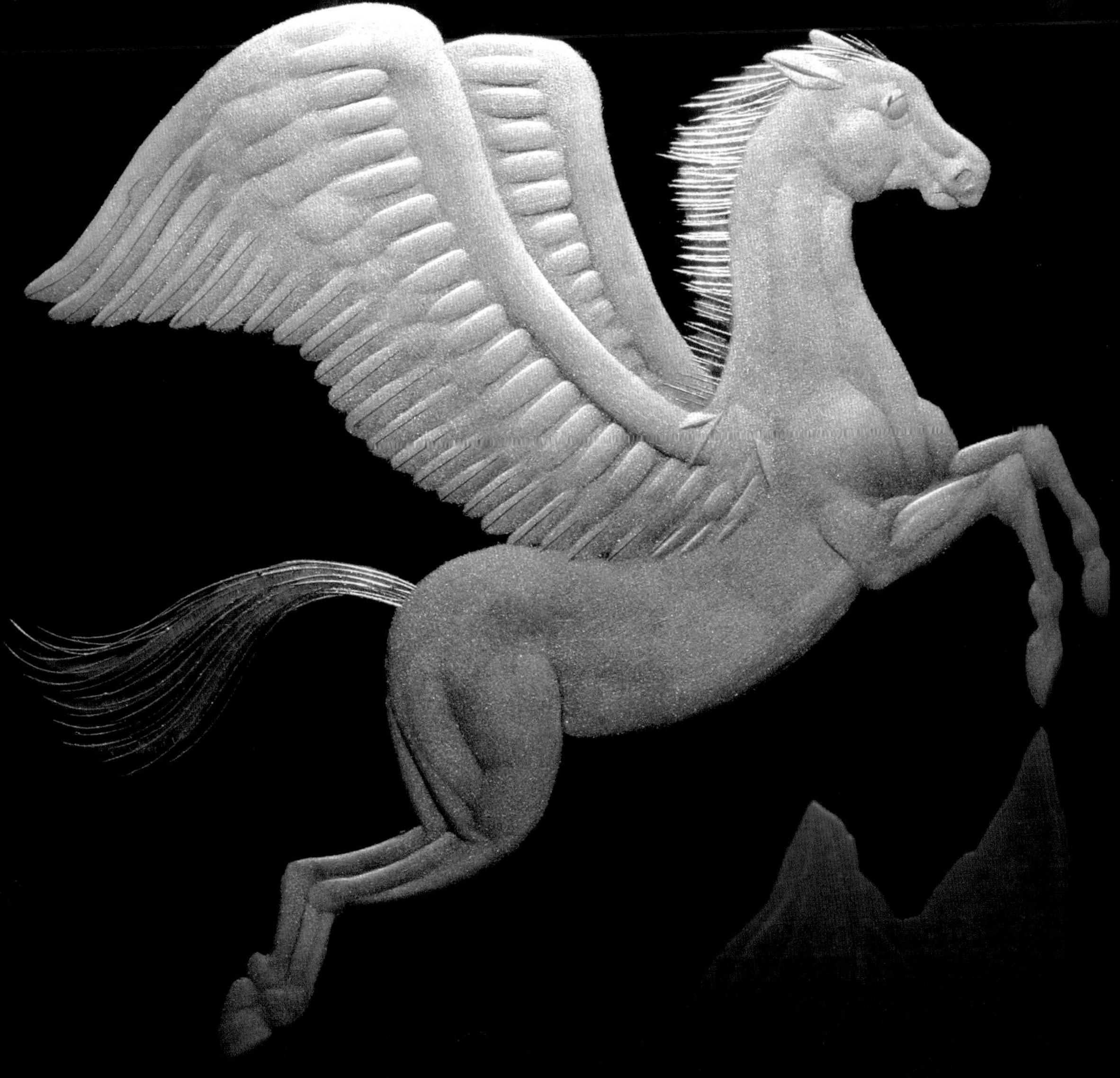

Colin Terris

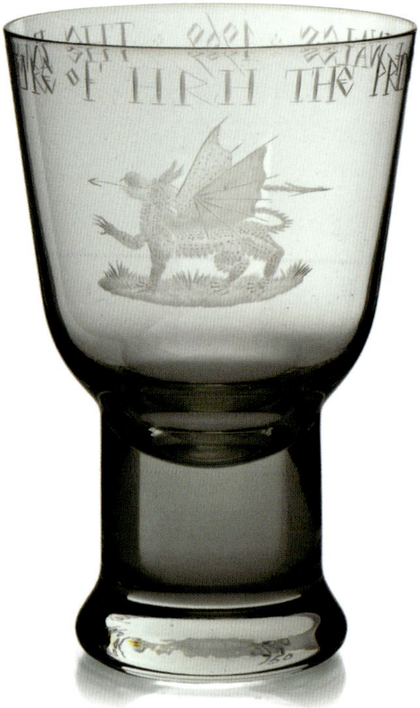

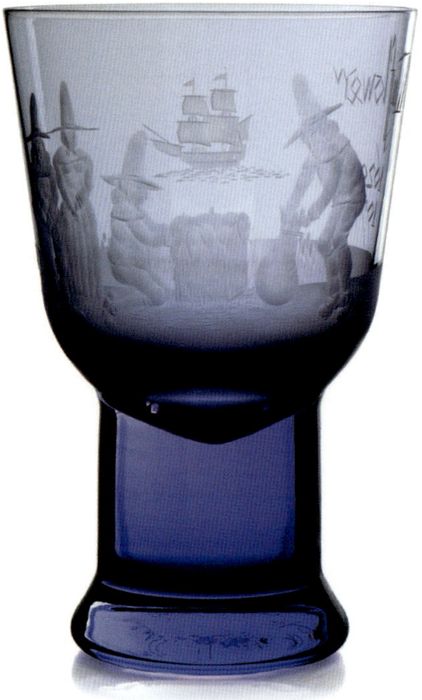

Colin Terris MBE was born in Kirkcaldy in 1937, and studied calligraphy and glass engraving under Helen Monro Turner at the Edinburgh College of Art. He graduated in 1960, and worked as an engraver in Norway for a year. After training as an art teacher, he taught art and ran an engraving studio in Lower Largo.

In 1968, George Mackie, a Director of Caithness Glass, asked him to open and run an engraving studio at the company. After joining, he recruited a number of other experienced engravers. Together, they produced high quality engraved designs, and also developed sandblasting techniques and designs that were used to decorate the majority of the company's 'engraved' works. He also worked with closely with experienced paperweight maker Paul Ysart, and launched the legendary 'Planets' series in 1969 that kick-started the company's highly prolific and successful paperweight department. By 1973, he had become the public face and lead designer for the entire company. As well as designing and making paperweights, he also contributed many designs for table and decorative wares from the 1970s–90s. From the 1980s–90s, he inspired and ran a team of innovative designers and makers including Helen MacDonald and Alastair MacIntosh. He retired in 2002, and died in 2006.

Top left: An 'Investiture of H.R.H. The Prince of Wales' commemorative Dunnet goblet, designed and cut by Colin Terris in 1969, numbered 116 from an edition of 150, and signed on the foot, 5.75in (14.5cm) high. Bottom left: A 'Mayflower Anniversary 1650-1970' Dunnet range Amethyst goblet, designed and cut by Colin Terris in 1970, numbered 9 from an edition of 12, and signed on the foot, 5.75in (14.5cm) high. Right: A unique display object titled 'Lute', designed and executed by Colin Terris using copper wheel engraving and a diamond point in 1973, 8.25in (21cm) high.

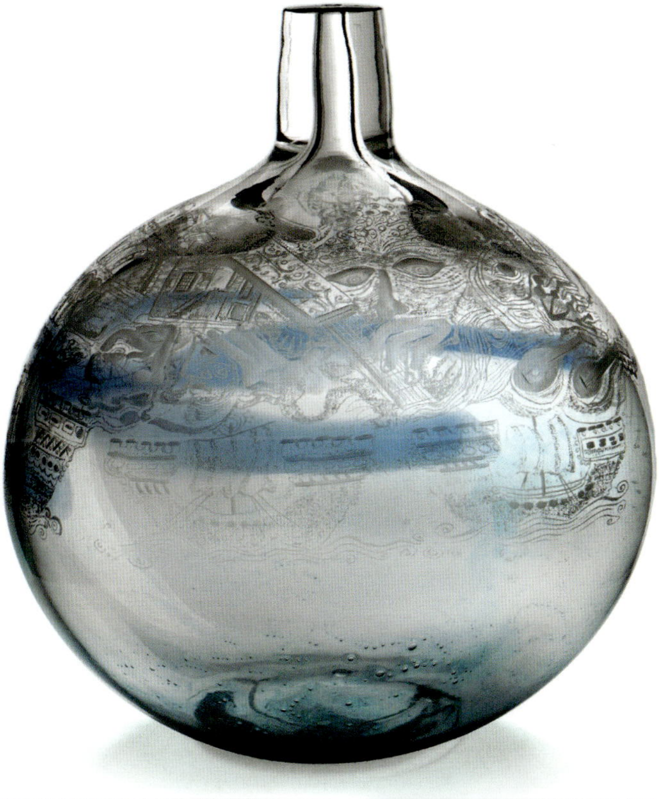

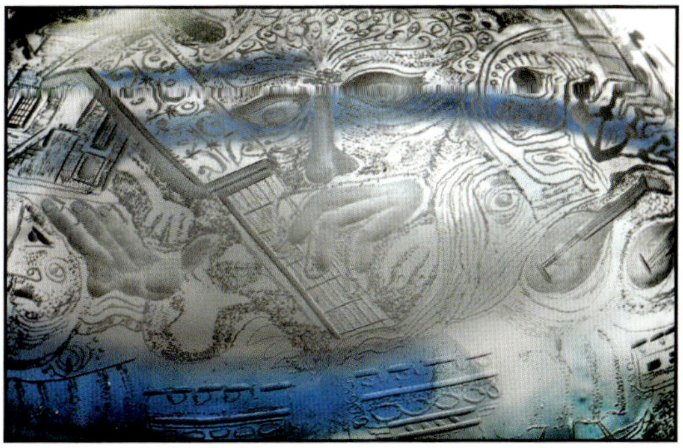

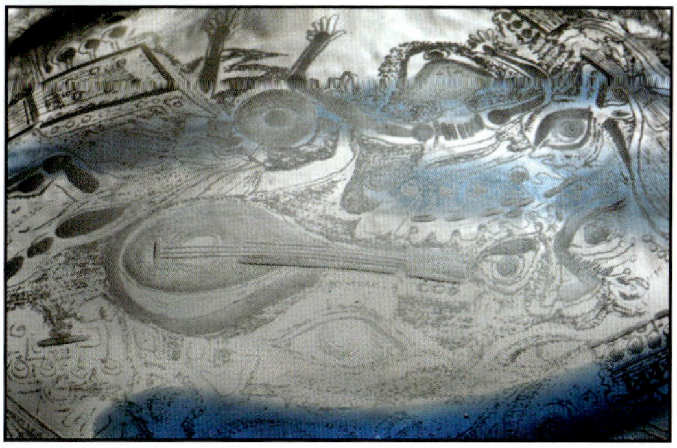

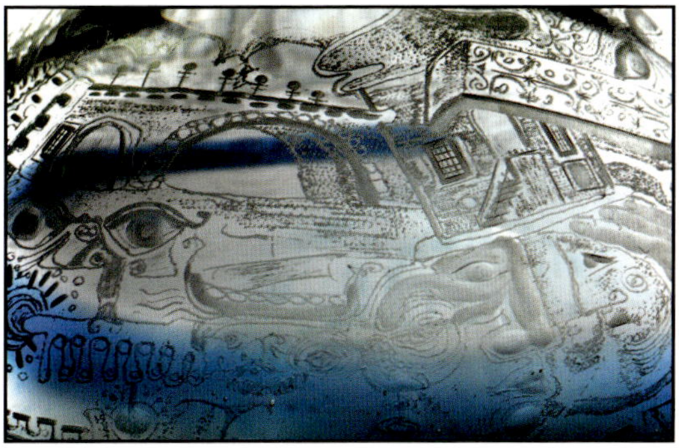

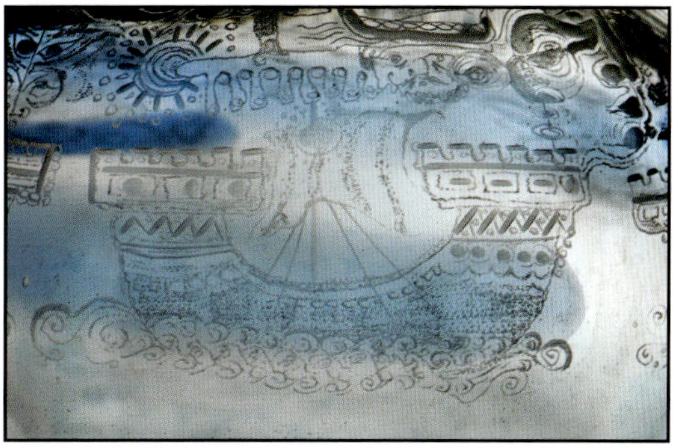

David Gulland

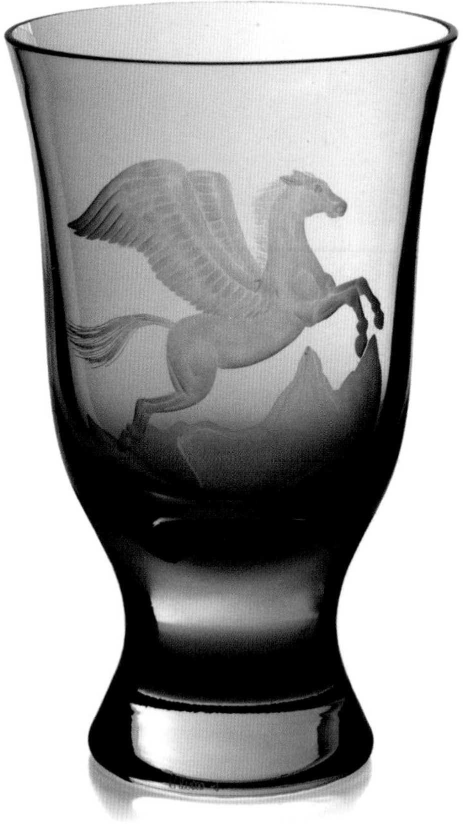

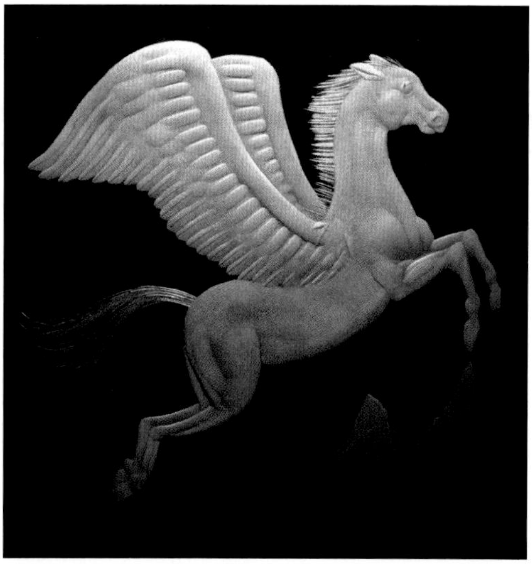

David Gulland was born in Edinburgh in 1934 and studied glass design and engraving under Helen Monro Turner at the Edinburgh College of Art. After graduating, he was awarded a post-diploma scholarship, and travelled and studied widely in Germany and Italy from 1956–57. He then taught art in Edinburgh and Kirkcudbrightshire and worked as a freelance copper wheel engraver. After three years working on Fair Isle in the Shetlands, in 1970 he was recruited by Colin Terris to join the engraving department at Caithness Glass. He was the second experienced engraver to join the team, following Anne Robertson.
He worked there until 1977, producing a number of copper wheel engraved designs, frequently on the goblet form on the left which was designed by Colin Terris specifically for engraved designs. Gulland's works include the 'Birth of Venus' of 1972, based on Botticelli's painting, a set of four goblets with designs of different flowers in a limited edition of eight from 1973, and the 'Shakespeare Set' from 1974, shown on the right. He also engraved windows and door panels for St John's Scottish Episcopal Church in Dumfries. After leaving Caithness Glass, he became a freelance engraver.

Top left: A 'Pegasus' copper wheel engraved goblet, designed and cut by David Gulland in 1973, numbered 6 from an edition of 8, and signed on the foot, 8.75in (22.25cm) high. Bottom left: A detail of Pegasus against black, showing Gulland's attention to detail in the mane and the muscles, and the sense of movement he gave this mythical horse. Right: A 'Shakespeare Set' of four goblets sandblasted and copper wheel engraved by David Gulland in 1974, each signed and numbered 1 from an edition of 8 on the foot, 5in (12.5cm) high. Clockwise from top left: 'A Midsummer Night's Dream', 'As You Like It', 'Twelfth Night', and 'The Merchant of Venice'.

CUT & ENGRAVED

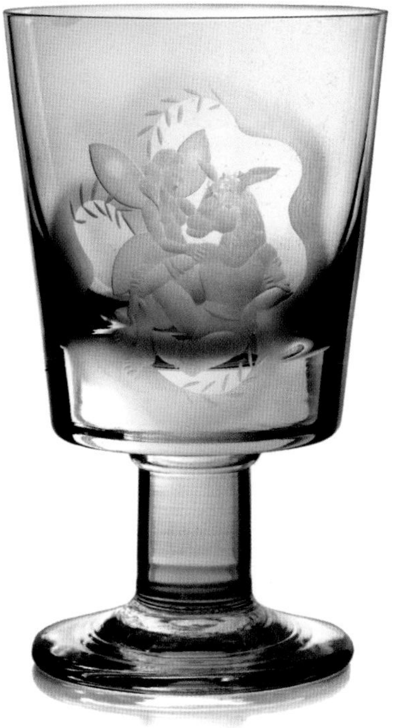

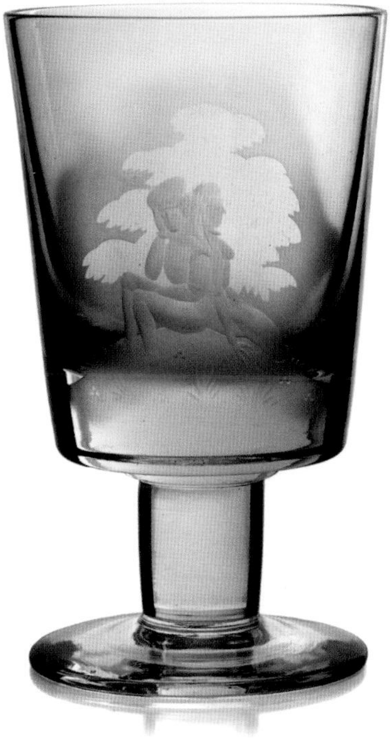

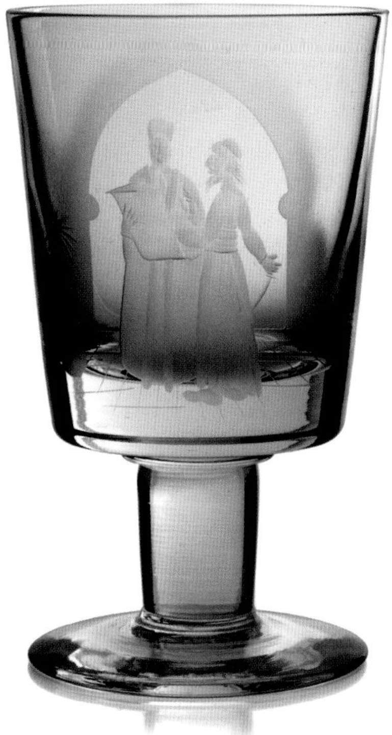

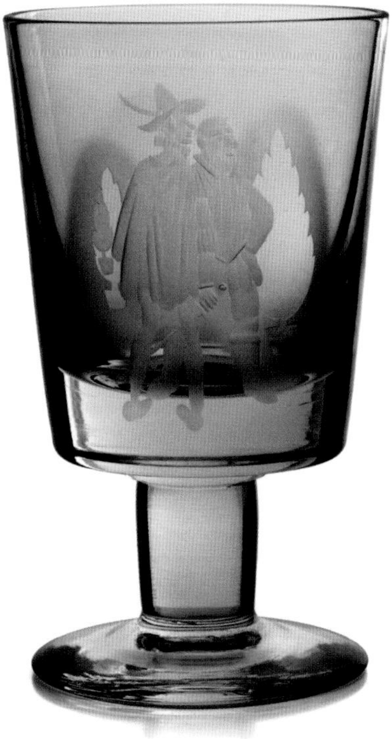

Denis Mann

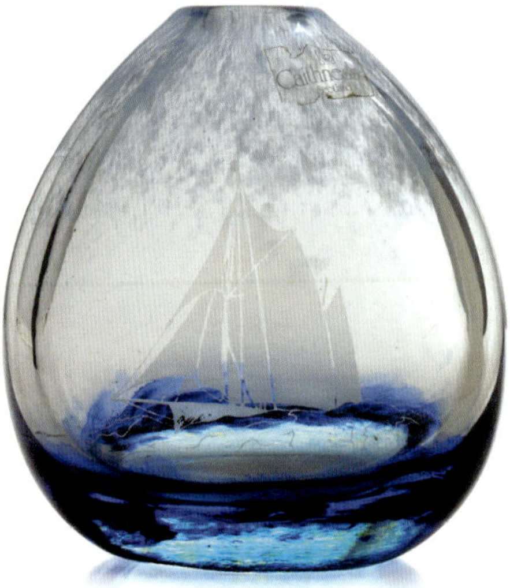

A Georgian Yacht freeblown vase, no.CT374, with a sandblasted design of a boat, from the Seascapes range designed by Denis Mann, c1984, 4.75in (12cm) high. The range also included Thames Bawley, Medieval Cog and Norse Longship.

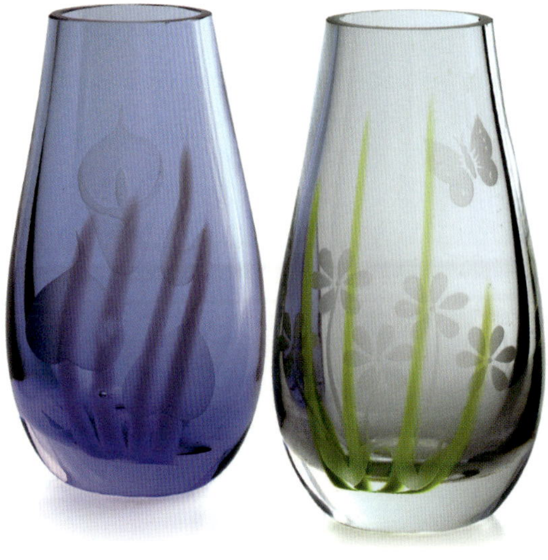

A Jack in Pulpit vase, no.CT365, and a Pink vase, no.CT366, from the sandblasted and hot-worked Floral Range, designed by Denis Mann, c1983, 5.25in (13.5cm) high. Other designs in the range included Daisy, Bluebell, Daffodil, and Snowdrop.

Denis Mann was born in Perthshire in 1935, and studied glass design and engraving under Helen Monro Turner at the Edinburgh College of Art. He developed a particular love for, and skill in, copper wheel engraving. After graduating, he served in the R.A.F., before becoming an art teacher. In 1970, he was invited by Colin Terris to join the rapidly expanding engraving department at Caithness Glass.

Many of his designs are of animals, usually depicted in their natural habitat. Typical of this was his designs for the sandblasted 'Woodland Series', which included 'Squirrel', 'Blue Tit', and the classic design 'Autumn Leaves' (see p.102).

His most famous design was the BBC 'Mastermind' trophy. Engraved annually by him since 1972, each design is slightly different. He also designed the form, which was given the number CT60, and it and a smaller version numbered CT4035 (see p.52), became amongst the most prolifically produced shapes made by the company. Many thousands of examples, typically with sandblasted wedding or anniversary designs, have been produced over three decades. Mann left Caithness Glass completely in 1998 to become a freelance copper wheel engraver and glassmaker based in Wick. He has since designed and produced the trophies for the 'Junior Mastermind' and 'Celebrity Mastermind' BBC series, as well as undertaking commissions for private, corporate and public clients, including sandblasted Millennium commemorative panels for St Joachim's Chapel in Wick.

Right: A freeblown vase with a copper wheel engraved design of a pheasant in flight on the front, and a tree on the back, designed and cut by Denis Mann, the base engraved 'DENIS MANN CAITHNESS PHEASANT 150', 4in (10cm) high.

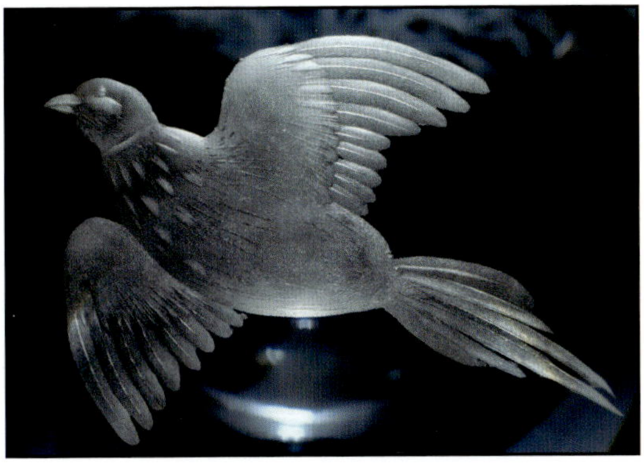

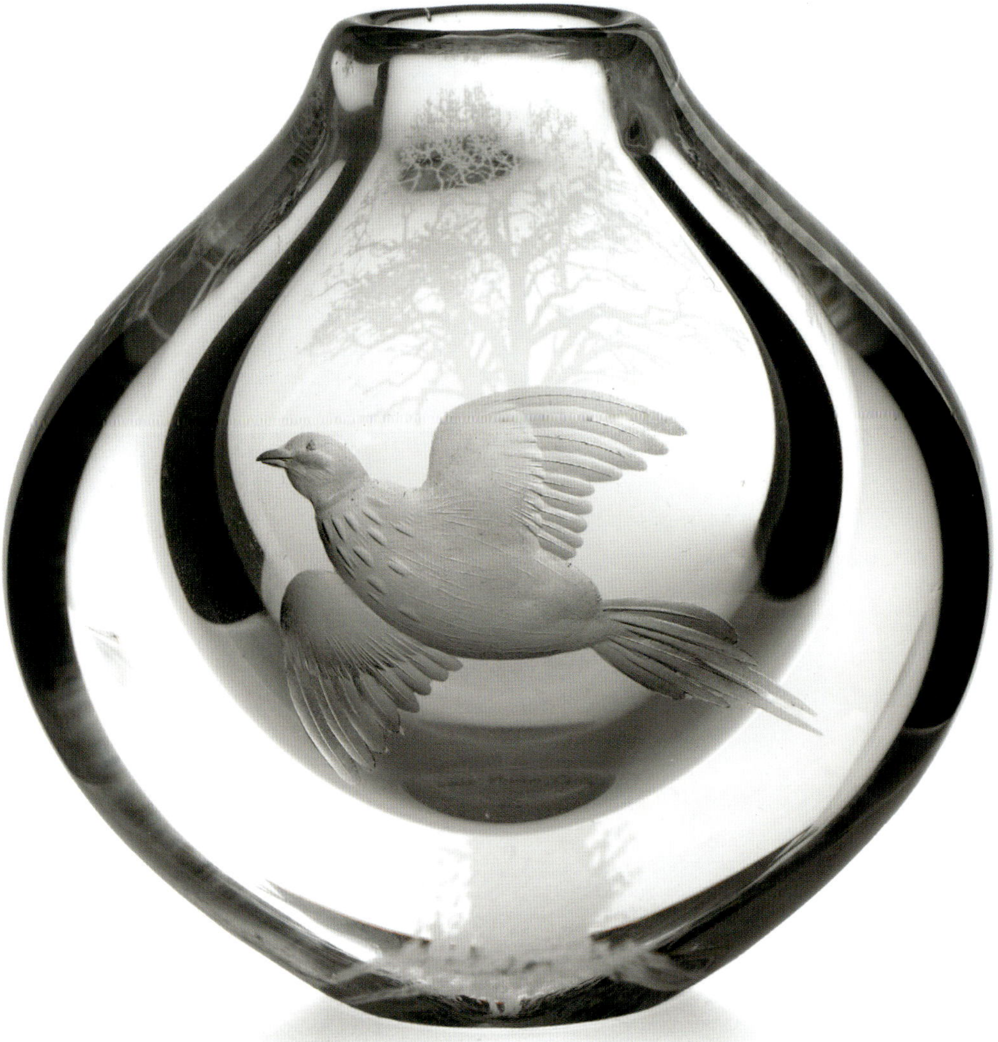

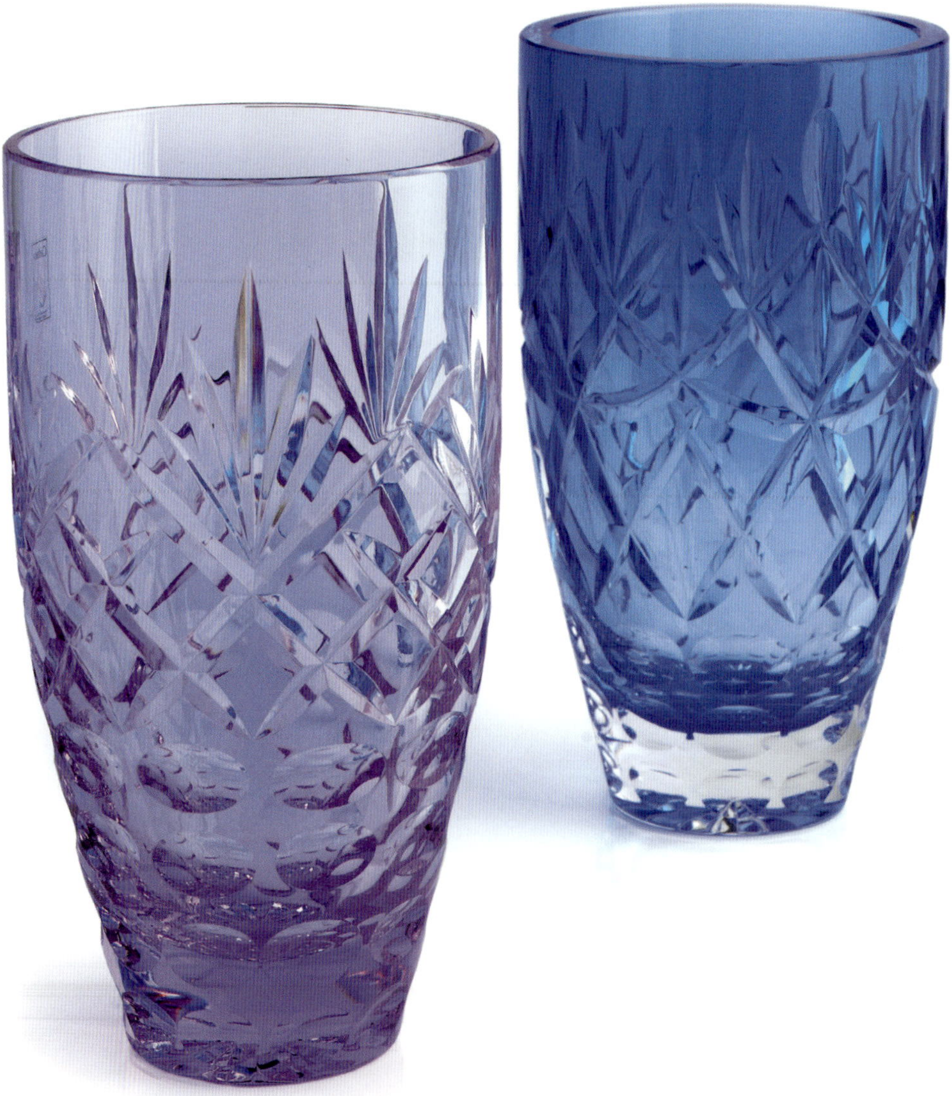

Two 1990s Floral Vases, no.B106CA14, in Lavender and Brancaster Blue, from the Norwich Giftware Collection, 8in (20.5cm) high. These vases were from a number of ranges of primarily colourless decorative and table wares cut with very traditional designs. Launched in 1987 following the company's acquisition of the King's Lynn Crystal factory, they were marketed under traditional names including Priory and Brampton Court. Some shapes were designed by Colin Terris, with cuts being designed by the King's Lynn factory manager John Dawe. The crystal cased Brancaster Blue colour was introduced in 1992, with these vases costing £34.95 each. The Canisbay range (see p.41) was also cut and sold as the Helmsdale range.

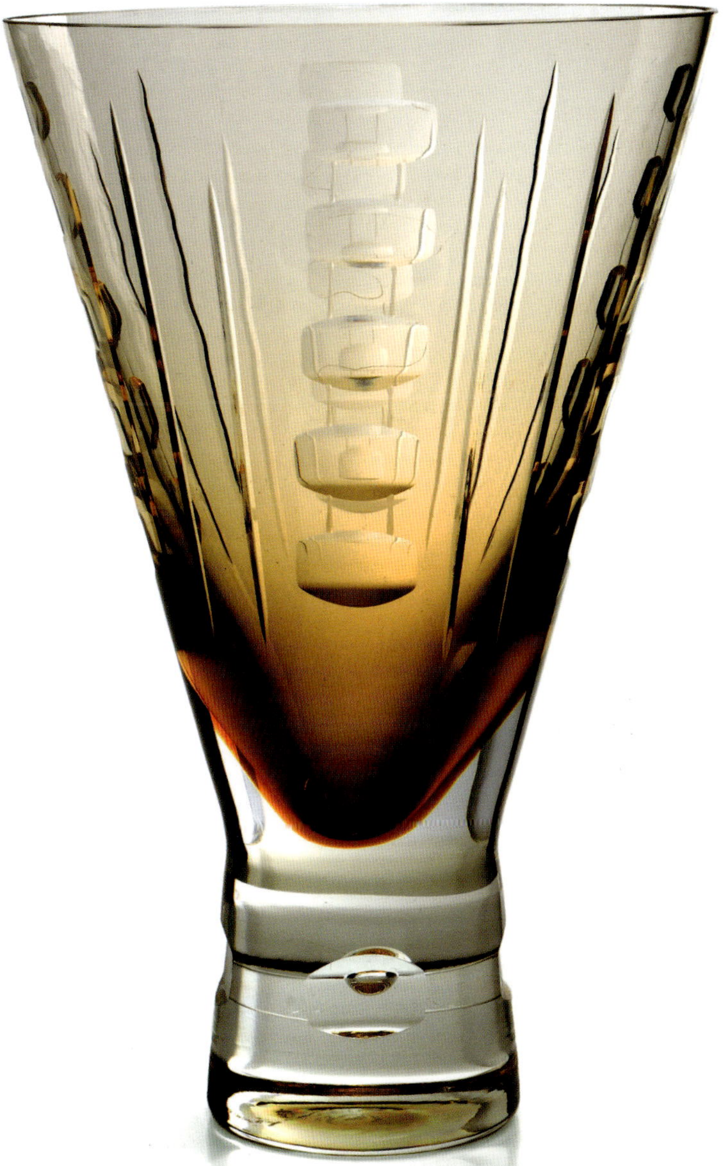

A Manhattan vase, no.8151, in Gold, from the Art Deco range designed by Helen MacDonald in 2002, 10.25in (26cm) high. The angular, cut Art Deco range was inspired by a visit to an Art Deco exhibition. Elements from the style used include geometric lines, dots, dashes and sunbursts. The range comprised this vase, a low and a higher conical footed bowl, and a 'Los Angeles' cylindrical vase and bowl. Looked down on from above, the cuts on the conical bowls appear like a sunburst. Colours were either graduated Gold or Kingfisher, and were kept light in tone. The range was launched in 2003 and was produced for over a year. Despite the price (this vase cost £75), the range was very successful, particularly in the US.

Sandblasted Designs

The highly prolific and successful engraving department at Caithness Glass was founded at Wick by Colin Terris in 1968.

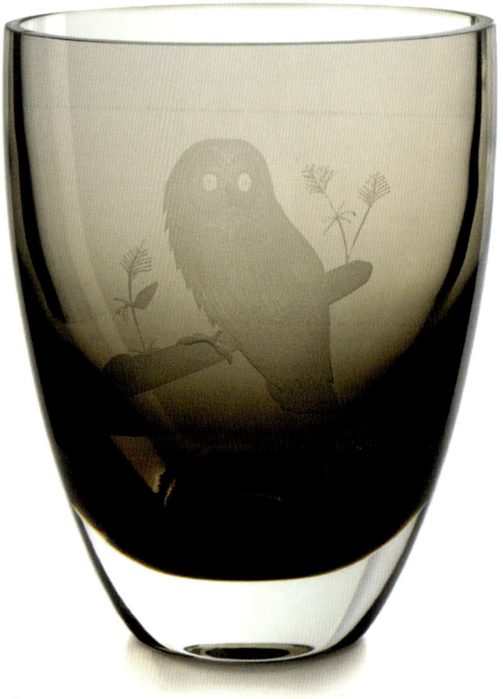

Although diamond point and copper wheel techniques were used, the majority of production was sandblasted. An engraver took a tracing of a master design drawing, applied Plasticine to the reverse, stuck it to a vase, and then rubbed a point over the lines of the design. This left a residue of Plasticine on the glass, which was drawn over in ink and covered with protective tape. A lamp was then placed behind the glass to enable the inked lines to be seen through the tape. A scalpel was used to cut away areas of tape corresponding with different elements of a design, such as the eyes or branch on the owl pattern (no. CT140, designed c1969) shown here. The element with the deepest sandblasting was removed first. The exposed glass was then sandblasted away, leaving a frosted effect. The areas still covered by tape would be protected. Each element was treated in subsequent stages, until the design was finished. Fine details, such as the sprigs on the branch, were added finally using a diamond point. As the design was traced each time by different designers, and

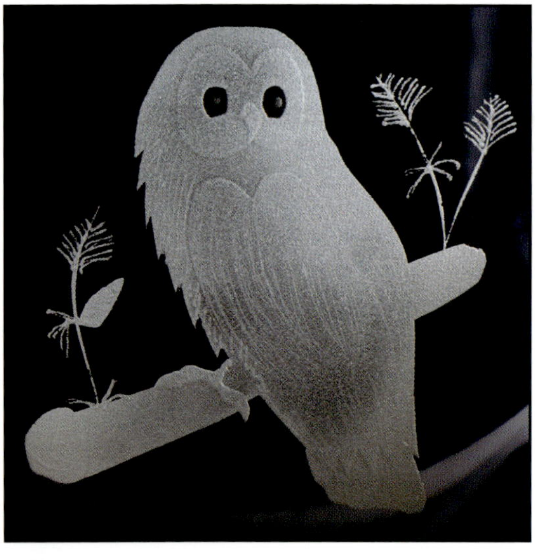

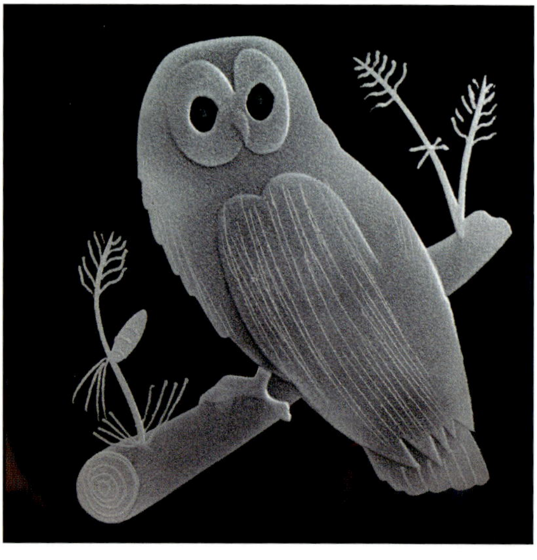

Engravers and sandblasters often signed their work on the base with their initials, and included:

Willie Bain
Christine Beaton
Catherine Burns
John Brown
Peter Brown
Keith Budge
Alison Coghill
Elaine Coghill
Douglas Cowie
Steven Davidson
Gordon Hendry
Lorraine Keith
Helen MacDonald
John MacDonald
Irene McCoughie
Marjorie McCoughie, *later MacKinnon*
Maureen O'Sullivan
Alec Reid
Carol Robbie
Anne Robertson
Jenny Robertson
Margaret Robinson
Annabel Smith
Alan Sutherland
Lorna Sutherland
Elaine Swanson
Sheila Tait
John Taylor
Ellison Talbot, *later Sutherland*
Andrew Webster
Carol Webster
Cora Will

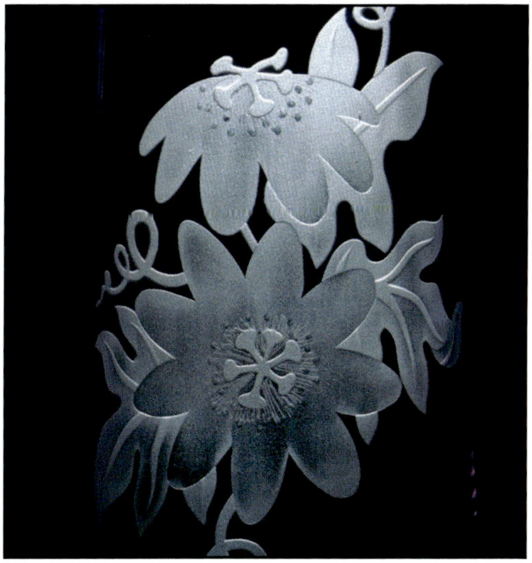

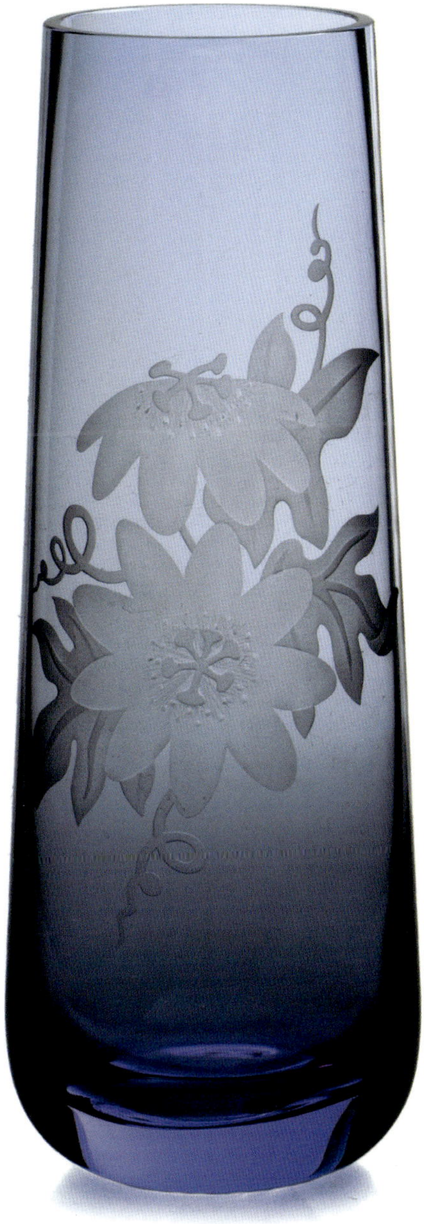

cut and sandblasted slightly differently each time, variations resulted, as seen with the owl (left). The different stages of sandblasting also created depth, as seen with the passionflower design above, and between the owl and branch on the left. If the body had an open top, a sheet of paper bearing the design could be placed inside the vase, and the design could be inked onto the exterior. Above: A 1980s vase, shape no.4096 from the Stroma range, in Amethyst, designed by Colin Terris, with a sandblasted pattern of passion flowers, 9.25in (23cm) high. Although there is a sense of perspective between the flowers, leaves and stalks, the petals of the flowers themselves are flat. The pattern on this unsigned vase was executed in four stages.

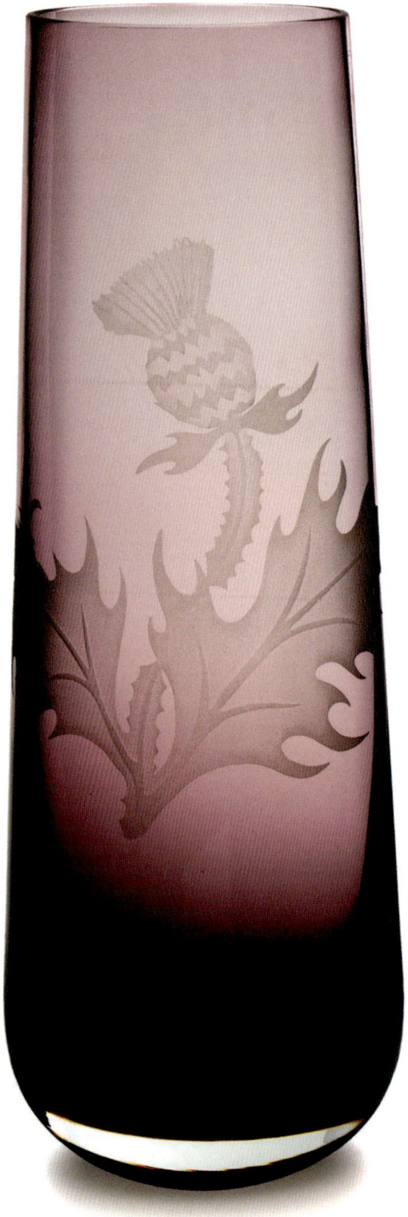

A 1970s-80s vase, shape no.4096, in Heather, with a sandblasted design of a thistle, designed by Colin Terris or David Gulland, 9.25in (23cm) high. This popular and patriotic motif is simple, enabling it to be sandblasted onto a form rapidly. Designs like this made superb gifts, or souvenirs of a visit to a Scottish glass company, particularly in the Heather colour.

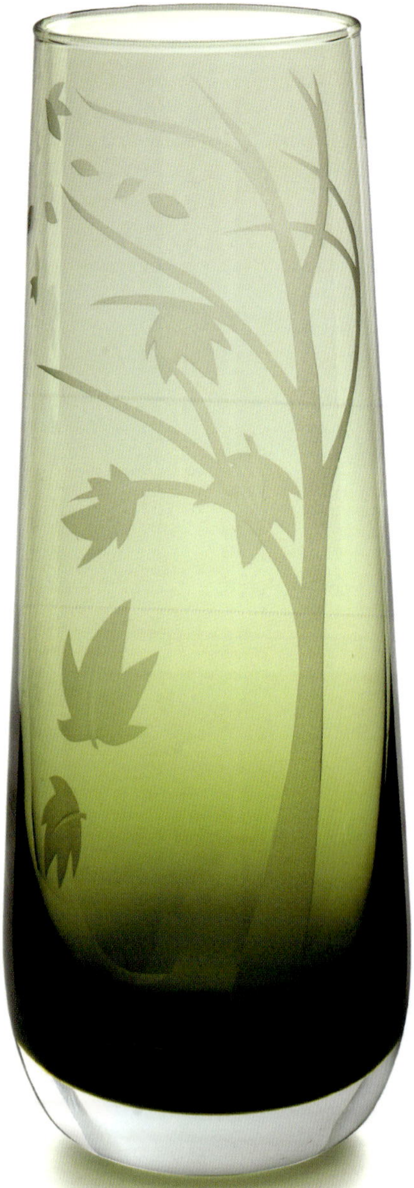

A 1970s vase, in Moss, sandblasted with the Autumn Leaves design, no. CT147, from the Woodland Series designed by Denis Mann in 1970, 9.25in (23cm) high. Very popular and produced for decades, Autumn Leaves is a classic design. Like Romeo & Juliet opposite, the leaves and tree are applied all around the body to give a sense of depth and perspective.

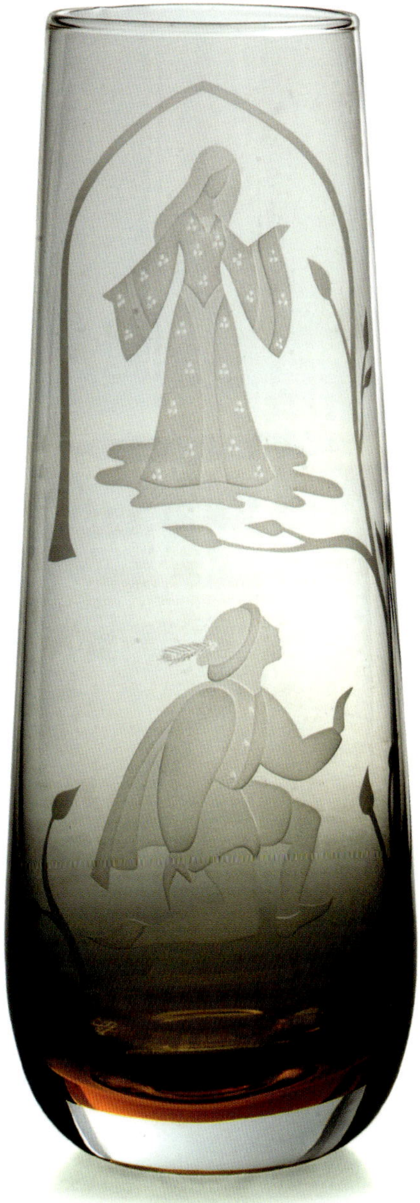

A 1990s vase, in Harvest Gold, sandblasted with the Romeo & Juliet design, no.CT117, from the Shakespeare Vases series designed by Colin Terris c1969, 9.25in (23cm) high. A popular wedding gift, this design was produced for decades. Later examples were produced with a screen-printed stencil, so lack the depth and detail of earlier pieces.

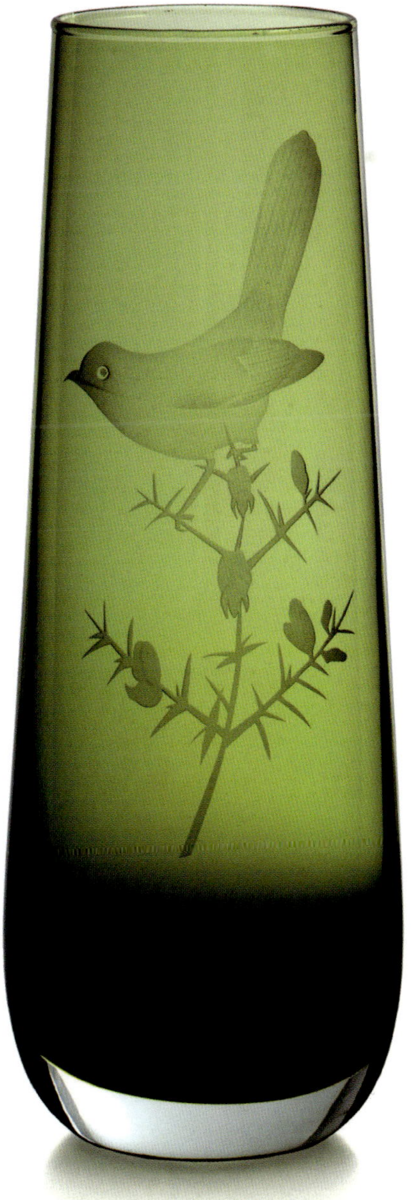

A 1970s-80s vase, in Moss, sandblasted with the Warbler design, no.CT183, designed by Denis Mann c1972, 9.25in (23cm) high. Mann's original pattern was converted from wheel engraving to sandblasting by Gordon Hendry c1976. Although nearly all sandblasted designs bore design numbers with a CT prefix, not all of them were designed by Colin Terris.

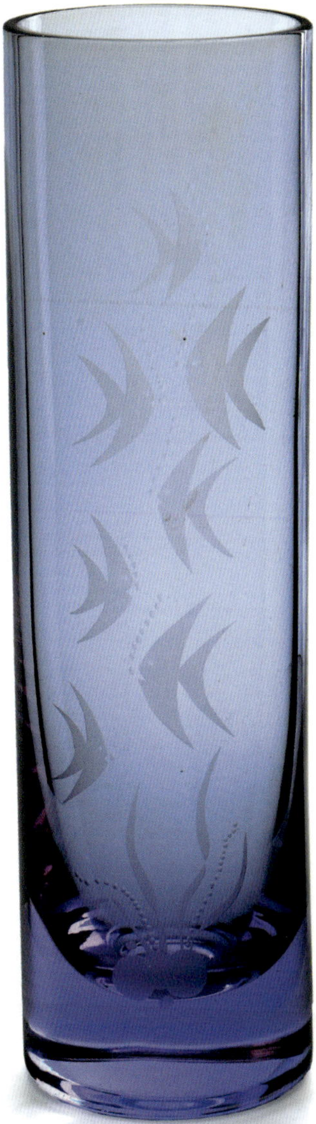

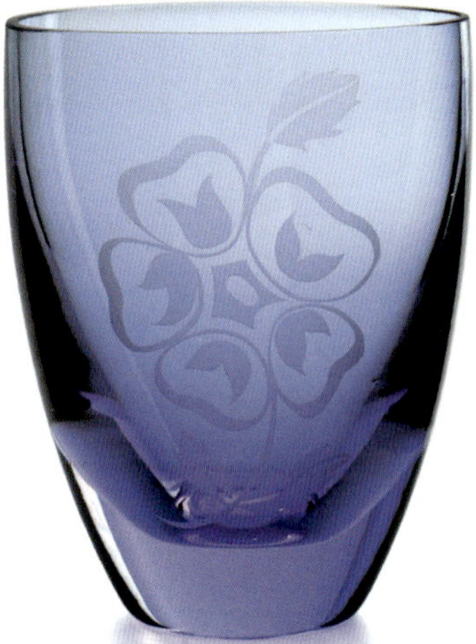

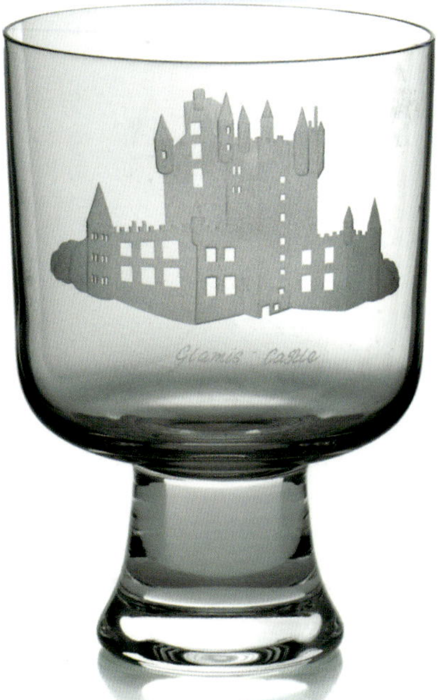

A 1970s vase, in Amethyst, sandblasted with the Angel Fish design, no.CT127, probably designed by Colin Terris c1969, 9.25in (23cm) high. This is a surprisingly modern and abstract treatment of fish under water. More realistic and naturalistic themes of animals, buildings or plants were more common, as they had a greater appeal with the company's target market.

Top: A 1970s-80s Barrel Vase, no.4019, sandblasted with the Rose design, no.CT134, designed by Colin Terris c1969, 5in (12.5cm) high. Bottom: A Chalice, no.CT120 designed by Colin Terris c1969, sandblasted with the Glamis Castle design by Colin Terris, 6in (15cm) high. This form was designed specially for sandblasted or engraved motifs, hence the large bowl.

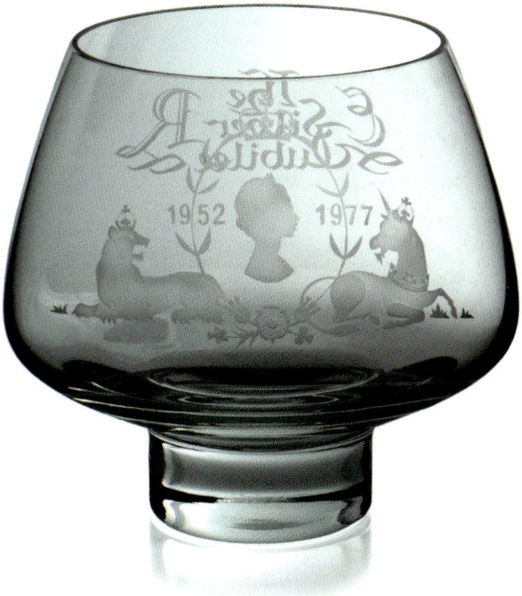

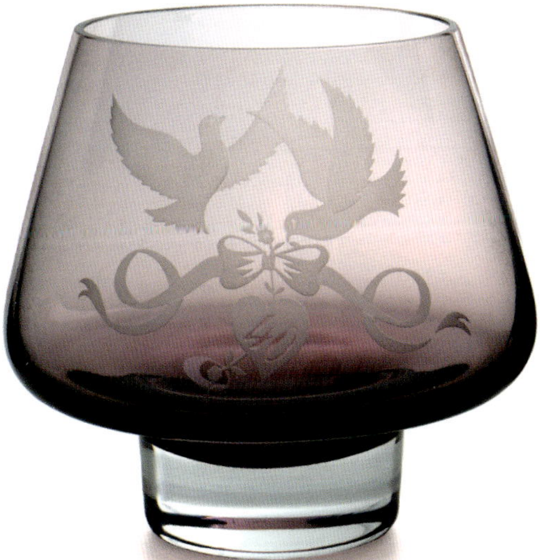

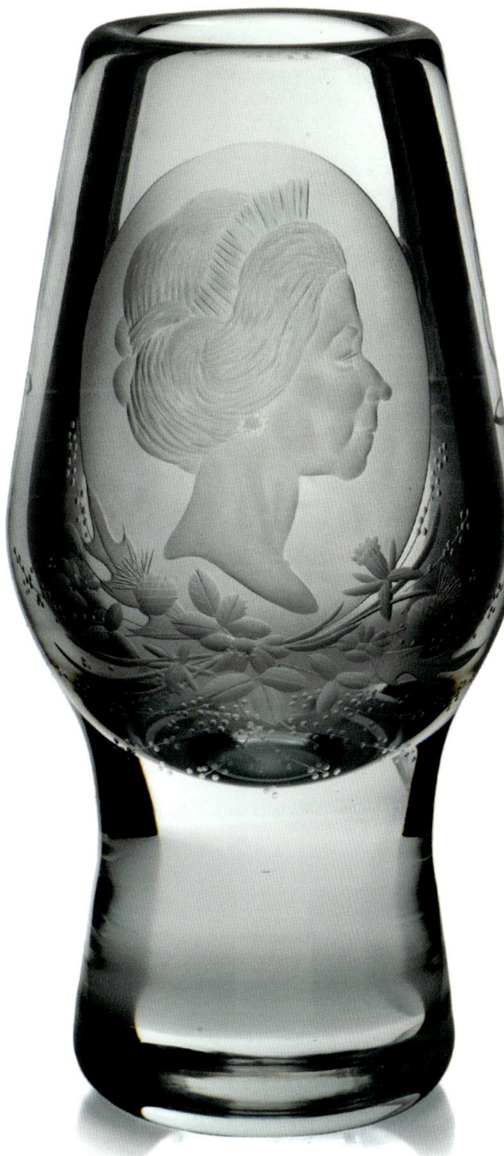

Top left: A commemorative limited edition Silver Jubilee bowl, no.CT60, designed, cut and sandblasted in 1977 by Colin Terris and signed 'CT 216/250', 7in (18cm) high. Bottom left: A no.4035 bowl in Heather, with the sandblasted 40th Wedding Anniversary design, no.CT100, designed by Colin Terris c1970, 5.25in (13.5cm) high. Right: A limited edition commemorative Silver Jubilee goblet, designed and cut by David Gulland in 1977, signed 'David Gulland 1/25', 7in (18cm) high. Many royal commemoratives were produced and were commercially highly successful. Some were produced in limited editions using a variety of techniques. As part of the Celebration range, wedding or anniversary bowls were popular, and were made in vast quantities.

Colours, Labels & Boxes

Five original colours were developed in 1960 by Domhnall ÓBroin, and comprised Peat, Heather, Loch, Moss, and Soot. Colour tones vary depending on how the batch was mixed. After ÓBroin left, tones were often less muted. Twilight was the result of an accident mixing Loch during the early 1960s. As the batch could not be wasted, it was used and the colour was preferred over Loch, which it eventually superseded. The later colours of Emerald (launched in 1986), Kingfisher, and Harvest Gold were developed by Alastair MacIntosh. Many colours were used for decades, and some were periodically reintroduced. Moss was revived in the early 2000s for a range produced in Poland, but had a different tone. Oban, Spinningdale, and Flamenco were produced with coloured rods imported from Kügler (later Friedrich Farbglashütte) in Germany. Boxes and labels allow dating to a period only.

Heather
1961–2000s

Moss
1961–2000s

Twilight
c1962–90s

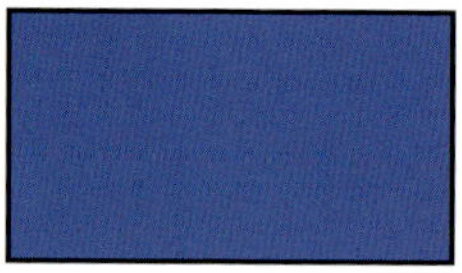

Loch
1961–70s

Peat
1961–2000s

Soot
1961–2000s

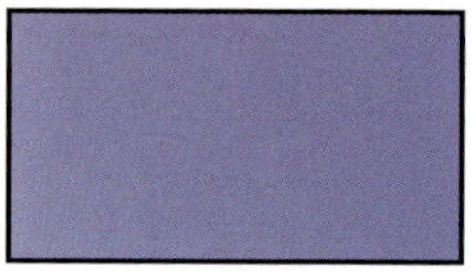

Amethyst
1970–2000s

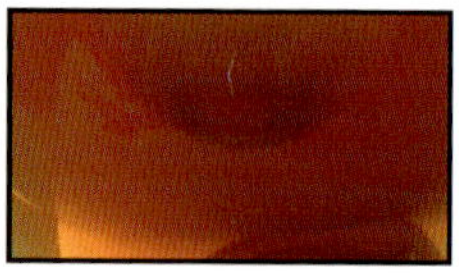

Harvest Gold
1989–2000s

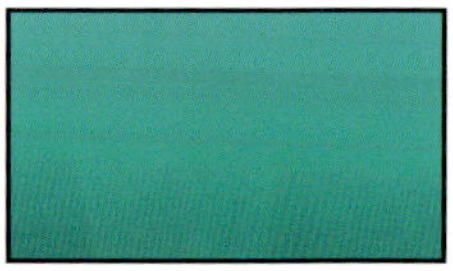

Kingfisher
1989–2000s

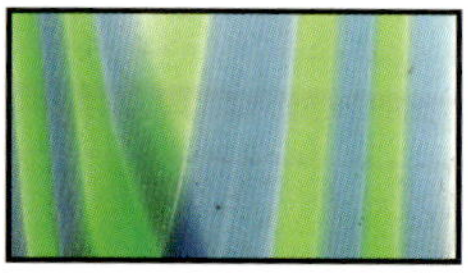

Oban
1970s-80s

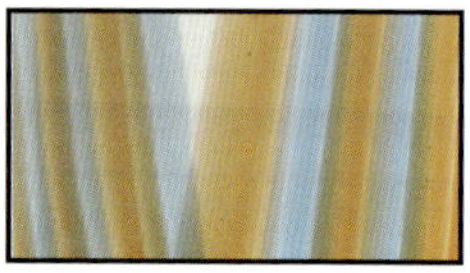

Oban
1970s–80s

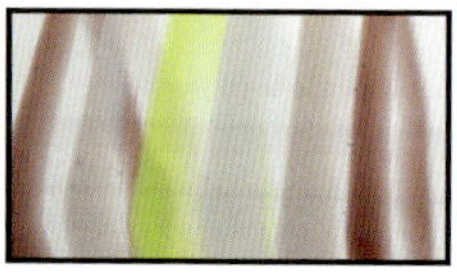

Oban
1970s–80s

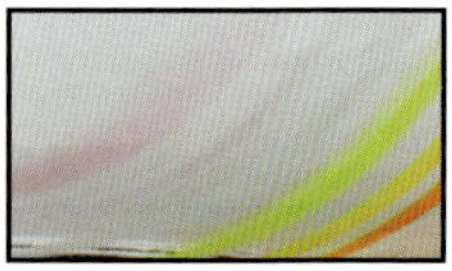

Oban Rainbow
1980s

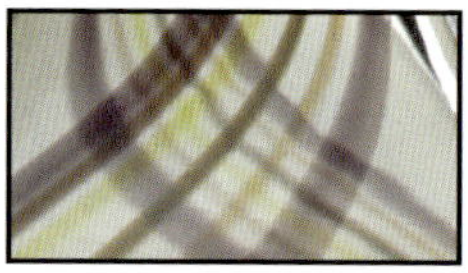

Spinningdale
1980s

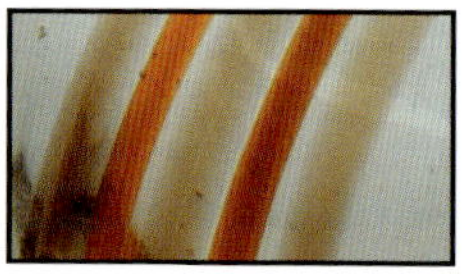

Flamenco
1990s–2000s

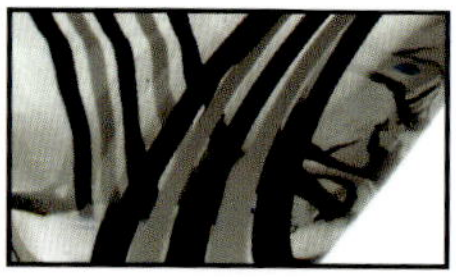

Flamenco
1990s–2000s

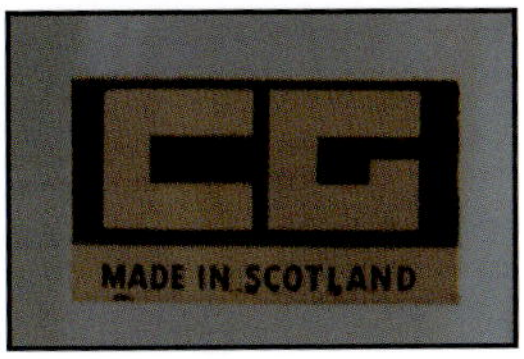

Early 1960s Label

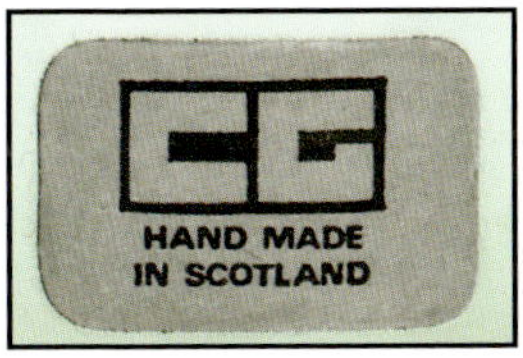

Late 1960s-70s Label

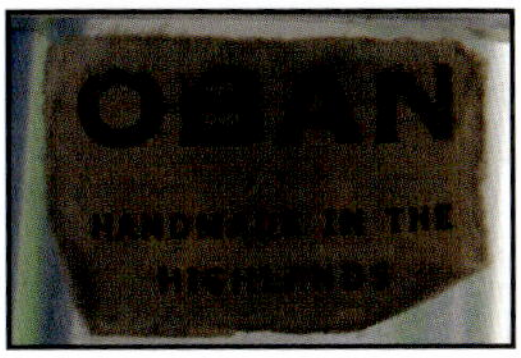

1970s Oban Range Label

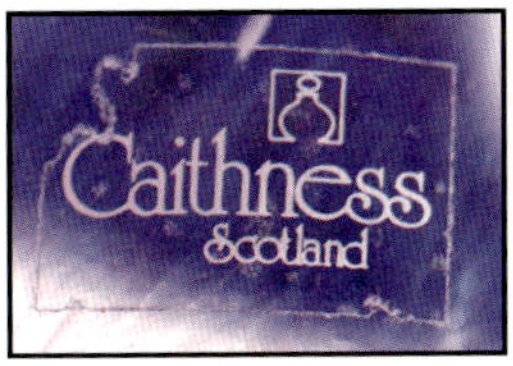

1980s Label

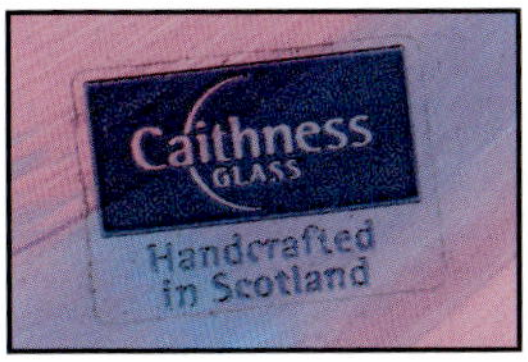

2000s Label

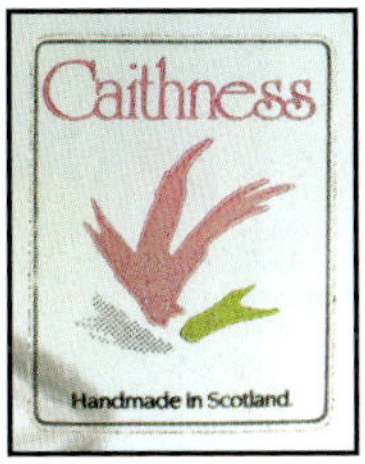

1990s–2000s Label

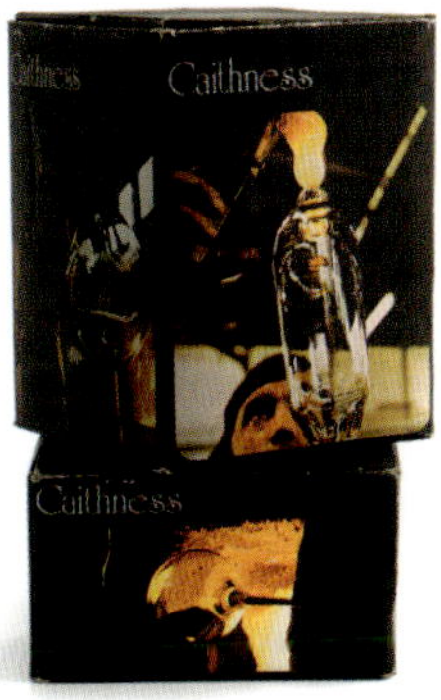

1970s–80s Box

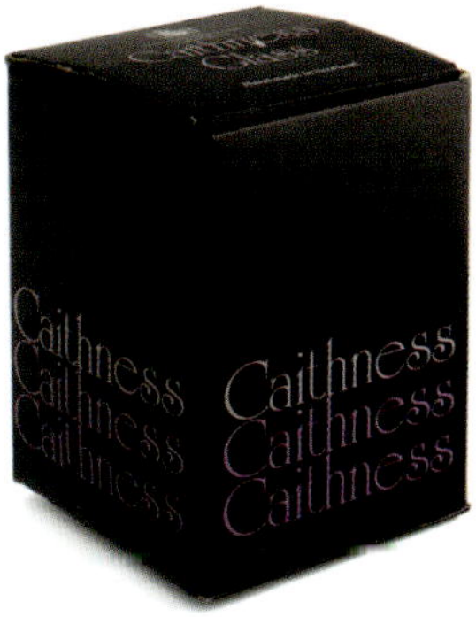

1980s Box

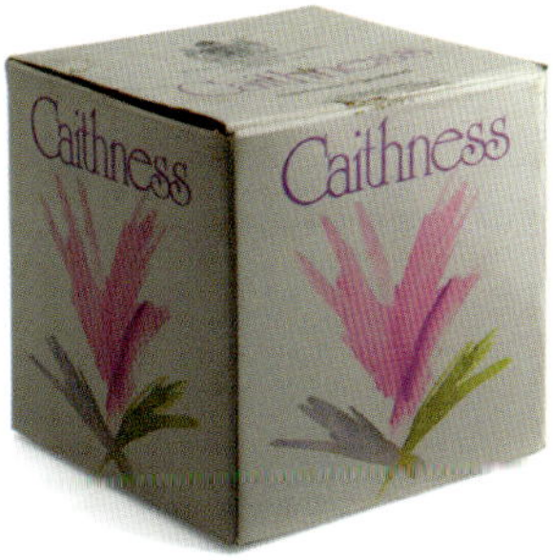

1990s–2000s Box

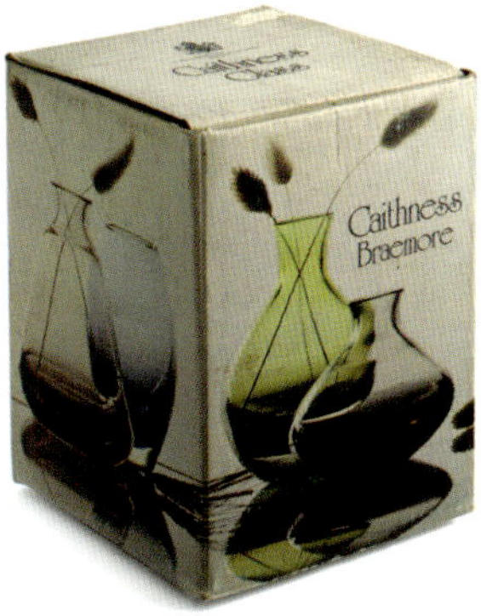

1980s Braemore Range Box

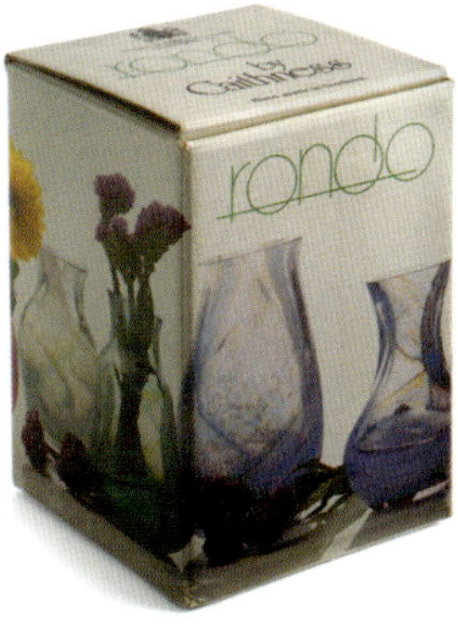

1990s Rondo Range Box

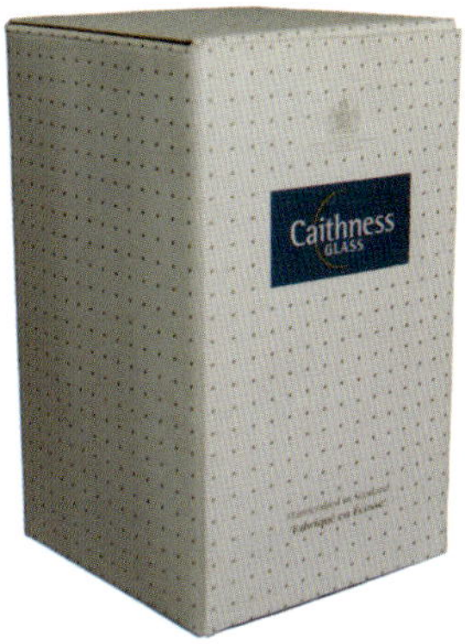

2000s Box

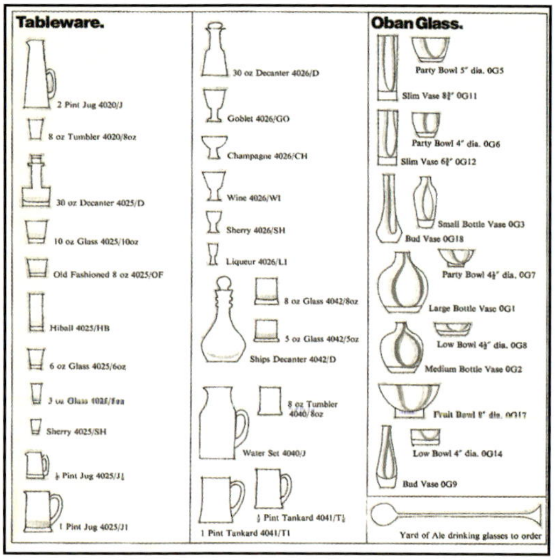

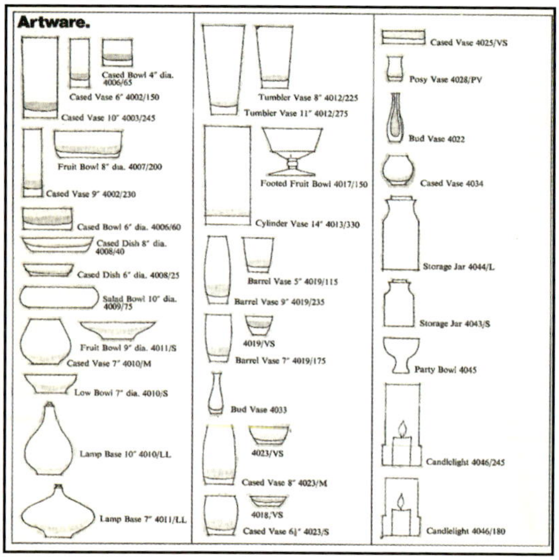

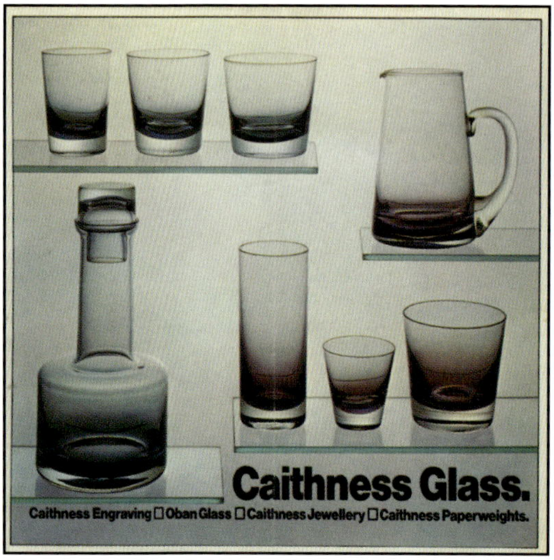

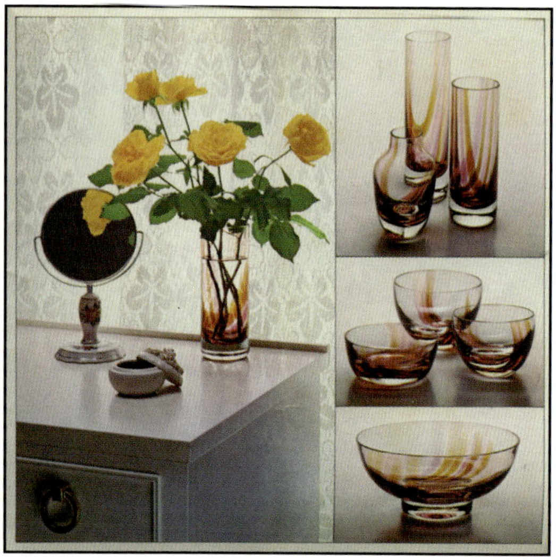

This was the first full colour, professionally produced catalogue distributed by Caithness Glass, and was devised by the Managing Director, Alistair Mair. It followed a catalogue of black and white photographs of engraved and sandblasted designs produced in 1970. It folds open to show six full colour photographs of ranges produced by the company. The front cover is shown on the bottom left, and ranges shown comprise cylindrical and other fruit bowls, the no.4040 water jug and matching glasses, the Lybster and Morven decanters and glasses, the no.4017 fruit bowl and some vases designed by Domhnall ÓBroin or Colin Terris, sandblasted designs on goblets and vases, a paperweight, and the Oban and jewellery ranges. The back displays line drawings of shapes and ranges (both pages shown above), and gives information about the company and the ranges shown.

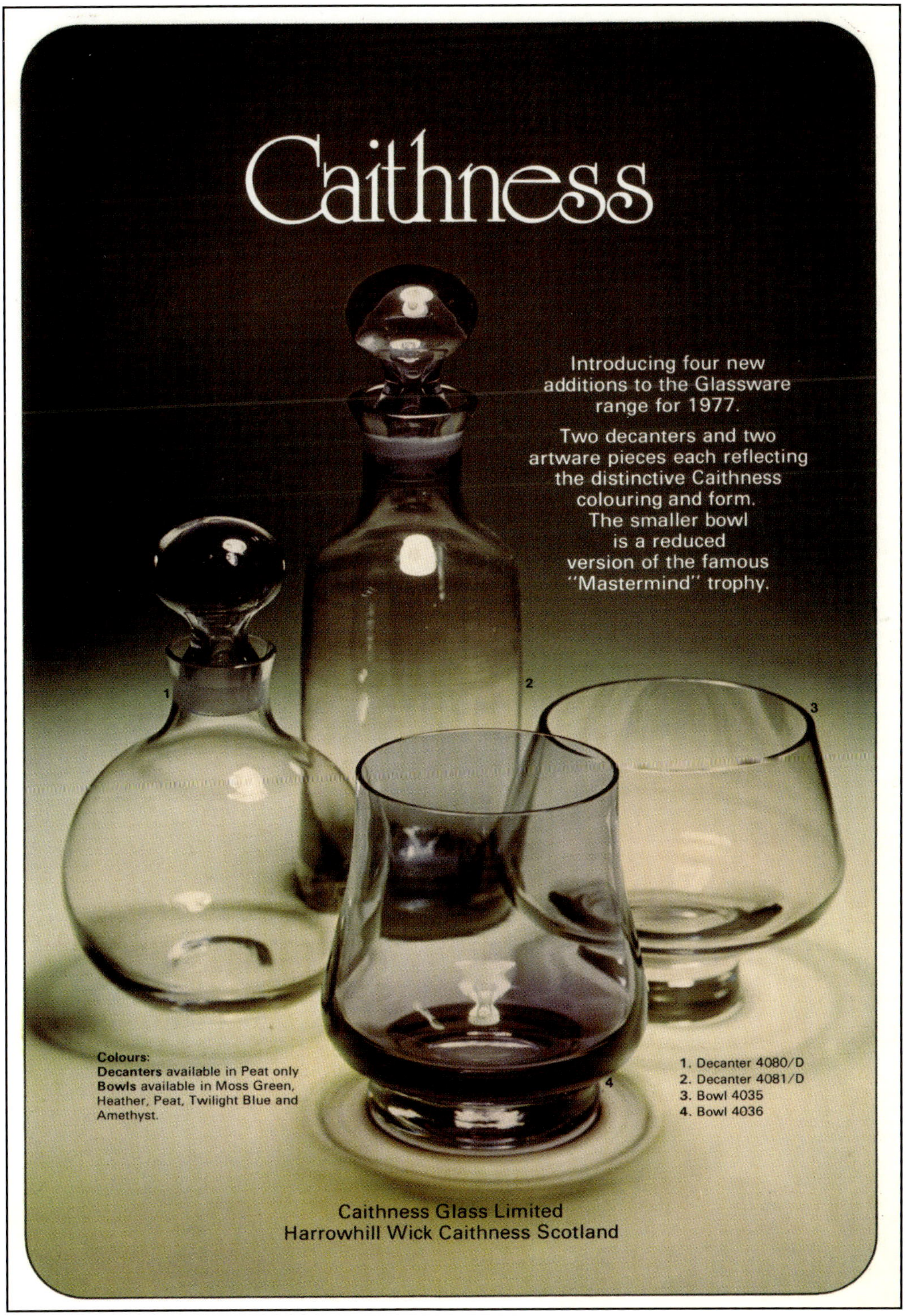
Caithness
Introducing four new additions to the Glassware range for 1977.
Two decanters and two artware pieces each reflecting the distinctive Caithness colouring and form. The smaller bowl is a reduced version of the famous "Mastermind" trophy.
1
2
3
4
Colours:
Decanters available in Peat only
Bowls available in Moss Green, Heather, Peat, Twilight Blue and Amethyst.
1. Decanter 4080/D
2. Decanter 4081/D
3. Bowl 4035
4. Bowl 4036
Caithness Glass Limited
Harrowhill Wick Caithness Scotland

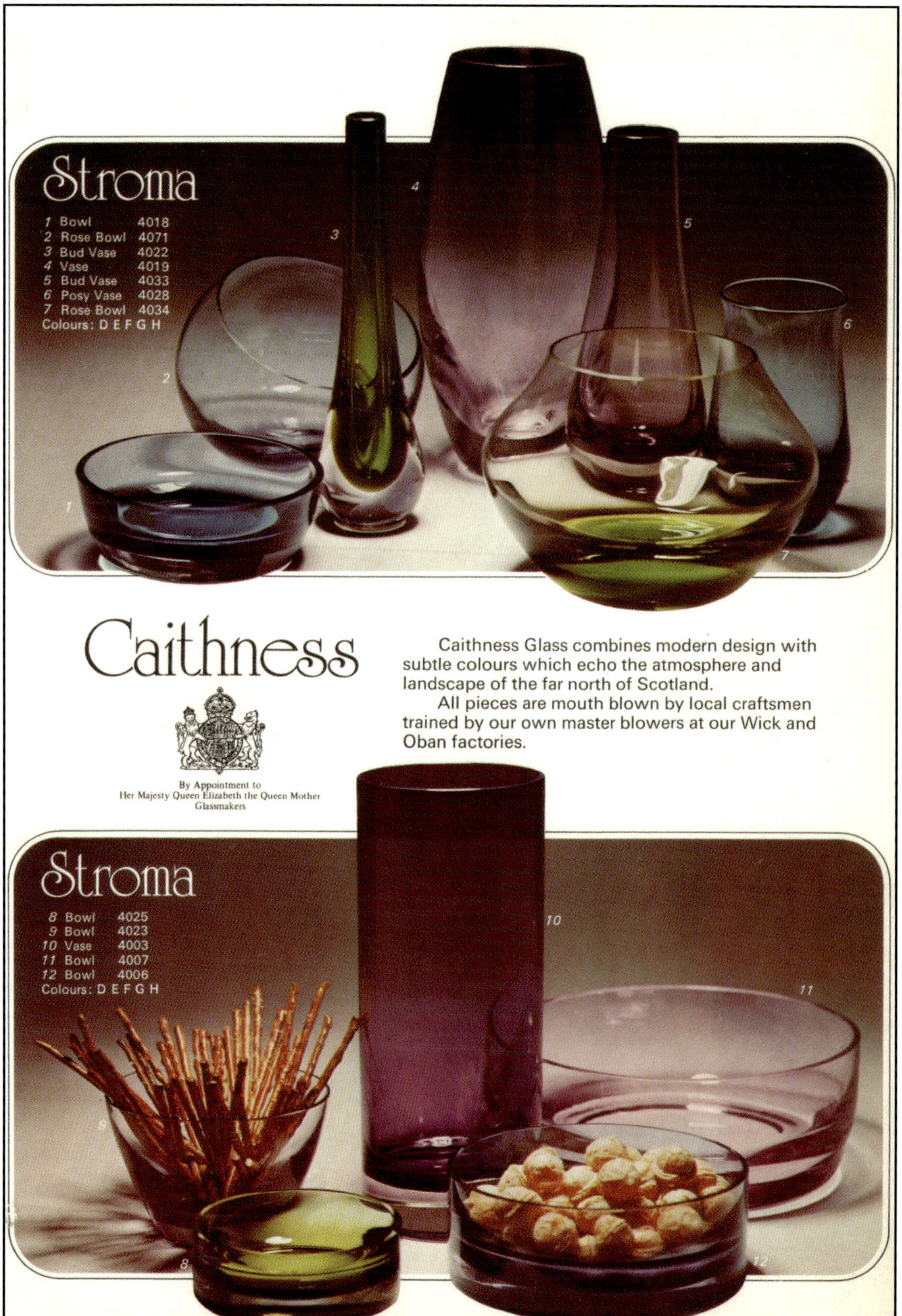
Stroma
1 Bowl 4018
2 Rose Bowl 4071
3 Bud Vase 4022
4 Vase 4019
5 Bud Vase 4033
6 Posy Vase 4028
7 Rose Bowl 4034
Colours: D E F G H
Caithness
Caithness Glass combines modern design with subtle colours which echo the atmosphere and landscape of the far north of Scotland.
All pieces are mouth blown by local craftsmen trained by our own master blowers at our Wick and Oban factories.
By Appointment to
Her Majesty Queen Elizabeth the Queen Mother
Glassmakers
Stroma
8 Bowl 4025
9 Bowl 4023
10 Vase 4003
11 Bowl 4007
12 Bowl 4006
Colours: D E F G H

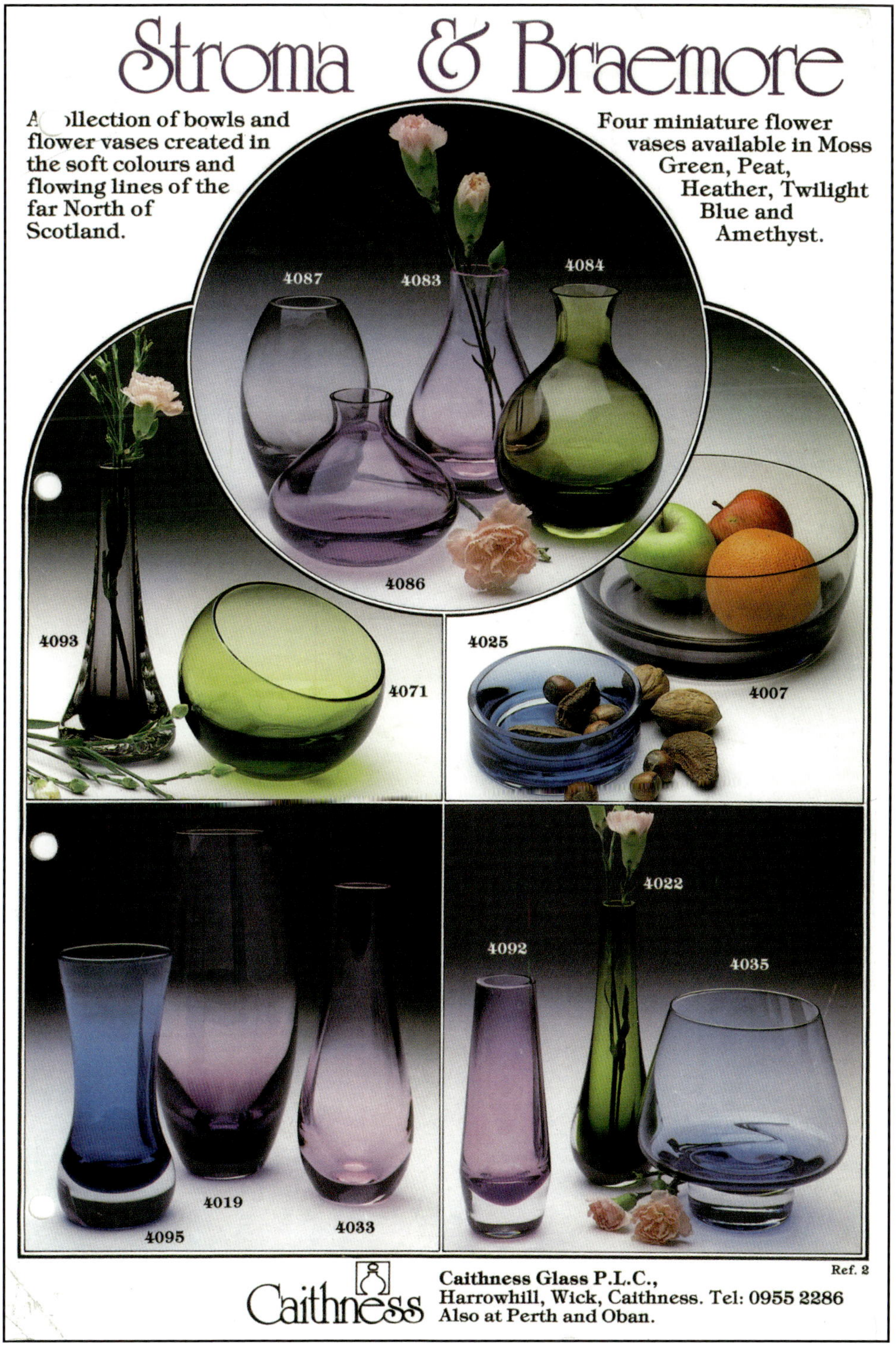
Stroma & Braemore
A collection of bowls and flower vases created in the soft colours and flowing lines of the far North of Scotland.
Four miniature flower vases available in Moss Green, Peat, Heather, Twilight Blue and Amethyst.
4087
4083
4084
4086
4093
4071
4025
4007
4022
4092
4035
4095
4019
4033
Ref. 2
Caithness
Caithness Glass P.L.C.,
Harrowhill, Wick, Caithness. Tel: 0955 2286
Also at Perth and Oban.

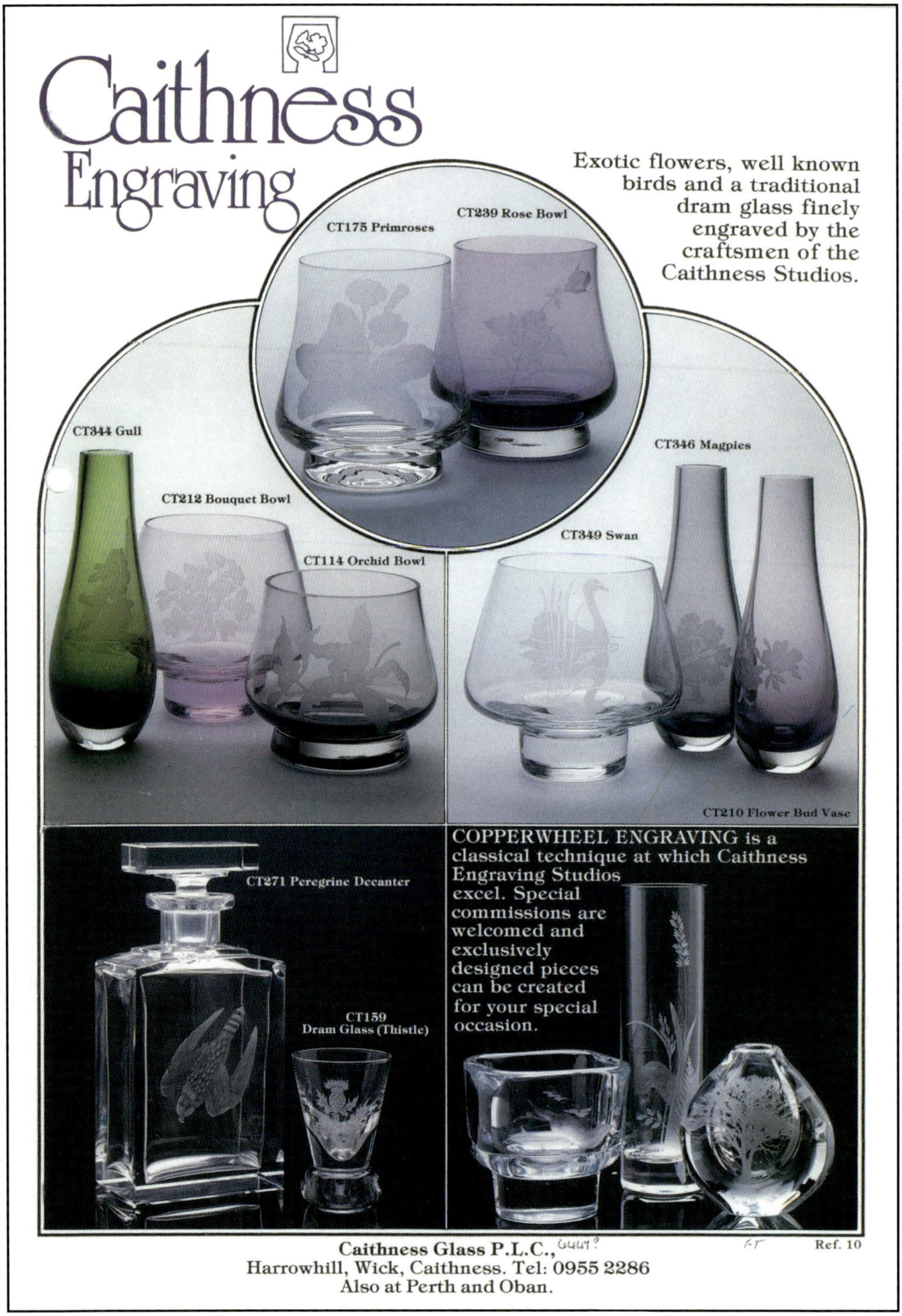
Caithness
Engraving
Exotic flowers, well known birds and a traditional dram glass finely engraved by the craftsmen of the Caithness Studios.
CT175 Primroses
CT239 Rose Bowl
CT344 Gull
CT212 Bouquet Bowl
CT114 Orchid Bowl
CT346 Magpies
CT349 Swan
CT210 Flower Bud Vase
CT271 Peregrine Decanter
CT159
Dram Glass (Thistle)
COPPERWHEEL ENGRAVING is a classical technique at which Caithness Engraving Studios excel. Special commissions are welcomed and exclusively designed pieces can be created for your special occasion.
Caithness Glass P.L.C.,
Ref. 10
Harrowhill, Wick, Caithness. Tel: 0955 2286
Also at Perth and Oban.

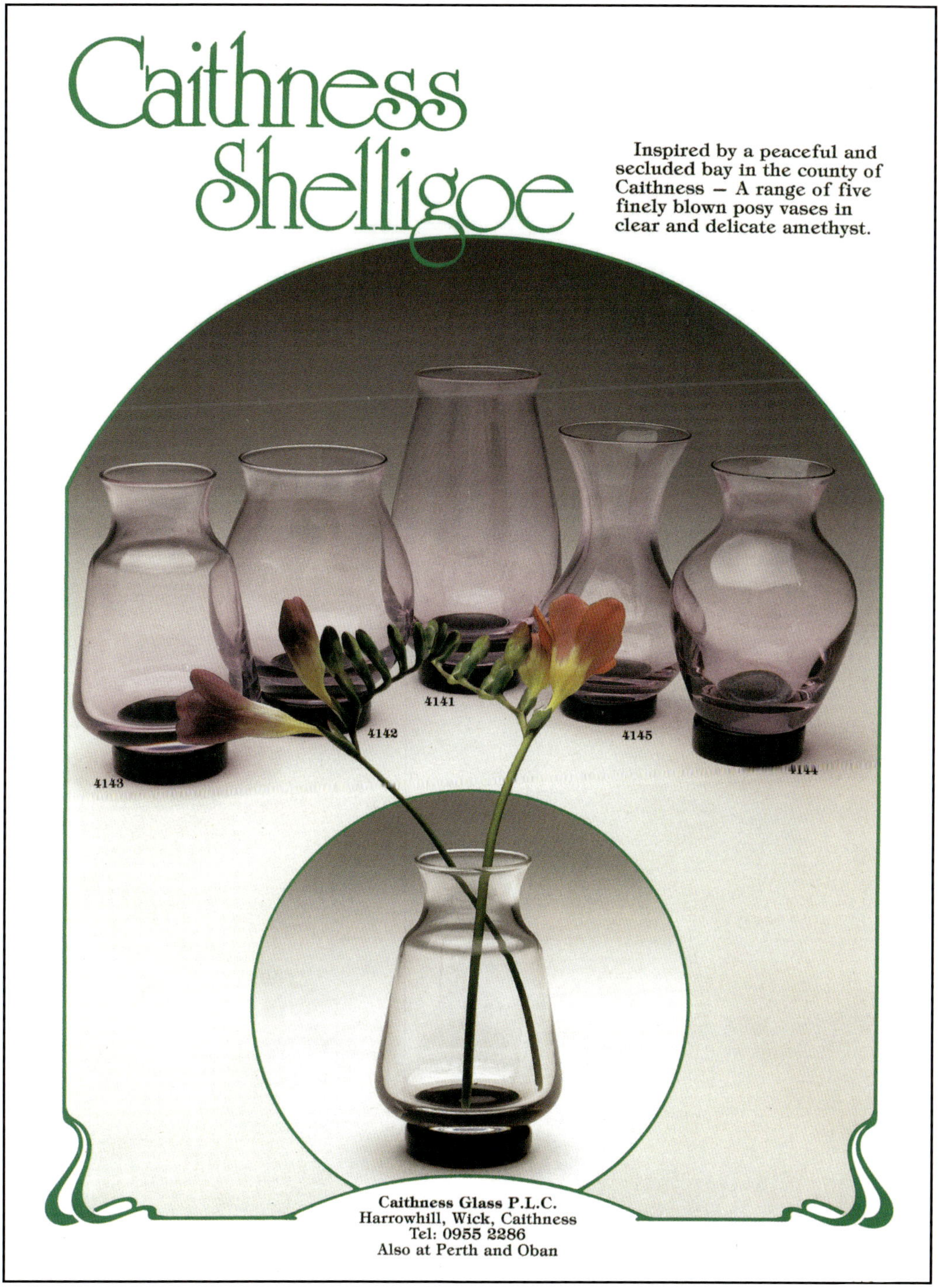

The Shelligoe range revived the 'black foot' element of Domhnall ÓBroin's early 1960s Scaraben range (see p.41). Like Scaraben, Shelligoe was not produced for long.

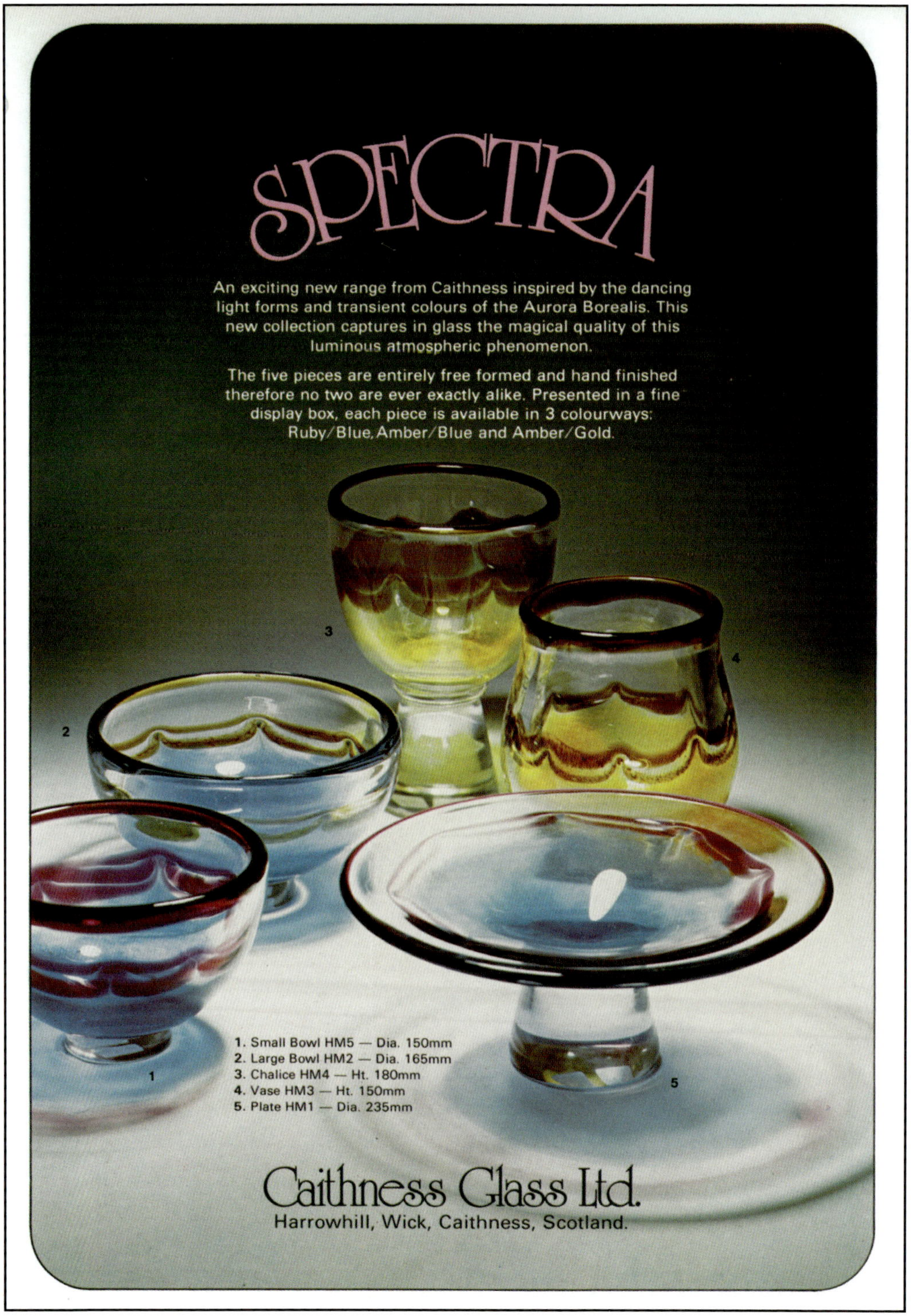
SPECTRA
An exciting new range from Caithness inspired by the dancing light forms and transient colours of the Aurora Borealis. This new collection captures in glass the magical quality of this luminous atmospheric phenomenon.
The five pieces are entirely free formed and hand finished therefore no two are ever exactly alike. Presented in a fine display box, each piece is available in 3 colourways: Ruby/Blue, Amber/Blue and Amber/Gold.
3
4
2
1
5
1. Small Bowl HM5 — Dia. 150mm
2. Large Bowl HM2 — Dia. 165mm
3. Chalice HM4 — Ht. 180mm
4. Vase HM3 — Ht. 150mm
5. Plate HM1 — Dia. 235mm
Caithness Glass Ltd.
Harrowhill, Wick, Caithness, Scotland.

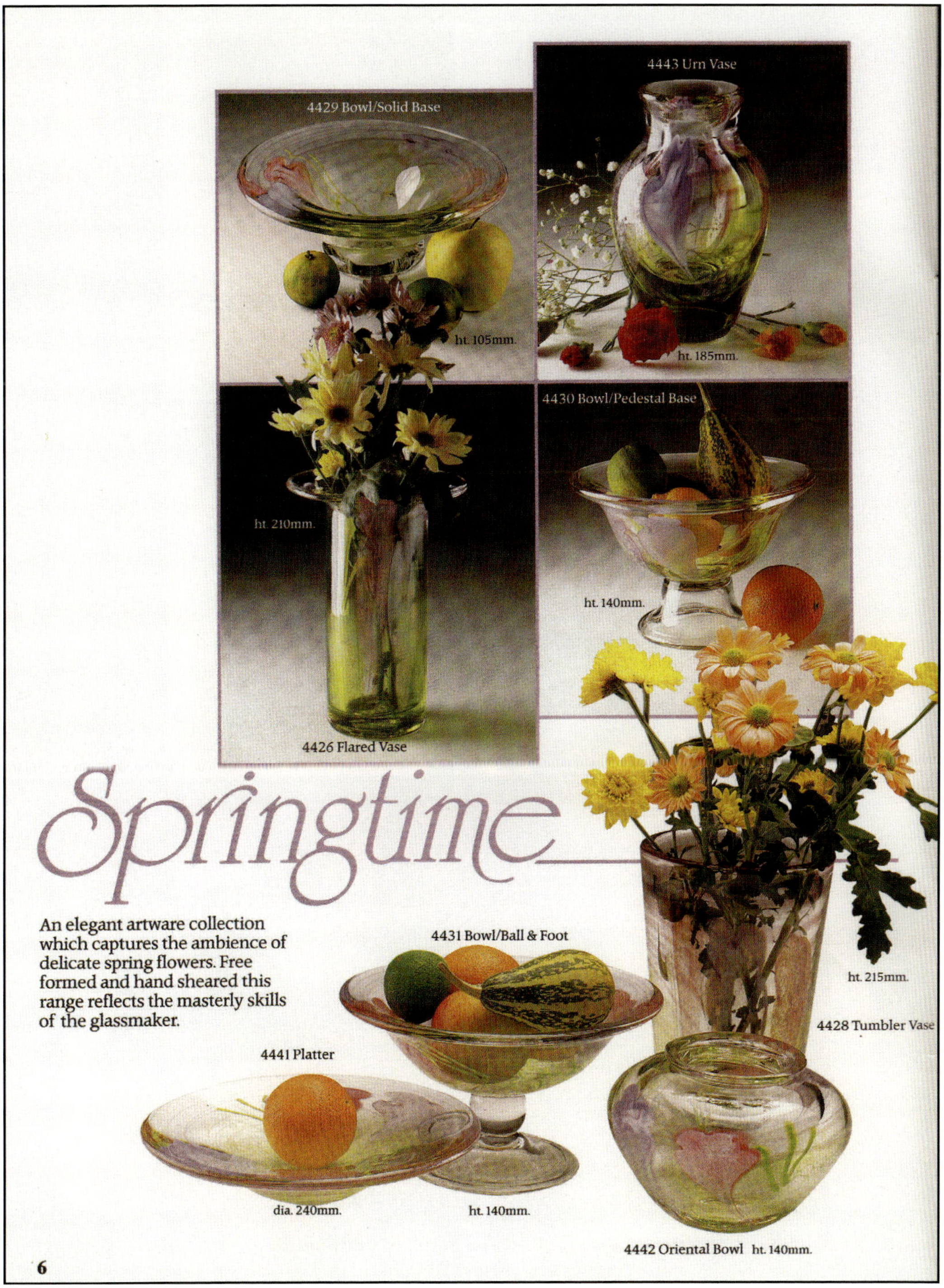
4443 Urn Vase
4429 Bowl/Solid Base
ht. 105mm.
ht. 185mm.
4430 Bowl/Pedestal Base
ht. 210mm.
ht. 140mm.
4426 Flared Vase

Springtime

An elegant artware collection which captures the ambience of delicate spring flowers. Free formed and hand sheared this range reflects the masterly skills of the glassmaker.

4431 Bowl/Ball & Foot
ht. 215mm.
4428 Tumbler Vase
4441 Platter
dia. 240mm.
ht. 140mm.
4442 Oriental Bowl ht. 140mm.
6

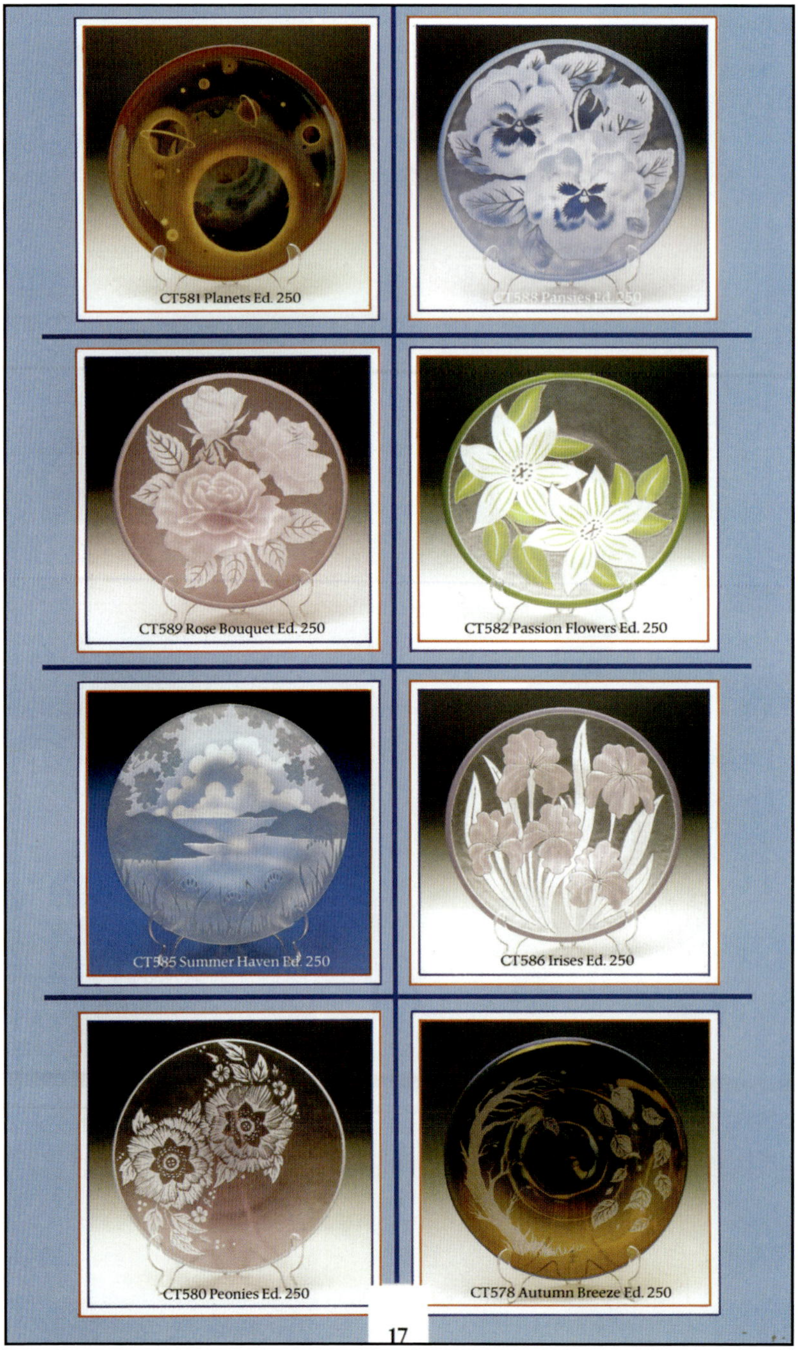

Designed by Helen MacDonald, there were twelve plates in the Cameo Collection. The four designs not shown comprised no.CT583 'Poppies', no.CT587 'Oriental Dragon', no.CT579 'Elephant Trail' and no.CT584 'Seascape'. Each design was produced in a limited edition of 250 pieces, and each piece was sold in a special presentation box with a display stand.

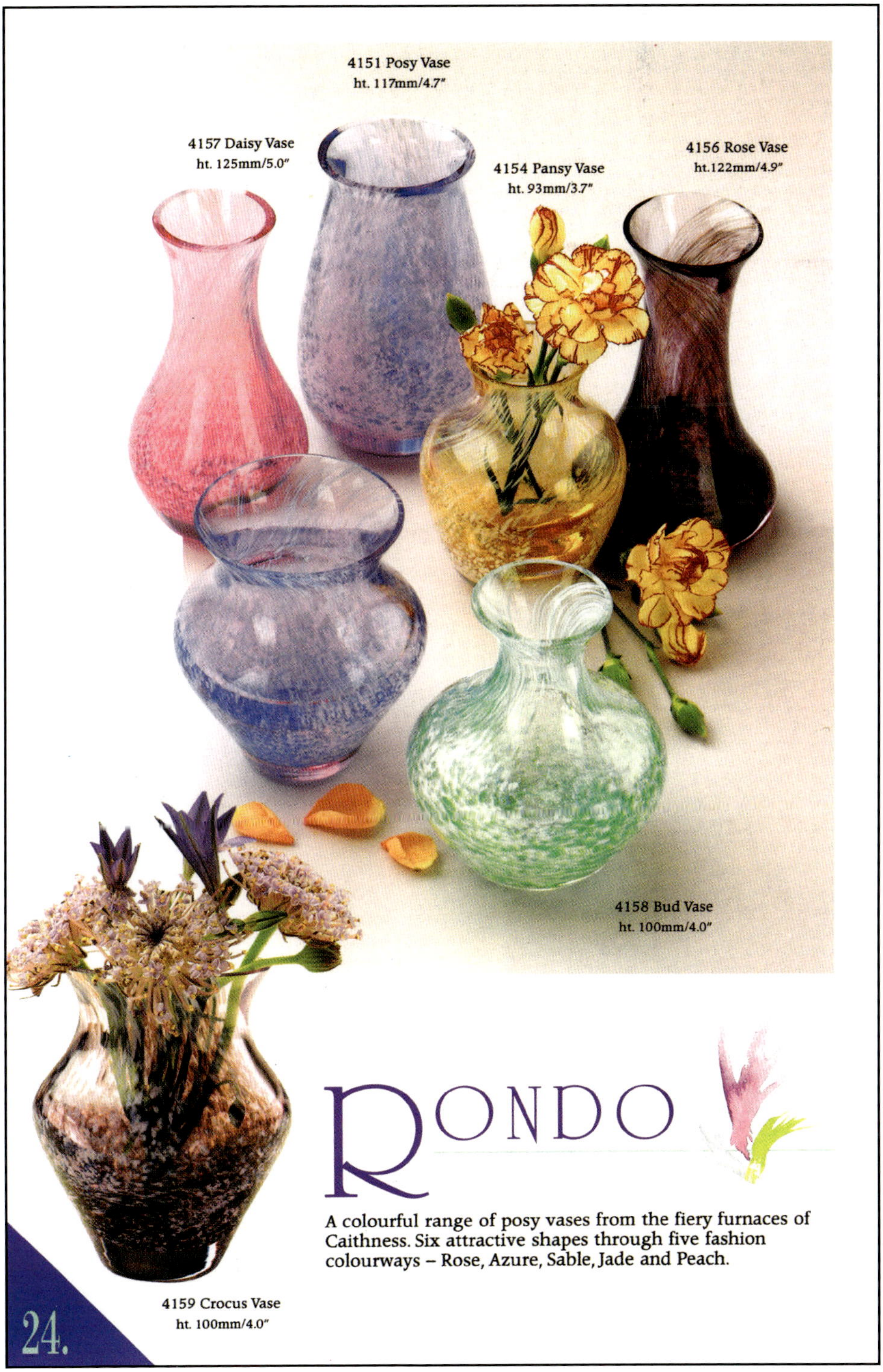
4151 Posy Vase
ht. 117mm/4.7"

4157 Daisy Vase
ht. 125mm/5.0"

4154 Pansy Vase
ht. 93mm/3.7"

4156 Rose Vase
ht.122mm/4.9"

4158 Bud Vase
ht. 100mm/4.0"

RONDO

A colourful range of posy vases from the fiery furnaces of Caithness. Six attractive shapes through five fashion colourways – Rose, Azure, Sable, Jade and Peach.

4159 Crocus Vase
ht. 100mm/4.0"

24.

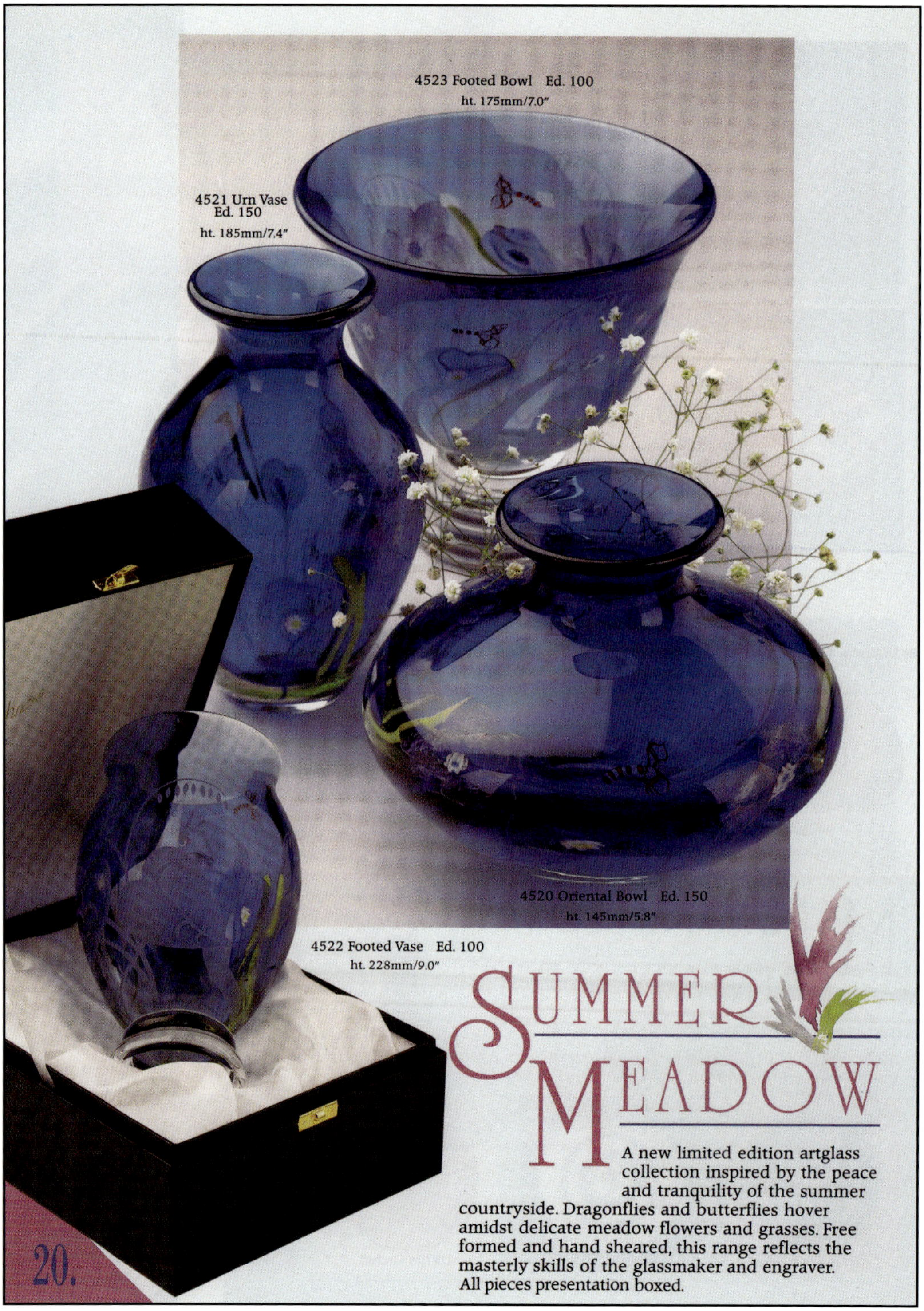

4523 Footed Bowl Ed. 100
ht. 175mm/7.0″

4521 Urn Vase
Ed. 150
ht. 185mm/7.4″

4520 Oriental Bowl Ed. 150
ht. 145mm/5.8″

4522 Footed Vase Ed. 100
ht. 228mm/9.0″

SUMMER MEADOW

A new limited edition artglass collection inspired by the peace and tranquility of the summer countryside. Dragonflies and butterflies hover amidst delicate meadow flowers and grasses. Free formed and hand sheared, this range reflects the masterly skills of the glassmaker and engraver. All pieces presentation boxed.

20.

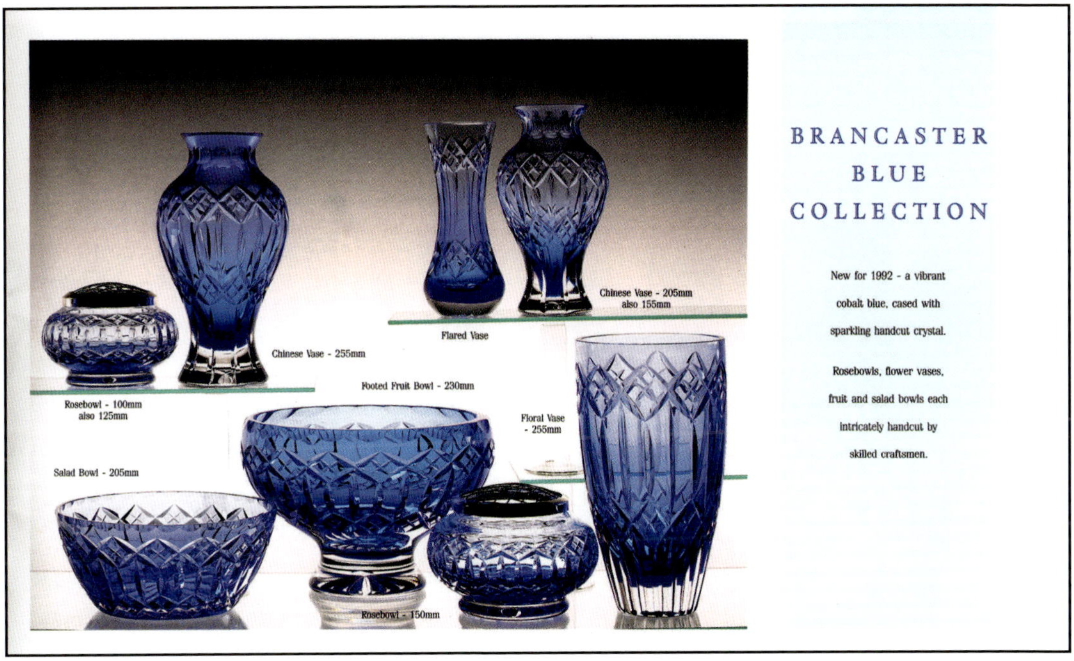
Chinese Vase - 205mm
also 155mm
Flared Vase
Chinese Vase - 255mm
Rosebowl - 100mm
also 125mm
Footed Fruit Bowl - 230mm
Floral Vase
- 255mm
Salad Bowl - 205mm
Rosebowl - 150mm
BRANCASTER
BLUE
COLLECTION
New for 1992 - a vibrant
cobalt blue, cased with
sparkling handcut crystal.
Rosebowls, flower vases,
fruit and salad bowls each
intricately handcut by
skilled craftsmen.

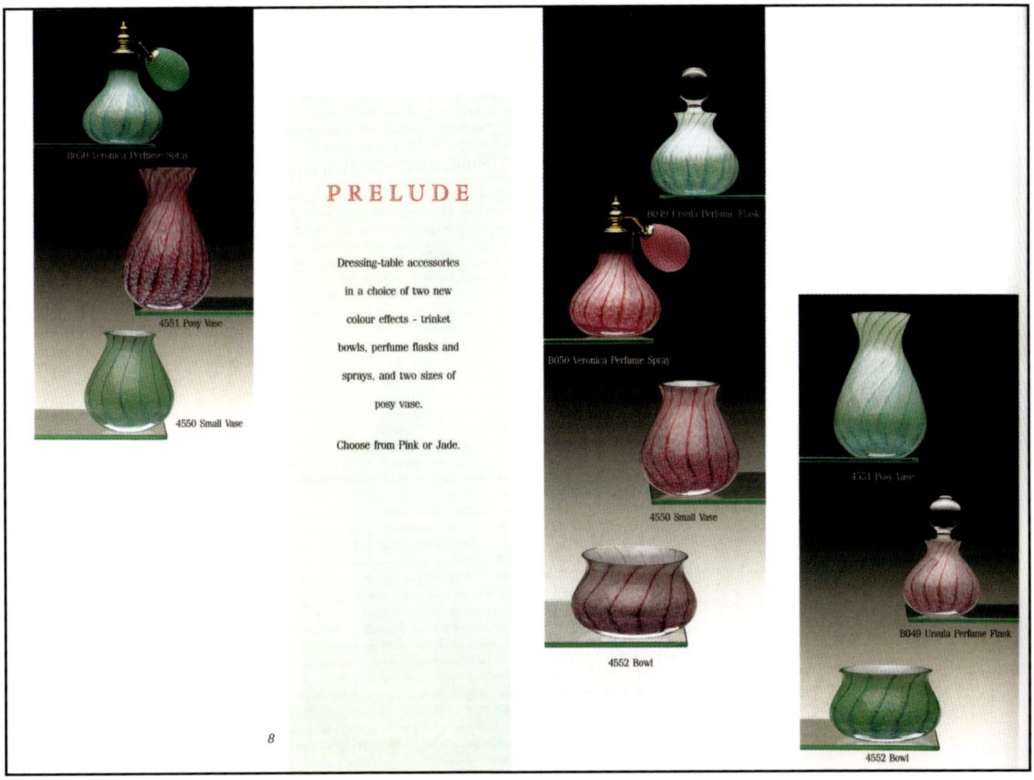
B050 Veronica Perfume Spray
4551 Posy Vase
4550 Small Vase
PRELUDE
Dressing-table accessories
in a choice of two new
colour effects - trinket
bowls, perfume flasks and
sprays, and two sizes of
posy vase.
Choose from Pink or Jade.
8
B049 Ursula Perfume Flask
B050 Veronica Perfume Spray
4550 Small Vase
4552 Bowl
4551 Posy Vase
B049 Ursula Perfume Flask
4552 Bowl

7660
Bud Vase
Ht.98mm

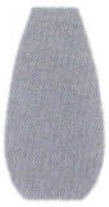

7664
Teardrop Vase
Ht.210mm

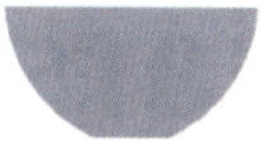

7663
Bowl
Dia.178mm

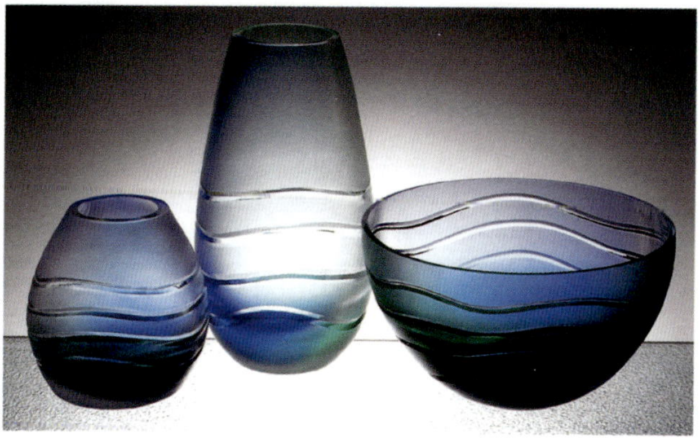

aqua nova

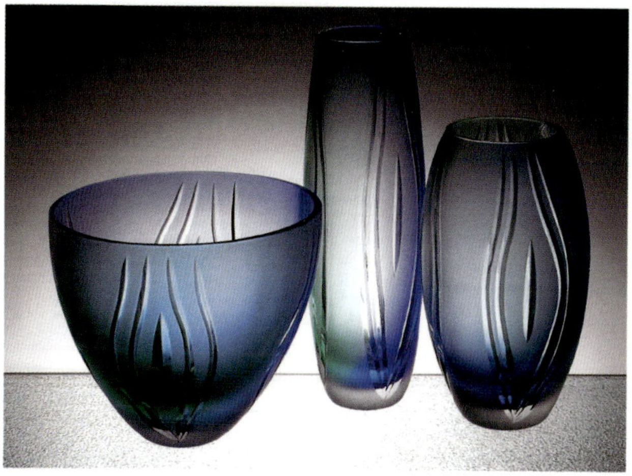

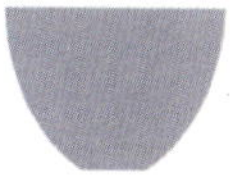

7665
High Bowl
Dia.170mm

7661
Tall Flower Vase
Ht.237mm

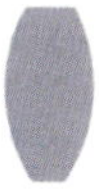

7662
Posy Vase
Ht.160mm

7

tempest

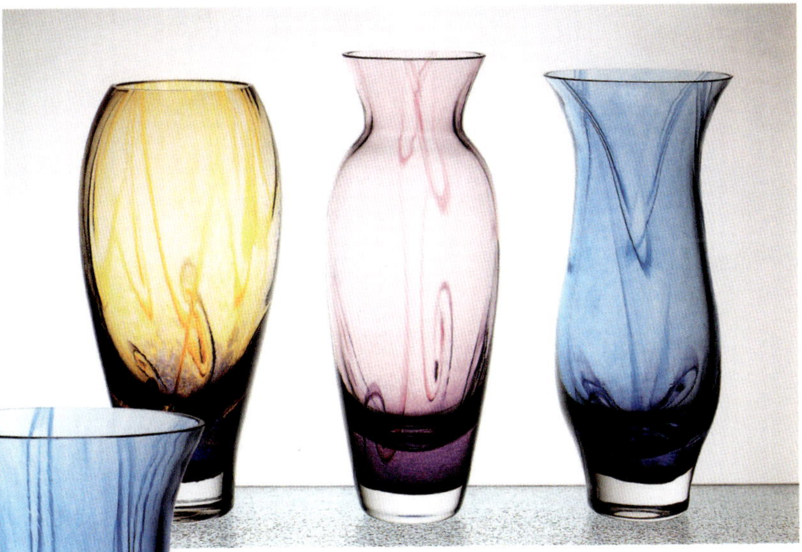

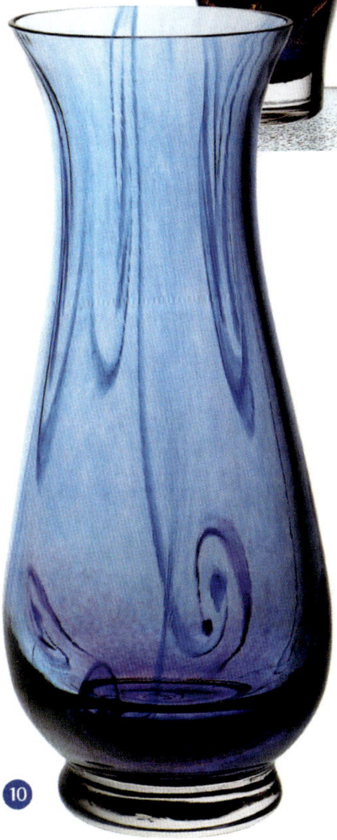

10

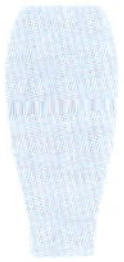

7022
Flower Vase
Ht. 220mm

7023
Spray Vase
Ht. 235mm

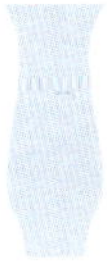

7024
Tulip Vase
Ht. 225mm

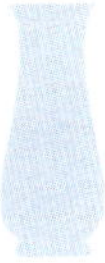

7021
Bouquet Vase
Ht. 230mm

Tempest colour options – Gold, Ruby and Indigo

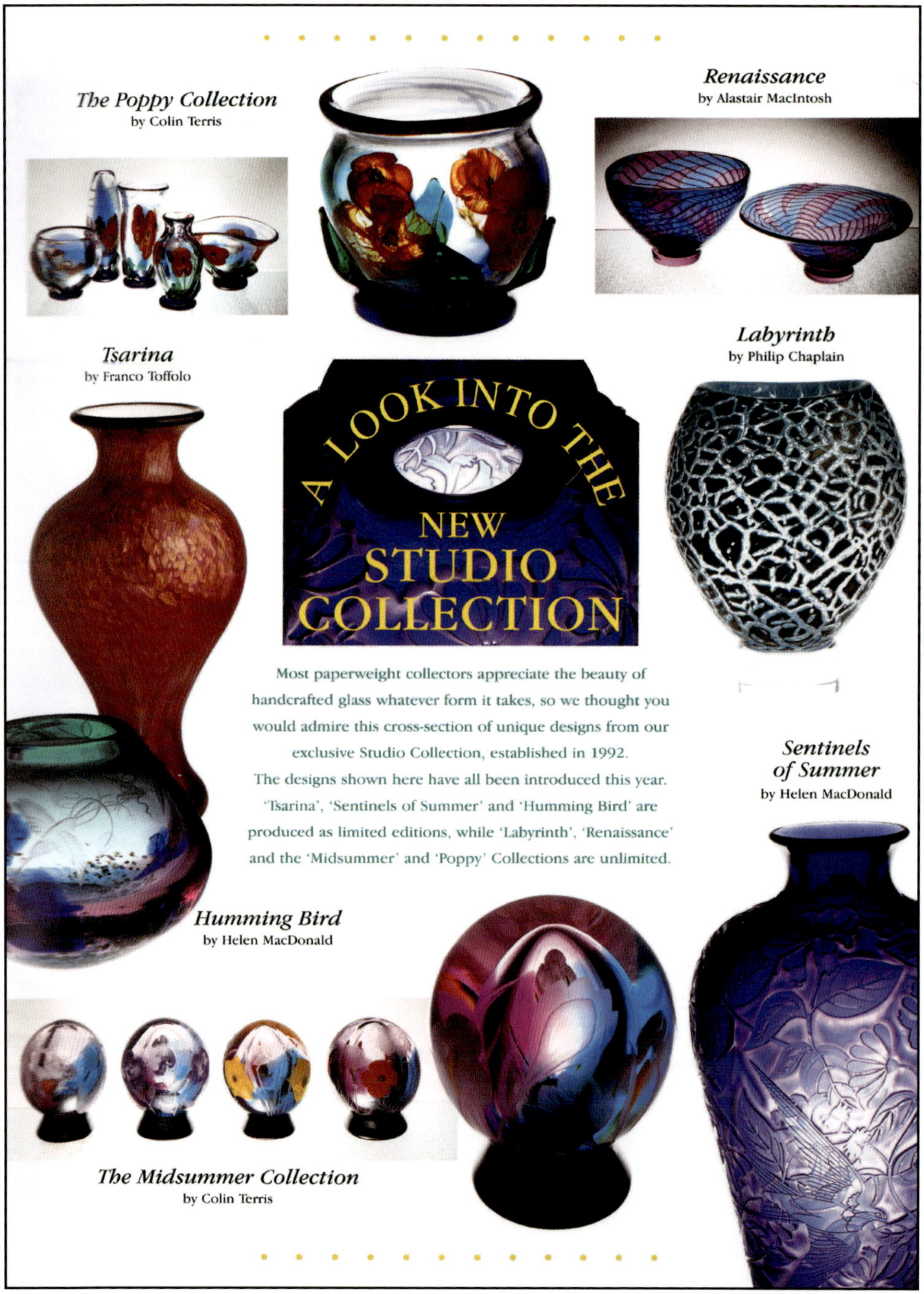

The Poppy Collection
by Colin Terris

Renaissance
by Alastair MacIntosh

Tsarina
by Franco Toffolo

A LOOK INTO THE NEW STUDIO COLLECTION

Labyrinth
by Philip Chaplain

Most paperweight collectors appreciate the beauty of handcrafted glass whatever form it takes, so we thought you would admire this cross-section of unique designs from our exclusive Studio Collection, established in 1992.
The designs shown here have all been introduced this year. 'Tsarina', 'Sentinels of Summer' and 'Humming Bird' are produced as limited editions, while 'Labyrinth', 'Renaissance' and the 'Midsummer' and 'Poppy' Collections are unlimited.

Sentinels of Summer
by Helen MacDonald

Humming Bird
by Helen MacDonald

The Midsummer Collection
by Colin Terris

Sentinels of Summer was produced in a limited edition of 15 pieces, each costing £2,000 in 2000. Tsarina was produced in a limited edition of 150 pieces, each costing £275 in 2001, and the Hummingbird vase was produced in a limited edition of 25 pieces, each costing £495 in 2000. All were part of high end ranges produced around the millennium.

back **Orchids Bowl** CT716 Dia.190mm/7½" **Highland Cattle Bowl** CT733 Dia.190mm/7½"

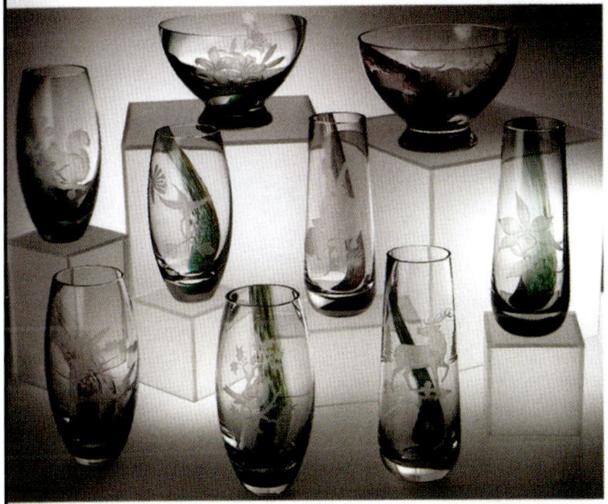

middle **Squirrel Barrel Vase** CT737 Ht.200mm/9" **Hummingbird Barrel Vase** CT715 Ht.200mm/8" **Rabbits Straight Vase** CT756 Ht.230mm/9" **Orchids Straight Vase** CT719 Ht.230mm/9"

front **Swallows Barrel Vase** CT757 Ht.200mm/8" **Robin Barrel Vase** CT760 Ht.200mm/8" **Stag Straight Vase** CT738 Ht.230mm/9"

N Dolphin Straight Vase

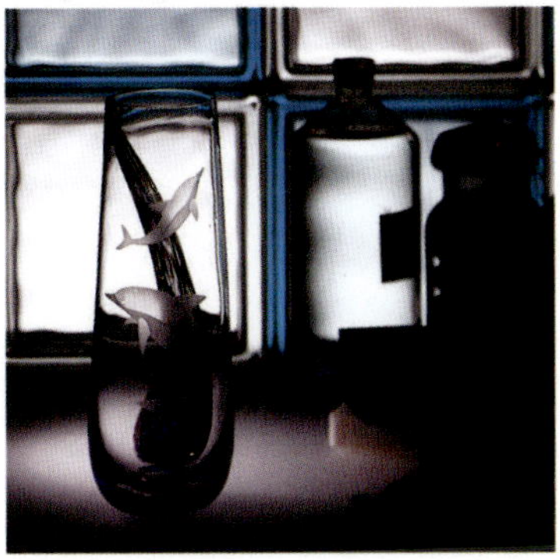

Images

The intricate skill of the engraver eloquently captures the theme of wildlife against the swirl of a coloured backdrop representing the native landscape. Each piece is mouth blown and hand engraved. A perfect gift, and very collectable.

clockwise from top

Dolphins Bowl
CT710
Dia.190mm/7½"

Otter Bowl
CT755
Dia.190mm/7½"

Otter Straight Vase
CT700
Ht.230mm/9"

Angelfish Straight Vase
CT728
Ht.230mm/9"

Salmon Straight Vase
CT736
Ht.230mm/9"

N Dolphin Straight Vase
CT768
Ht.230mm/9"

Dolphins Barrel Vase
CT702
Ht.200mm/8"

Owl Bowl
CT734
Dia.190mm/7½"

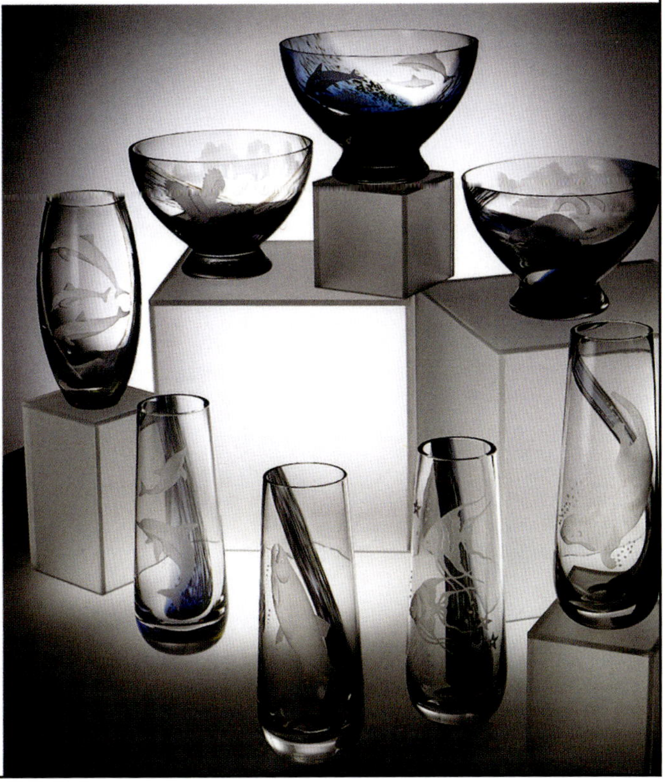

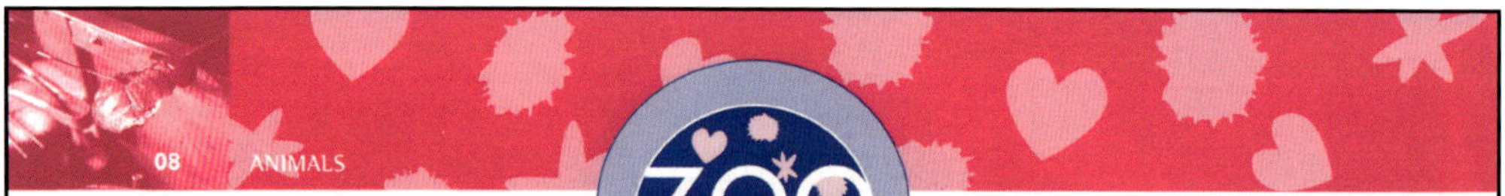

Zoo

Zoo is the stylish new range of glass animals designed by Sarah Peterson. Using strong colours and simple shapes each animal has its own distinctive style and personality. Bold colours and delicate stencil patterns link the range, allowing you to create your own personal zoo. Highly collectable and perfect for gifting.

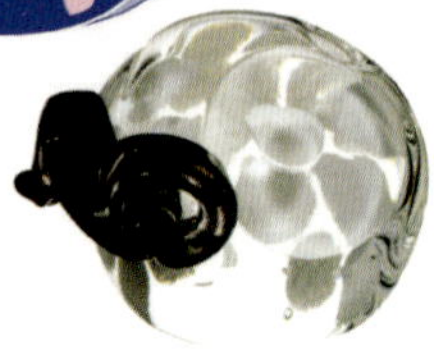

Baa the Ram
A02004 SP
Ht. 65mm/2½"

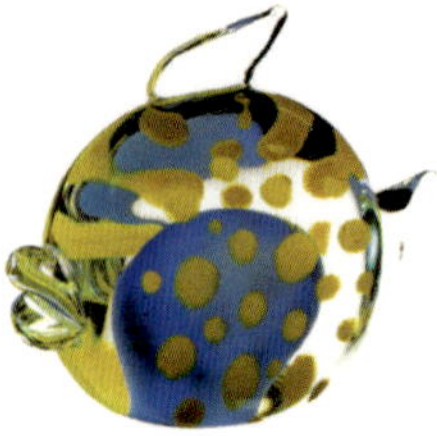

Bob the Fish
A02001 SP
Ht. 90mm/3½"

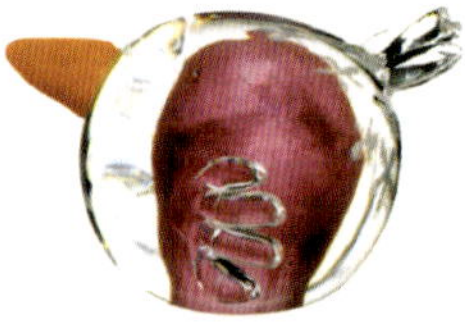

Boing the Bird
A02002 SP
Ht. 85mm/3⅓"

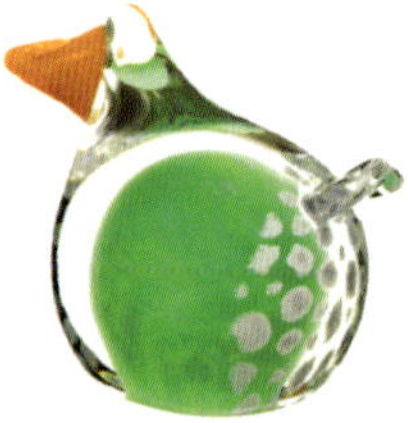

Bombay the Duck
A02003 SP
Ht. 90mm/3½"

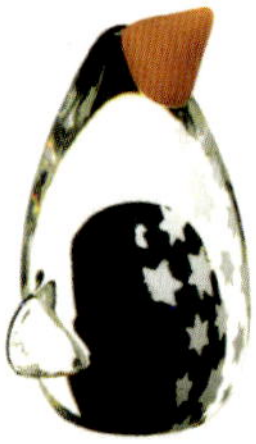

Shuffle the Penguin
A02005 SP
Ht. 120mm/4¾"

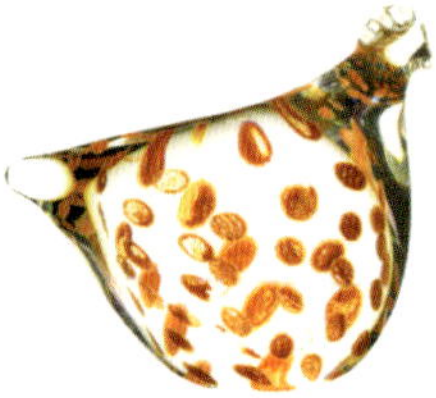

Speckle the Hen
A02006 SP
Ht. 80mm/3"

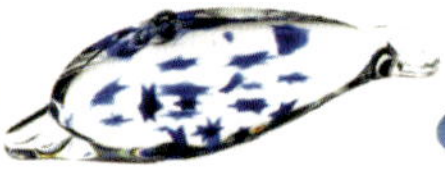

Splish the Small Dolphin
A02008 SP
Length 130mm/5"

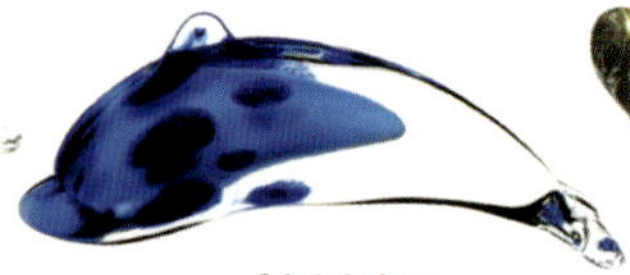

Splash the Large Dolphin
A02007 SP
Length180mm/7"

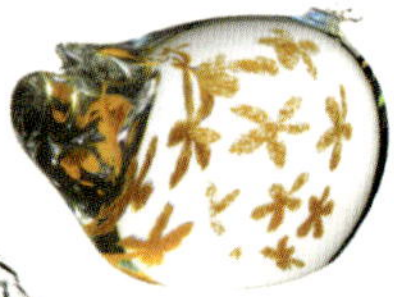

Truffle the Pig
A02010 SP
Ht. 55mm/2"

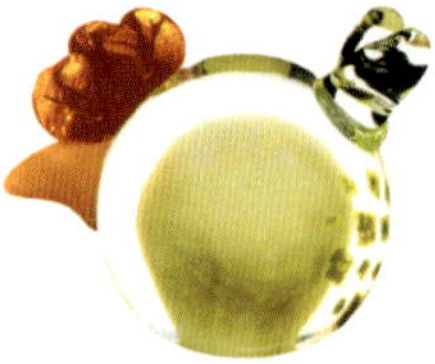

Tikka the Chicken
A02009 SP
Ht. 85mm/3⅓"

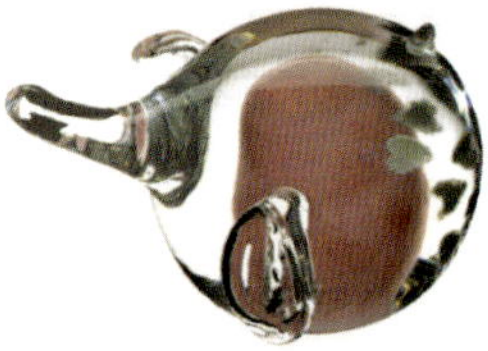

Trumpet the Elephant
A02011 SP
Ht. 70mm/2¾"

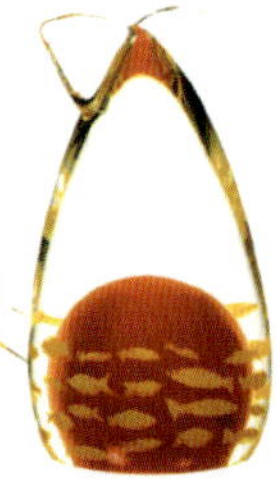

Whiskers the Cat
A02012 SP
Ht. 120mm/4¾"

The Zoo range is handcrafted at our Caithness Glass studios in King's Lynn (England) and Perth (Scotland).

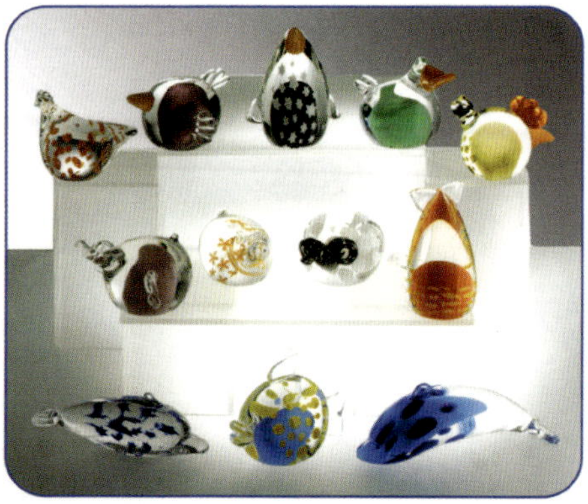

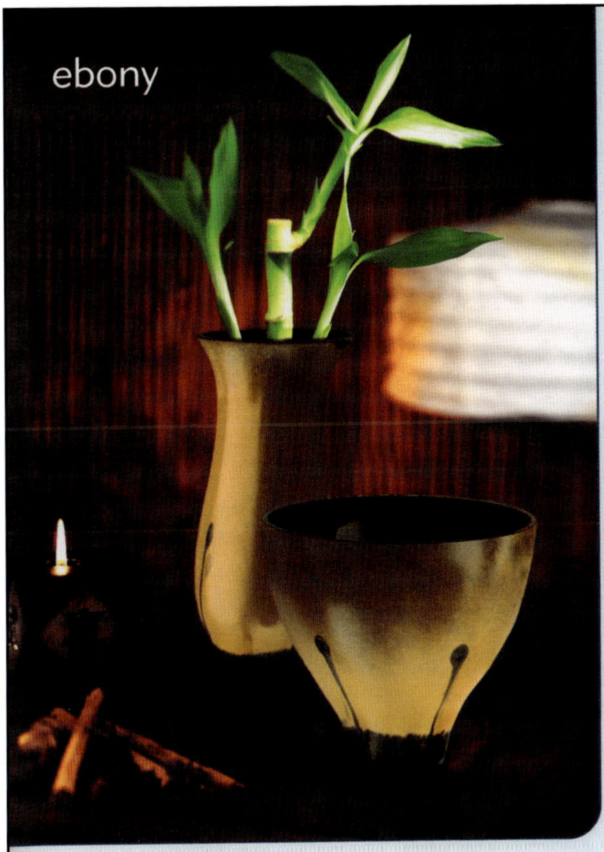

Elegant art **nouveau** inspired shapes set against a flame red or neutral sand exterior create a dramatic statement when teamed with the black interior. A collection that includes a large vase and planter has been styled to give an oriental feel.

Colour options: **Flame** and **Sand**

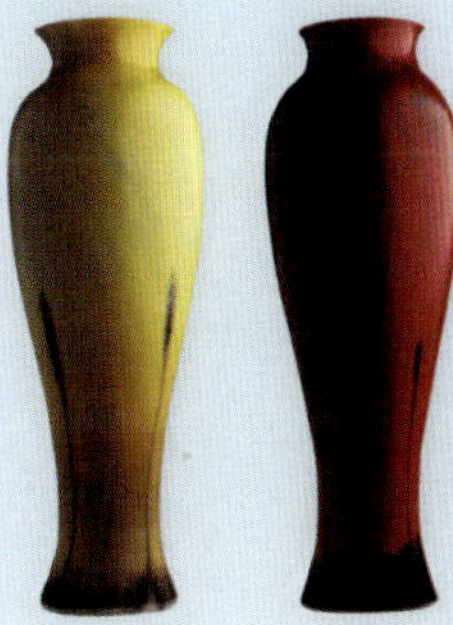

sand flame

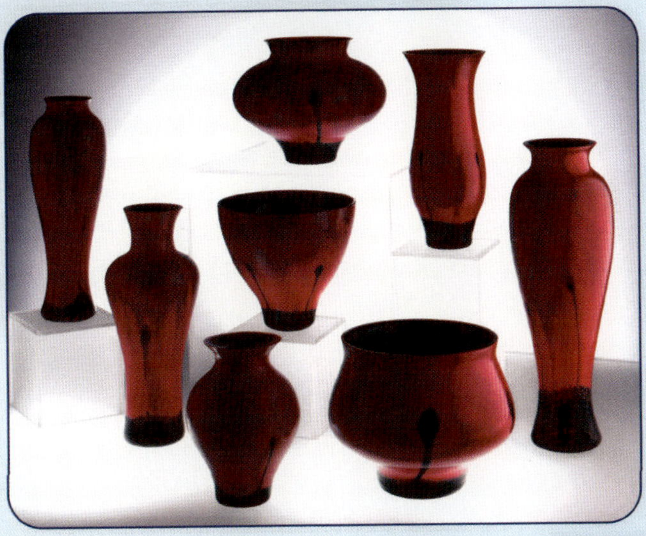

left to right
Chinese Vase
6654
Ht.250mm/10"

Tall Vase
6651
Ht.250mm/10"

Bulb Vase
6653
Ht.150mm/6"

Fruit Bowl
6650
Dia.150mm/6"

Tulip Vase
6658
Ht.150mm/6"

Planter
6657
Ht.145mm/5¾"

Flared Vase
6655
Ht.225mm/8¾"

Large Chinese Vase
6659
Dia.310mm/12½"

artglass 11

Designer Biographies

These biographies are of selected designers who worked for Caithness Glass and whose designs are included in this catalogue. For biographies of Colin Terris, David Gulland, and Denis Mann, please see pages 92–97.

Gordon Hendry

Born in Wick in 1959, Hendry joined Caithness Glass as a trainee glass engraver in 1975. He worked in that department until 1982, when he was made redundant when the department was halved in a cost cutting exercise that focused on quantity rather than quality. He then studied Illustration and Printmaking at Dundee Art College, before taking a postgraduate position at Central St. Martins College of Art & Design in London from 1987-89. He was a freelance illustrator from 1987 onwards, with clients including DC Thomson and the Oxford University Press. He rejoined Caithness Glass as a designer at Wick in 1995. He specialised in developing designs into a final product, working closely with glassmakers. He worked in this role, and as a designer at the Perth factory from 2001, until he left the company in 2007.

Helen MacDonald

Born in Caithness in 1958, MacDonald joined Caithness Glass in Wick in 1974 as a trainee glass engraver after leaving school. She studied under David Gulland and Denis Mann, and became one of the most skilled engravers in the department by 1979. Her specialities included sandblasting and copper wheel engraving techniques. In 1985, she transferred to the Perth factory to continue her work with engraving, specialising in commissions and commemorative designs. She also became Colin Terris' assistant, and produced her own designs. In 1991, she began designing paperweights, and she was appointed Lead Designer in 2003. After producing many art glass and paperweight designs, she left the company in 2007.

Alastair MacIntosh

Born in Falkirk in 1951, MacIntosh studied glass design at the Edinburgh College of Art under glassmakers Ken Wainwright and Andrew Scott. He graduated in 1974, and was the technician at the college until 1979. He then took the same role at the Paisley College of Technology from 1979–81. From 1981–87, he ran his own glass studio in Falkirk, producing decorative wares, perfume bottles, and paperweights. He joined Caithness Glass as a designer in 1987 and became involved in many aspects of product design and development, and the development of colours. During the late 1980s, he worked with King's Lynn Crystal, where his practical technical knowledge proved invaluable. His first paperweight design was produced in 1988, and he produced decorative designs (including the best-selling Images range) from the 1990s until his departure from Caithness Glass in 2003.

Sarah Peterson

Born in 1972, Peterson joined Caithness Glass in 1987 and worked in the factory shop in Perth. She progressed from there to being a glassmaker's helper, to being a glassmaker in her own right. In 1994 she left to study for a degree in ceramics and glass at Buckinghamshire University, returning to Caithness Glass in 2000 to become a Design Developer. By 2008, she had become the lead designer for the company after its relocation to Crieff. Peterson has also produced designs for Dartington Crystal, the current owners of Caithness Glass. She is now producing designs, paperweights, and sandcast sculptures at the company's new factory in Crieff.

About This Catalogue

This catalogue is intended to be a basic introduction to the history and production of Caithness Glass across four decades after it was founded in 1961. As such, not all of the many thousands of designs the company and its team of talented designers and glassmakers produced over the years can be included. The focus is on the founding of the factory, the life and work of its co-founder and first designer Domhnall ÓBroin, and on selected designers and ranges produced from the late 1960s until the early 2000s. Paperweights, which have already been covered in depth by numerous publications, are not included. It is also worth bearing in mind that, like many smaller studio glass companies, experimentation was rife. Some designs were produced on different forms, in different colours, or in different styles (or in any combination of these), and unique and special commissions were undertaken. As such, it would be impossible to cover every design and its variations produced. I hope that the contents are enjoyable, educational, and helpful.

Acknowledgements

Mark Hill would like to thank Helen MacDonald, Alastair MacIntosh, Gordon Hendry, Alistair & Mary Mair, Peter Holmes, and Sarah Peterson for so generously giving their time to pass their expertise and experiences at Caithness Glass on to me. Domhnall ÓBroin's daughter Emer has been a true staunch supporter throughout, and her kind help and wealth of information and stories about her father and his work have been invaluable. I'd like to thank Richard Halliday of Dartington Crystal for permission to reproduce Caithness Glass catalogues. I must also thank Andrew Nowson for supplying scans of some extra catalogues, and Steve Adams for extra photography of pieces in Emer ÓBroin's collection. On the subject of photography, I can honestly say that my bookalogues would not be worth doing without Graham Rae's formidable photographic skills and talent. His bonhomie and sense of humour also always makes working with him fun. In the same way, I'm indebted to Ali Scrivens of TJ Graphics for her design help and pre-press work. I also couldn't have done this without support, advice and editorial brilliance from Tracey Smith and Judith Miller. Last, but certainly not least, extremely big thanks to Graham Cooley for coming up with the idea, lending me his catalogue archive, and for his friendly, knowledgeable support and help. And many thanks, of course, to Philip Reicherstorfer for everything and more.

Graham Cooley would like to thank Emer ÓBroin for her unstinting support and help, and also say that this is "*For my delightful daughter Beth, who one day will inherit more glass than she can shake a stick at! I blame the parents.*"

Select Bibliography

Catalogues, 'Reflections' magazines, and promotional literature, produced by Caithness Glass from 1970-2004.
'20th Century British Glass', by Charles Hajdamach, Antique Collectors Club, 2009.
'20th Century Factory Glass', by Lesley Jackson, Mitchell Beazley, 2000.
'Caithness Paperweights', by Colin Terris, Charlton Books, 2004.
'Maestro of Crystal: The Story of Miroslav Havel', by Brian Havel, Currach, 2005.
'Scotland's Glass: 400 Years of Glassmaking 1610-2010', by Shiona Airlie & Brian Blench, Cortex Design, 2010.

Readers are also encouraged to visit www.scotlandsglass.co.uk, run by Frank Andrews, for further information.

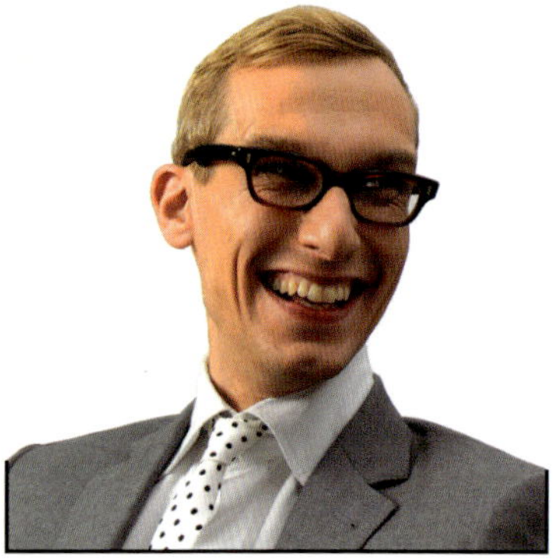

Other books by Mark Hill...

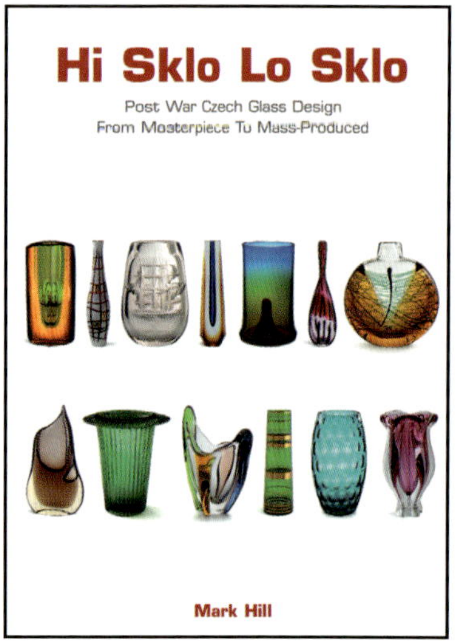

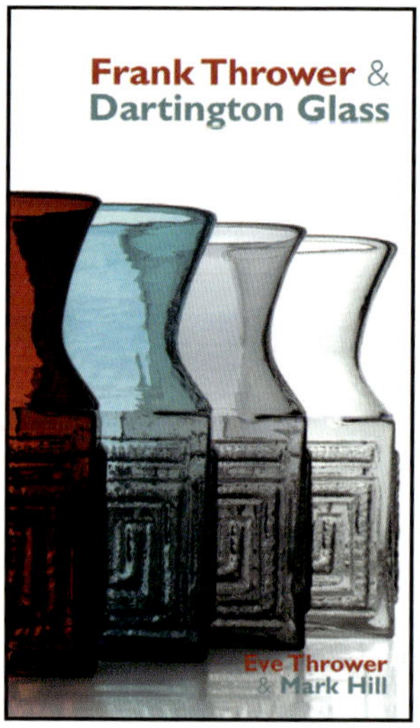

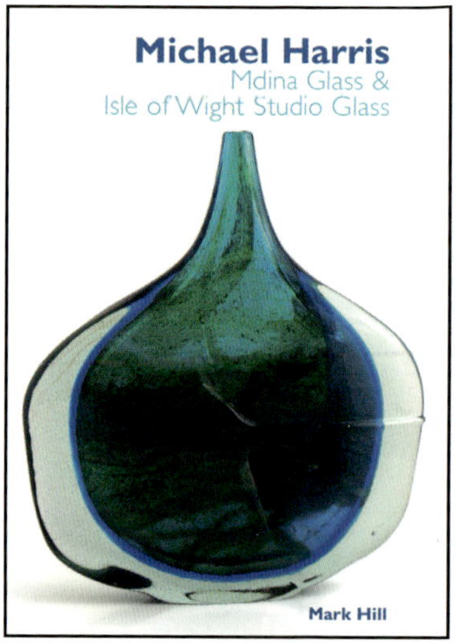

Hi Sklo Lo Sklo: Post War Czech Glass Design From Masterpiece to Mass-Produced
Softback, 148pp – £20

Frank Thrower & Dartington Glass
Softback, 112pp – £12

Michael Harris: Mdina Glass & Isle of Wight Studio Glass
Softback, 160pp – £25

Fat Lava: West German Ceramics of the 1960s & 70s
2nd Edition, softback, 160pp – £18

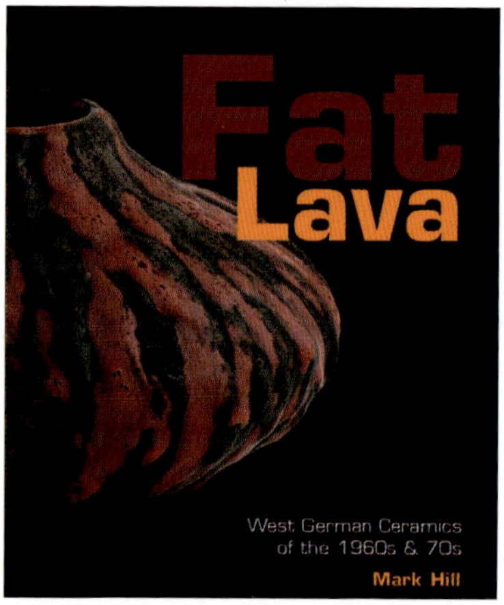

To buy your copy and learn more...

visit: www.markhillpublishing.com
email: books@markhillpublishing.com

Mark Hill Publishing
antiques & collectables

*All prices exclude postage and packing.

Caithness Glass: Loch, Heather & Peat - Price Guide

Page	Value
4	£20–30
6	£10–15
7	N.P.A.
8	N.P.A.
9	N.P.A.
10	N.P.A.
19	£70–100
20	£100–150
21	£10–15
23	£25–35
24	£30–40
26	£30–50
27	£15–20
28	£15–40
30	£20–30
31	£8–12
32 TL	£3–7 each
32 BR	£10–15
33	£70–100
34 TL	£30–40
34 BR	£50–70
35	£70–100
36 BL	£10–15
36 TR	£30–40
38 C	£25–35
38 L	£8–12
39 SET	£400–600
40 TL	£15–20
40 BL	£15–20
40 R	£25–35
41 SET	£40–60
42 PAIR	£250–350
43 PAIR	£150–200
44 TL	£10–15 each
44 TC	£5–8
44 TR	£20–30
44 BL	£25-35
44 BR	£20-30
45 SET	£70–100
46	£30–80
47	£70–150
48	£80–120
49	£15–40
50	£120–180 each
51	£20–50
52 TL	£20–30
52 BL	£10–15
52 TR	£30–40
52 BR	£30–40

Page	Value
53 TL	£25–35
53 BL	£30–40
53 TR	£20–30
53 BR	£30–40
54 BL	£15–20
54 TR	£15–20
55 TL	£80–120
55 BR	£80–120
56 L	£15–20
56 R	£25–35
58	£20–40 each
59	£20–120 each
60	£100–150 each
61	£15–25 each
62	£8–12 each
63	£8–25 each
64	£70–100
65 L	£15–20
65 C	£20–30
65 R	£20–30
66 L	£20–30
66 R	£25–35
67 L	£25–35
67 R	£20–30
68	£200–300
69	£150–200
70	£3–12 each
71	£3–12 each
72	£10–15 each
74	£70–100 each
75 L	£20–30
75 C	£30–40
75 R	£30–40
76	£30–40
77	£100–150
78	£80–120
79	£100–150
80 L	£30–40
80 R	£40–50
81 T	£80–120
81 BL	£50–70
81 CR	£30–40
82	£200–300
83	£150–200
84	£30–50
85	£200–300
86	£200–300
87	£150–200
88	£50–70

Page	Value
89 TL	£40–60
89 BL	£40–60
89 BR	£40–60
90 TL	£15–20
90 BR	£10–15
90 BL	£8–12
92 T	£150–200
92 B	£200–250
93	£400–600
94	£200–300
95 SET	£400–600
96 TL	£25–35
96 BL	£20–30 each
98	£20–30 each
99	£70–100
100	£20–30
101	£20-30
102	£20-30 each
103	£20-30 each
104 L	£15-20
104 TR	£15-20
104 BR	£10–15
105 TL	£30–50
105 BL	£5–8
105 R	£70–100

Notes

'N.P.A.' indicates that no price is available as the piece is unique and has not, and will not or cannot, be sold.

TL' indicates a photograph on the top left of the page, 'BR' on the bottom right, 'C' in the centre, and so on.

Where a wide range is given for a group photograph, the value of each item depends on the colour or the size. The higher end of the range applies to scarce colours and/or larger pieces.

Errata & Additional Information

p10 The Primavera Gallery was founded in 1946 in Sloane St, London, by Henry Rothschild to showcase the best in British and other art and craft. It soon became highly important, and helped launch or develop the careers of Bernard Leach, Lucie Rie, Ray Rinch (at Winchcombe Pottery), Harry & May Davis (at the Crowan Pottery), and the Cole brothers (at Rye Pottery). The 1950s saw exhibitions of fine textiles, furniture, glass, and folk art and craft from Peru, Mexico, Crete, Russia, and other countries. The company is now based in Cambridge and continues to showcase the work of the best British artists, designers and craftspeople.

p11 The furnace was supplied by Sismey & Linforth, not Sismey & Lindforth

p12 The factory opened in October 1961, not June 1961, with 20 employees, 8 of whom were apprentices. Each apprentice attended a glassblowing course at Foley Technical College, Stourbridge.

p13 The photograph on the bottom right shows Tom MacBeath and Chick Young in front of the Sismey & Lindforth furnace, not the mechanical lehr.

p14 The glass on the shelves behind ÓBroin also includes trial ranges and shapes.

p46 The cylindrical Cased Vases were originally named 'Lochalsh' by ÓBroin. The 10inch (25.5cm) high example cost £2 9s 6d in 1966. Loch Alsh is an Inner Hebridean sea inlet between the Isle of Skye and the North-Western Highlands.

p52 Bottom right: this is a cut down version of the taller lampbase on p55, and was thus made using the same mould.

p98 The manager of the King's Lynn factory was John Dowe, not John Dawe.

p106 Emerald was launched by 1996, not 1986.

Read Mark's blog at: www.markhill.net

books@markhillpublishing.com
www.markhillpublishing.com

This version dated 22nd February 2011